#439
2002

RY
2

DATE DUE

JUL 0 8 2003
JUL 1 9 2003

WITHDRAWN

DEMCO

the boy on the green bicycle

Men
Me and You

the boy on the green bicycle

a Memoir

Margaret Diehl

MEADOWLARK LIBRARY
LEWIS, KANSAS 67552

SOHO

Copyright © 1999 by Margaret Diehl
All rights reserved.

Published by
Soho Press Inc.
853 Broadway
New York, NY 10003

Library of Congress Cataloging-in-Publication Data

Diehl, Margaret, 1955–
The boy on the green bicycle : a memoir / Margaret Diehl.—1st ed.
p. cm.
ISBN 1-56947-149-5 (alk. paper)
1. Bereavement—Psychological aspects. 2. Grief. 3. Brothers—Death—Psychological aspects. 4. Loss (Psychology)
5. Diehl, Margaret, 1955– . I. Title.
BF575.G7D54 1999
818'.5403—dc21 99–12852
CIP

First Edition
10 9 8 7 6 5 4 3 2 1

To the memory of
James Hill Diehl
February 1, 1951 - February 27, 1965

Acknowledgments

I have many people to thank for their aid in the writing of this book. Gina Heiserman provided a brilliant first edit of the manuscript, and unfailing encouragement, Andree Pages, Lisa Schubert, Paula Sharp and Ann Beckerman offered insightful comment and sustained me with their friendship. Virginia Kelley, Elisa Rozov and Maritza Arrastia guided me through the psychological stress of writing about these events, and my husband Charles took me out to dinner when necessary. I would also like to thank my agent, Carol Mann for her help; and to thank a thousand times my editor Juris Jurjevics for his tireless efforts and his confidence in me. Lastly, I am grateful to my family for not complaining too much about having a writer in their midst.

Preface

WHEN WE WERE children, my brother Jimmy used to say to us younger ones, "I'm going to mangle you," and then chase us as we ran laughing up the back hill, excited by that word which seemed new-minted, but which could also be found in the dictionary, referring to an old-fashioned machine. Then when he died our mother would not let us see the body. "He's mangled," she said, meaning his face, ground into the highway so even our family doctor could not tell him apart from his best friend Grant.

And so was stolen the freshness of the world.

Our mother, of course, at the hospital knew which boy was which. Because the doctor was wrong, she saw them both, two fourteen-year-olds more handsome than most, Jimmy crisp-haired and blue-eyed, Grant silkier all over.

I didn't see. No parent would have let me see. I didn't really want to see except that I didn't believe. It wasn't possible, death. He must still be there, hiding under an eyelid, tucked into a curl of hair. He must still be there, laughing at how he tricked us, that triumphant teenage joy at the basement hall of horrors. Jimmy was a master at creating these on Halloween, decorating the basement with dimestore skulls glowing in the dark, chains rattling, recorded moans; and Johnny and I, first of all the neighborhood kids, allowed to put our hands into bowls of gooey stuff. "Mr. Englehart's brains."

Jimmy was an American boy the way they used to make them in the early 1960s. He played football, he had a dozen friends, he was a cartoonist specializing in gangsters and tough women smoking cigarettes. He taught Johnny and me how to wrestle, how to ride a bike, the meaning of such concepts as masturbation, murder in the first degree, taking the Fifth. He knew the names of prisons. He knew there actually were such things as prisons.

He taught us how to be sarcastic. He took extravagant delight in this device—you say the words the adults make you say but by your tone subvert them. He would perch on his bicycle or backward on a chair, drilling us. Over and over again, get the tone right, like learning French, the exact shade of disdain. We spoke, lifting our chins, carrying the words high on our tongues. That wide grin, as if his face were unzipping. His hands, when he was pleased, unable to not shimmy in the air, tracing warm arabesques. (I learned it well, sarcasm. Later I was amazed when it hurt people. It hurt me to banish that sneer from my voice. Sometimes I still use it, inaudibly. I say something I mean the opposite of with no inflection in my voice. I'm misunderstood, of course. It's a private joke. I'm talking to Jimmy.)

I was a little girl; he was my big brother. He did it well. The what he taught me not mattering so much as his love of passing things on, his expansiveness in a family where most of us were insular. Gathering the tribe of his siblings, talking, talking. I thought, listening to him—against my own doubts—that society, the wide world, the human race must be of interest. There was something of culture outside of books and our house, better than school.

I've watched myself grow up, become sophisticated, disillusioned, etc., while Jimmy remained a boy, at some point becoming A Boy. His memory a flat brightness like medieval art. In his madras jacket. My book of hours.

But more than a boy, of course, a person. The still-quick pain in recalling this disappeared person—unfinished? No. He was not unfinished, any more than everybody is. What hurts me is how much I couldn't know of him, being four years younger, and frightened besides. The later children in a family go through life always waiting to catch up; my mother used to tell me that someday the years between my siblings and me wouldn't matter. We'd be as equals. This isn't quite true, though I see what she means. But Jimmy is forever apart. Not older unless I am willing to be a child again, not younger because he can't be touched.

This is a book about grief, about death, and about the shadow of these things transformed in the imagination. I am reminded of the story *The Little Prince*, in which the picture of a snake eating an elephant is so striking. The drawing the prince makes is first mistaken for a hat. A jaunty hat, the kind you'd pick up in a thrift store, in 1970, when you were fifteen to wear with a tomboy, rakish thrill . . . I mean when I was fifteen. Grief is like that. It takes years, or decades, to digest, deforming you all to hell—yet the shape it makes is sometimes confusing, and can be worn at a tilt, romantically. Though I don't recommend it.

Jimmy as a teenager was fascinated by death. He knew all about the Red Death and the Black Plague, guillotines, quicksand, the Mafia. He read *Appointment in Samarra*, "The Pit and the Pendulum," the details of Egyptian burial rites. In ancient days, he told us, wives and slaves would die with their king. All buried with gold necklaces, embroidered robes, honeycakes.

Honeycakes. Wrapped in white linen, laid down gently beside the combed and perfumed head. How could the spirit not wake up to taste the sweets? As we did on Easter mornings, our beribboned baskets on the floor where an arm dangled.

I didn't think about death very often. It was something that happened to old people and animals. I killed a kitten once, when I was three, by shutting it up in my father's briefcase and carrying it around. Actually I didn't kill it, merely rendered it brain-damaged, so whenever it tried to walk, it fell over. My mother took it away. To the doctor, she said—and there to some happy home? My siblings told me the truth. "She's having it put to sleep.

You know what that means? I mean dead, and it's your fault." I remember running the picture over and over in my mind: the little gray kitten trying to walk, falling over, trying again. If it was up to me, I thought, I would have given it many more chances. But death for humans was almost obsolete; this was the 1960s, we had penicillin, the polio vaccine. Nobody would die anymore of TB, like mother's father had when she was a child. Our world was like a ladder, we kept climbing the rungs, *progress*, no time and place as fine as this, America in the second half of the twentieth century. Refrigerators and cars and TVs. Not death.

I ALWAYS ASSUMED it was to me the exotic event would happen. If one of us four siblings were taken, it could only be the wayward, out-of-touch child, the one who got left behind or who lost herself, running through long grass on top of the hill behind the house. In the stories it was always the solitary child who strays into the invisible landscape, the dreamy yet critical one who is chosen by those aesthetes of nonhuman society: I speak of course of fairies.

I wonder for how many of you that word evokes such buried wonder and longing as I feel or whether it has been entirely corrupted by Disney and sexual slang. The fairy folk, the Sidhe, cool-blooded amoral sharers of our earth. They who are mostly water and sky, perhaps the spirit of vegetable or mineral matter, the Celtic elderly. Fairies are what you believe in when every bush looks like a house, when a streambed or flowerbed make you want to lie down and sleep, when every berry and acorn, every firm blossom seems like food, and you compulsively arrange them on plates made of leaves. I saw what was there in our big suburban yard: the habitations, the delicacies. Perhaps my mother, intensely dreaming her house, tuned my mind to the passionate labor of such a making. I could not compete with her, so I ranged outward. I was in the woods, on the soft bosom of moss.

Fairies are cool, their passions aslant. They are the souls of nature and the muses of art with no traffic in the workaday world. They can be kind, as kindness is a pleasure, but are not bound to be; and even the kind ones take wickedness lightly. They don't love as we do yet feel an odd attraction to the mortal, to the lonely child bursting with ordinary affection. She is to them a creature enduringly strange, and they capture her as we might want to capture a unicorn.

One

WE WERE A family of six. My father worked in publishing in New York, my mother took care of us. Our house was big, twenty-two rooms if you count the maze of windowless chambers, what used to be servants' rooms, on the third floor. We had seven bedrooms and seven baths, halls long enough to play soccer in, a wine cellar, the dungeons, and an attic. The house sat on a plateau halfway up hilly Union Street, two pretty acres of roses, tulips, and flowering dogwood, green lawn, and a curving strip of young woods. A Mediterranean-look beige stone rectangle with a red roof, it was immense, imposing, though not quite beautiful. Not a house so much as an edifice.

We moved in when I was seven. After my parents bought the house, during the long months of renovation—we weren't allowed to see—I imagined it as the old house the children move into in the first chapter of the story. Or else it was one of the palaces in fairy tales, built overnight: the palace of silver and gold, the palace of diamond and pearl. Gradually I was disabused of my more extravagant fantasies—no silver, gold, diamond, pearl, no visible magic—but held on to an inchoate hope.

My parents were southerners. My mother grew up in Memphis and then Houston after her father died, my father in Wilmington, North Carolina. My parents were liberal Democrats, book lovers, jazz lovers, who came north to be with their kind. Yet they were not like the people in New Jersey; I was always aware of that. It was somewhere else my mother's voice acquired its languor, its you-alls, where she learned songs like "Summertime," which she sang to us at bedtime. (My mother couldn't carry a tune, but I didn't mind. Her voice wandered around the melody with its own plaintive charm, producing none of the excitement of music on the beat but something more intimate and curious. Something like my mother, who though sociable was also eccentric and fond of solitude. Who would wander around her enormous house all day, making and fixing, planning, arranging, talking to herself in a low, contented murmur.)

It was somewhere else she had been a young lady of prominence, a thousand people attending her wedding. Her mother's brother, Gus Wortham, was one of the wealthiest and most powerful men in Houston, the founder and chairman of American General Insurance Company. Uncle Gus—no, I confess, we called him Uncle Bubber—had been like a father to her since her own father died. He was like a grandfather to us now. We were required to talk to him when he called, that hearty, yet oddly shy Texas voice full of an affection I found mysterious. How could he be our family if he was so far away? If we barely saw him? He came through New York on business maybe once a year—short, big-stomached man, smiling—we went to Houston in those early days only twice. Bubber lived in a white house with pillars, which I couldn't believe he was serious about, and the servants cooked fried chicken, biscuits, and rice. All of us sitting formally around the table, being served from the left. The two black people slender, straight, very dark, selves rigidly contained behind impassive faces. Yet I had heard their low sweeping laughter in the kitchen.

Bubber also had a ranch an hour or so out of town. He'd take us kids riding in an old car over the flat dusty ground, through the droning masses of Black Angus cattle. Then he was happy, turning the wheel with big sloppy moves, stopping and starting—a man in his seventies, born in the horse-and-buggy days. Sometimes the car couldn't move at all, bovine faces pressed up to the windows. I was nervous, but Bubber would sound the horn and the lumbering creatures would list sideways, hooves scrabbling. Driving a car through cows. That was what the man liked to do. He sat down low in his seat, legs spread to accommodate his belly, ten-gallon hat riding his small head.

I liked going to the ranch. I also liked riding the elevator to the top of his office building, being ushered into the enormous, plush CEO's office, where he sat daintily behind a massive desk. He had sad brown eyes, silver hair, small hands and feet, a big nose. A sweet, old-southern-man smile. When you know nothing of business or the world—and I was an exceptionally unworldly child—there is a clean, unguilty satisfaction in being related to power. I didn't want to grow up and be a CEO, or marry one; I merely wanted him there, in his distant office. It was my parents who had to suffer the lost possibility of being his heir—my father who quit a job working for Bubber, a job that would have made him, eventually, very rich, in favor of books; my mother who had to wrestle with the idea that if she'd been born a boy . . .

If she'd been born a boy, she'd have done what my father did, giving up the insurance business for something more artistic. She left the South of debutantes and the Junior League for the bohemian life in New York City, and when I was little she was still energized by her escape. The natural inclination of a child to think that wherever she lives is the right place, the only place, was bolstered for me by my parents' relief, their self-congratulation at having left the South. And my mother's pleasure in her power: grown-up, her own mother and mother-in-law far away. She told me once that thirty-six is the perfect age, and I remember her at thirty-six, slim wand of beauty, that drawl in her voice that spoke of magnolias and hammocks on front porches even while she was crisp and efficient, buttoning our snowsuits, fixing lunch, doing all the mother-things with no sign of strain. More than that: with glory. She had the stamina and vision of an artist; and we were her raw materials. Her children and her house. I knew that very young—resented it—envied it—fell inside it and became both object to myself and rebellious sorcerer's apprentice. Writer. Putting her in my book now as she once put me in my life, the big dark lamps of her eyes shining.

We all knew New Jersey was the right place to be, the progressive place, the normal place, yet I liked the South. Its warmth, perfumed air, servants. Servants—so brilliant in their performances, like the movies (I was brought a Coke in a frosted glass on a silver tray!), so smart and evil-minded in private. I knew it wasn't fair to them, being servants—that's why you couldn't like the South, though we had a maid in New Jersey as well, it was confusing—but even in their wickedness, their manners were so supple, like well-oiled leather, so soft. And they weren't fooled by the adults of my family: they saw everything, and I could see it, too—even if I didn't quite understand—in the lively glinting roll of eye and lip.

Bubber took care of us. His yearly stock gift raised our income considerably above what it would have been on Daddy's salary alone; he created trust funds for us kids. It's also the case that my parents knew how to live on a certain sum of money as if they had twice as much.

My mother always told me we weren't rich—not as rich as the so-and-sos who lived down the block—and I knew this was so, but she had the gift of creating an atmosphere of luxury. She bought Persian rugs, Danish teak, green leather chairs, colorful paintings with mythological themes, abstract sculpture. On the coffee table a huge hunk of gnarled driftwood and a silver cigarette box, on the dining-room wall a pair of china climbing cats painted with blue and lavender flowers. Crystal whiskey decanters, gleaming mirrors and chandeliers, vases of fresh flowers, books. At least a thousand books. She bought them, he bought them, he brought them home free. Poetry, philosophy, history,

novels, art books, and books on witchcraft and the occult. My mother was probably the only person in Montclair with *Magick in Theory and Practice* by Aleister Crowley on her library shelf.

But more than what she owned, what was notable about my mother is that I never sensed any fear or doubt regarding money. There was always enough—not for everything we wanted, certainly, not for a pony or a swimming pool—but enough; and if more was needed, if an emergency arose, there was always that rich old man in Texas. My mother felt safe, so I did, too. More than safe: I felt elect. My mother told us almost daily what superior children we were, so intelligent, beautiful, talented, good, destined for the highest success. Success which would occur not without some effort, but without serious competition. Our defeats in school, my defeats in social life, she waved away as having to do with the temporary status of being children. She insisted that when I grew up I would conquer the field without difficulty. I would dazzle while the girls I now deferred to at school would be revealed as the ordinary creatures they really were. (This made me anxious, a little sad; I didn't want my friends to lose their charms.)

I loved safety, privilege, and comfort as only the introverted and physically clumsy can. I was intoxicated by the romance of my mother's hopes for me. I knew she wasn't telling the whole truth. Mommy, who drilled into us the importance of honesty, wasn't honest about the nature of the world. Not a deliberate dishonesty. She was telling me what she passionately wanted to be true, and that passion, as much as anything, snared me. I would live in her heart's desire as if in the branches of a flowering tree. Yet I was aware, how could I not be, of a different, grubbier world passing just beneath my nose.

My mother in her late youth still had chivalric ideals, and I learned early about honor and nobility, particularly as they come down to us through the myth of the South and through literature. The former was never stated—it drifted in on her voice—the latter reinforced every time she made a selection at Brentano's. I think of the legend of Robin Hood, of King Arthur and the knights of the round table; of the high-minded collies of Albert Payson Terhune.

She believed in the religion of books in a way that is perhaps not possible anymore. For her generation books were the way out—of small towns, provincial cities, of closed-in families and social repression. The transition from a lonely child's love of books to an adult's respect and reverence for them was more seamless for her than it will be for any succeeding generation. I can't imagine it will be true in the future that people are judged by whether they have many books in their house but that was how my mother judged people. That was how I judged them until fairly recently. I felt dizzy in a house with no books. No company. No anchor. No *life*.

When she didn't have guests, my mother read to me at night. She would sit in a chair by my bed, *The Green Fairy Book*, or *The Yellow Fairy Book*, or *The Blue Fairy Book* on her lap. She encouraged my belief in fairies. She told me she believed in them, too. I didn't realize she meant something different than I did. That she meant she was once a bookish lonely girl in Memphis, Tennessee. That now, as a mother, she was still bookish, still lonely. I took her literally.

Mommy. Her long neck bent, the smooth cap of her dark hair,

her dark eyes, her calm, which is almost preternatural. The power she spreads around herself, shining like feathers. It is motherhood that gives her such power, but I don't know that. Or I know it but not how small it is in the clamorous world. There is no world but this house, what happens in this house, and one moss-green path away.

Most fairy tales are about a child being rescued. The youngest or kindest or most beautiful, or, in the modern stories, the child with imagination. Sometimes the child is an orphan, as in the novels of the great Victorian writer George Macdonald. The Princess Irene, who climbs the stairs of her father's castle and finds rooms she never knew about, in one of which a beautiful white-haired woman sits by a fire, awaiting her. The boy Diamond, in the tale *At the Back of the North Wind*, who is the son of a coachman and sleeps in a tiny room with holes in the walls where the cold comes in. One night North Wind herself comes to visit; she is a grand and gracious lady; she gathers him in her arms and tucks him into her long hair, where he's not cold at all, carries him along in her travels across the sky. That long, thick hair, that ocean of hair, hair as in the other story, the one about a princess whose hair won't stop growing until it threatens to cover the whole kingdom with its tresses. Easier than riding on a winged horse, or balancing on a flying carpet to cling to the ropes of a woman's long hair.

North Wind comes for Diamond again and again, tapping at his window, and when the boy is convinced she is only kind, she takes him out to sea to watch her sink a ship. "This, too, is what I am," she says, as the sailors drown. "If you will know me, you must know this."

None of my siblings believed in magic the way that I did. None of them had this hunger for stories, especially stories of journeys, quests, transformations. Something becoming, or revealed as, something else. Animal to human, and vice versa. Straw to gold. I would stop listening for a moment at that moment in the reading, savor a sensation of exquisite pleasure, as I would feel later discovering the conceits of Shakespeare or Donne, the imagery of Yeats, any effective metaphor. This to that. *This* to *that*. It hardly mattered what the thises or thats were, as long as the two were in the proper balance. What I liked best sometimes were the silly changes, the ones where no one gained or lost, there was no particular, or moral purpose, just a surge of sparkly energy. The Oz books were full of that sort of abundant, not-quite-random change, magic simply out there, how life proceeded.

I didn't think my mother would mind if I joined the fairies. Though she was so careful about warning us not to talk to strangers, never get in anyone's car, etcetera. Though she made such a point of how she loved us, would do anything for us, give her life, etcetera. Yet she couldn't mind if I went off, because she was the one who read me the stories. Who confessed that she, too, had longed to be, and wasn't, taken.

How could she sit there and talk so nostalgically—yet so calmly—about it? Her childhood, when she lay in bed at night waiting for Peter Pan to step in through the window? Thrilling low tones in her voice, her eyes dreamy. As if it were possible that she could have been as I was, an actual child. I knew all adults believed this; I imagined it as a kind of mass delusion. The world had begun when I was born, my mother fully created as this tall, long-necked beauty. All the grown-ups fully created, in their shoes and girdles, suits and briefcases. With their pasts like picture postcards. Or else, for the sake of argument, if she really had been a child—that cute, dark-eyed face I saw in the photographs, chubby cheeks, smile, big soft bow in her hair—then her belief that she would be taken by the fairies was a sad mistake. I could barely imagine the grief of that: to have experienced this joyous anticipation, lying in bed in your springy flesh, being loved from afar by the invisibles, in the light of their gaze—then to realize you were mistaken. They didn't want you after all.

She'd never had a chance. She was fated from the beginning to grow up and become my mother. It was more important that I be born than anything else she had wanted; and I was going to have what she'd been denied. It was me the slim boy would come for, stepping across the window frame. The inexorable logic of my feeling led me to a frightening knowledge: My mother's whole life was in service to mine. How could she possibly forgive me?

I lay quietly listening, and hid myself.

Mommy read me "Sleeping Beauty," "Cinderalla," "Snow White." The liquidity of her voice was like the milk of the moon poured down shining on my bed. She talked about princesses taken to the dance, about dresses made of bluebirds' feathers. And as she spoke something in her soul came forth—it was a beautiful girl, a girl of glass who had been shattered into a thousand pieces, each piece sewed back together so she was flexible, she could bend and twist, but was still shattered. She glittered but there was a whiteness in the glass; it was cloudy.

This girl, as she reads to me in bed: Nobody else knows her. Nobody else can see. I am so still, I barely breathe, coaxing her. I let my eyes drift secretly over her arm, shoulder, neck, the outline of her head. An alertness in my flesh, protective and excited yearning. Don't be afraid, girl. Come out, oh, come out.

The calmness with which she reads; my body under the crisp white sheets. We are traveling; we do this every night. My mother comes to me and we go down the river of the story. This I can trust: that she will come. But she is also the river of the story I want to dive into.

"Read me another one."

Sometimes she does, which is a great coup. I get more stories than the others because of the ones I choose. Johnny asks for a book called *Little Brown Monkey* every night for years, Charlotte and Jimmy are listening to Jules Verne. Only I stick to the true tales. Only I can make the girl come forth.

But eventually she closes the book, kisses me good-night. She has an adult life to go to, with my father. I tell my mother that I love her. "I love you, too," she says. Her voice doesn't quiver.

"But I love you," I insist, hanging my arms around her neck. Her neck is creamy and smooth, the scent of her skin, which is very mild, she barely sweats, overlaid with the expensive seductions of her cosmetics. Herbessence, by Jean Natè. She slathers it on every morning. She almost bathes in it. Her eyes look at me, those big dark orbs, and where I want to see the girl again, there is only her shiplike calm. She blinks, gets up to leave.

I'm alone in my big bed. I scissor my legs back and forth, or lift them up to bicycle in the air. I'm not afraid to be alone. I love the white field of my mattress which spreads out on either side, and above and below me. I enjoy falling asleep, how my consciousness rises, first, into the air, so I float around near the ceiling—in the far corner—as if at the top of a taut string. Then I plummet down into a tunnel; I fall and I fall. Sometimes I imagine the princes who slid off the glass mountains in the fairy tales, hundreds dying before the princess finds her match, and strangely I, too, am a prince; sometimes I think of Alice's rabbit hole. Sometimes it's not a fall but a drift sideways, a kind of loop like what a needle does when making a knot in cloth: that's the best, when you can taste that contact—sleep on your tongue—just as you dissolve. If I am ever afraid, and I sometimes am, of the dark window, or Dracula, or clothes on my chair, I get over it so as not to ruin the sweetness of night. Quiet, my room, my bed. But I don't understand what happens to love.

In the old house, when I was five and six, I would get out of bed at night, go looking for my mother. I'd find her in her sewing room, sitting at the machine under a cone of light. My mother sewed as some people write or paint, and I saw that fierce energy in her, that obsessive love of craft. Unfinished dresses and coats hung in her closet; she only wanted to do the impossible thing, copy the picture in Vogue, makeshifting a pattern, or fashion perfect buttonholes, perfect collars and sleeves. Then she grew bored. Then she wouldn't bother to hem the garment but would hang it up, go on to the next thing. I understand this now. But as a child, I wasn't sure. Ought I to be scared? I'd stand in the doorway as the machine whirred, as the needle bit down, traveling quickly through the cloth. My mother was very intent, her face sallow in the lamplight.

The floor was covered with paper patterns, glistening with pins. "Watch where you step," she said. In the corner, on a small bed, my younger brother slept, face turned to the wall. The old house was not so big; Johnny and Mommy had to double up.

I stood on one bare foot and then another, watched the steady progress of the needle, its chomping force. "Go to bed," she said without moving her eyes from her work. The paper patterns whispered, seemed to move slightly toward the small bed. The tousled curls of my brother's head were visible on the pillow; I was concerned. Was she in control of this sharp magic? What do mothers do when their children are asleep?

She was also thin, so thin. When I sat on the floor and looked up at her straight on, it looked as if she were standing sideways.

My mother was always making. Copies of designer clothing for herself, hand-smocked dresses for us. She made clothing for our dolls out of scraps of fine material so my Jackie Kennedy doll had a blue-and-white silk dress like my mother's with the same high neck and blue velvet sash. She sewed drapes for the living room and the dining room, and red velvet Christmas stockings, lined with red silk, decorated with cut-out felt toys and the letters of our names, silver bells jangling at the toes. She baked angel-food cakes and devil's food cakes, made chocolate mousse, pots de crème, crème brûlée. In all chocolate desserts, she taught me, you double the amount of chocolate called for. This was something, like the owning of many books, that defined one as a proper person.

At Christmas the downstairs was hung with holly, pine boughs, and mistletoe. She glued the Christmas cards we received to red ribbons and framed the fireplaces. She decorated our big tree with painted glass trumpets and drums, wooden Santas, Mexican tin ornaments, little birds that clipped onto the branches, and delicate glazed balls in crimson, yellow, and violet. Under the tree on Christmas morning, unwrapped, were our presents, arranged in intricate tableaus. Madame Alexander dolls in printed cotton dresses and white petticoats, Steiff animals, Lionel trains, chemistry sets, Erector Sets, books, bicycles—all of it right there, taken in at one glance, that was the idea: abundance, dazzlement—

I'm reminded of the tarot card, the seven of cups, where a man staggers back before an array of fairy gifts. The central gift is a woman, standing in a chalice, arms outspread in greeting, her head and upper body hidden beneath a cloth.

I wanted to do things as well as my mother, and that wasn't possible. She made perfect layer cakes, I made lumpy cookies. She sewed evening gowns of pale silk, I sewed a little cotton change purse in art class that she put in her drawer and never used. She promised me I would inherit her skills with age. I believed her—did I believe her? It didn't matter. I needed it now. Art was the shape of love; how could I disburse myself of feeling? I wooed her with my poems and pictures, and she received these graciously.

"Thank you, Margaret," her voice mild, drawling—that difference that seemed to swathe her in a private melody. Sometimes she talked of the South—afternoons in a hammock in the early Texas spring, the warm waters of North Carolina. I thought it was a made-up country, though I'd been born there. My first memory—of shafts of sunlight on a bed where I lay, my mother mysteriously absent, which I mull over, remembering voice, hands, scent, and locating a faith that she'd return from the wilderness of not-here: that had taken place in Texas. In the little house in Houston I'd seen in photographs. Still, the South was mostly a place inside her throat.

"Thank you," she always said, unfailingly courteous, yet so private. My love was a bat squeaking in the darkness. She knew I loved her, but she took it for granted. It was her love for me she thought I needed to focus on.

"I will always love you; I will always take care of you; nothing you can ever do will change my love."

"What if I killed somebody?"

"You wouldn't do that."

"But what if I did? It could be an accident."

"I'd be very upset. But I'd still love you."

"How do you know?"

"You'll understand when you have a child."

It was my love itself that sometimes led me into error. Once I found some lovely daffodils in the woods, nodding fresh yellow heads in little hollows of pine needles. I yanked the stems from the earth and presented my mother with a bouquet. She was in the kitchen, preparing something—this kitchen that she had designed herself, spacious, light, and clean, with its modern island, two stainless-steel sinks, two ovens. I gave her the flowers. She didn't scold me but became very upset, flinching to contain her distress—I remember the muscles of her back in motion, her weight resting heavily on her hands. She had planted those flowers specially to look as if they were growing wild. She had *strewn* them.

She didn't scold me. She didn't need to. Mommy's beautiful idea.

Even in the woods, there she is.

Two

I STAND OUTSIDE my sister's door: a soft, sticky child—hair dishwater blond—swelled with yearning. Oh, let me in please, I need to come in. Charlotte closets herself with Jimmy or her one girlfriend, the dark and timid Shelly. They climb up the ladder to the loft in her bedroom called the Nest. There they practice such mysteries as I longed to know.

Charlotte was a sprightly girl, beanpole and lively. She wore cowboy boots, a cowboy hat, a pearly, lowslung holster. She had long brown braids, thin as whips, and big brown eyes. Charlotte didn't unbraid her hair, once, for an entire year. Washed it still in its plaits, went to school. It grew denser and more matted, like a thicket. The braided pieces, twisting and twining, were the two sides of the ladder to the Nest, that ladder she could haul up, so the balcony hung in air. (I wanted her Nest. I wanted her dolls. I wanted her girlfriend, the dark and timid Shelley.)

The teachers complained about my sister never brushing her hair. My mother said, "She cries when I brush it, so I don't brush it." I wanted those snarled chestnut ropes. My mother always cut my hair in a pixie cut. Then, later, when I was allowed to grow my hair, it never reached the length or thickness of my sister's. I also loved Charlotte's hair unbraided, brushed and clean, its deep waves glinting in the lamplight as she sat in the library with Jimmy, one on either side of my mother. (Then I felt like the black boy, our maid Hattie's grandson, who used to ask to comb our hair, running his fingers through it as he murmured "So soft . . . so soft." His hands an exquisite pleasure, dry and sinewy, cool, making my scalp swim. Hattie angrily banging pots across the expanse of the kitchen.)

I sat hugging my knees in the shadow of the stairs as my mother read to my siblings. Jimmy's grave eyes, the blurred soft lines of his mouth. Charlotte's pink-and-white princess complexion, high cheekbones and pointed chin.

Jimmy and Charlotte swoop down the driveway on their two-wheelers, silver bells ringing, as I follow on my tricycle, pedaling furiously, lost in about thirty seconds. Lost. I ride my tricycle up and down a few feet of sidewalk. I know children get lost; I've heard about it.

I explore the shining square of my panic: It is very bright and terrible. I move across it like an ant, not yet swallowed up. The heavy branches and dark masses of leaves hide the façades of houses, shimmering and rustling with muscular indifference. My siblings long ago gone—whether minutes or hours I'm not sure. I hold very firmly in mind an image of their long legs flashing as they pedaled away, the trailing ribbon of their laughter.

A police car stops next to me and the policeman gets out. I'm surprised: It is just what my mother had predicted. If you get lost, find a policeman and ask him to help. I hadn't seen enough policemen in my four years to believe this would work. But here he is, squatting down to speak to me. Speaking nicely, not mad at all. He asks me my address and I don't know it. He leads me up to the nearest driveway and there she is, my mother.

All afternoon and evening my mother praises me for having the wit to be found. She acts as if I had conjured the policeman from my own brain. Meanwhile my siblings jeer at me for having gotten lost in the first place. "She didn't even know her own address. She didn't recognize our driveway. She was lost, Mom, right in front of the house." I find their position more tenable than my mother's.

Jimmy and Charlotte. Their curious faces over my crib—this picture I invent but I see it so clearly, bright eyes, glints of auburn in their hair when the sun catches it. Boy four, girl three. As I become more myself, a baby person, they become children, going off to school. Curious faces over my crib, what then? Did they play with me, pleasure beyond bearing, did they stop? Did I chase them, wanting more, whining, until they turned on me?

I was teased as a child. That's what we called it. My siblings would dance around me in circles, taunting, all three of them but especially the elder two, neighbor boys and any visiting children. Anyone coming to our house quickly learned the rules, and were glad, girls especially: *It's her*.

I've needed to ask my older cousins to reassure me I haven't invented it all. (My sister can't remember. Won't remember, I used to think, but now I believe her. Can't remember.) My cousins remember: Old fear stiffens their voices. What they were afraid of—what if I'm the next to be set upon?—it seems they are still afraid of; and this makes me strangely embarrassed. Even now, no one can bear to imagine being me.

I remember the leaping children, nimble and quick, and myself standing in the middle, rigid, flushed, skin tight with trauma.

Also the pleasure on the children's faces, that sharp dreamy excitement. Being locked in a toy jail we had in the basement, a small cage with bars . . . stripped naked in the bushes and left alone . . . laughter . . . flickering images. And I think about the word *teasing*; how it can mean something sexy, affectionate. I tease people that way myself, trying to keep it within limits though it wants to go further—but what I feel when I'm doing it is attraction and warmth. It comes naturally to hide that behind the veil of the tease.

You tease to make someone cry and there's still love in it, in a raw fascinated state. You want to see what's in them, the tears, the blood. You want to make sure it's not in you, to feel so light and cool, watching the squirming flesh. Yet still you love it, in your bent way. Is that the way a cat feels, playing with a mouse? Tease it, tease it—scoop it up, taste and savor the shivery body.

Those taunting circles are like a fire in my mind, the place where they happen still soft, as if melted or unmade. When I try to work with it, my body slides into panic. My anus hurts, my pupils dilate, the muscles in my neck and jaw become so tight spasms of pain ignite my nerves. The whole inner architecture of my body glows, and I fall through a hideous solitude, no connections made, nothing spoken, felt, or held.

Imagination. Dreams. That's where it comes from and that's where it goes, the madness flowing through me like an underground river. I hear my siblings' voices like the chattering of birds. Unintelligible, mocking, glinting with laughter. The voices of devils who are so beautiful.

IN MY MIND, I was the scapegoat, my sister the villain. Jimmy's role was more ambiguous. Often he was kind (especially as he got older), sometimes he was not. He was able to be more generous, being the eldest and the boy. Boys were better than girls, even though it was also true that our mother was better than our father.

Mommy was an oasis. Never angry. It was Daddy who got angry, whom we were so scared of. Nevertheless, or exactly because, or who knew why—boys were better than girls. There was something nasty in girls.

When I think of myself and my sister in childhood, I think of our bodies. Her body that I admired, coveted—her body chasing mine, on top of mine, pinching, poking, scratching, drooling saliva. Her smell, which made me feel sick to my stomach, her height, which was so unfair. Her exuberant restlessness. She always knew more, did more, the world belonged to her more.

Charlotte's body: eternal advantage. My body: soft, weak, defenseless, site of attack. My sister gave me nicknames, Booger and Blubber Baby, which she used every day for years. As an adult, until recently, I couldn't bear to hear these words spoken aloud, but as a child they caused only a flicker of resentment. What was harder then was hearing "Margaret" spoken by any female voice in our house. At school I was Margaret and I heard it neutrally, but at home to hear those syllables—in my mother's voice, children's voices, most of all the voices of my girl cousins—caused a pleasure so intense it was immediately shame. I had to wrap myself in six kinds of silence before replying.

I used to look in the mirror, trying to puzzle out Blubber Baby. I wasn't fat but was rather the only child in the family with rounded, pleasing limbs. At least to me they were pleasing; I ran my hand over my warm arms; I thought my sister, in contrast, looked like the stripped carcass of a baked chicken.

At school nobody called me fat and everybody knew who the fat kids were. It wasn't something you could get away with. I stood on the side with the normal ones always. I decided I must have another body, invisible in the mirror, that was fat. I kept trying to see this body. I'd sneak up on the mirror—walking sideways to it, gazing past, then quickly slewing my eyes around, hoping for a glimpse of the blubbery girl. I say hoping because I wanted to *know*. What was Charlotte talking about? Where was it, that ugliness? It had to be somewhere.

I couldn't see it. I saw Margaret, a rounded pretty child. I liked my face: eyes, nose, mouth, everything pleased me. This was reassuring in a way, and yet I could only conclude that if I didn't see what Charlotte saw, maybe nobody saw what I saw. I couldn't form any opinion, for example, as to how I was seen at school—couldn't rely on my image in the mirror. It could be that nothing in the world was truly as I saw it. I had to wait until I was told, and kids in elementary school don't tell you you're pretty. All I really knew was that they didn't see me as fat, because I wasn't teased. Most of the time I assumed they saw a girl without a face. A girl with regular features, nothing deformed or hideous, yet without that stamp of dependable selfhood. So I was quiet, expected nothing. And if somebody obviously liked me, especially a boy, that little piece of attention would briefly knit me a face.

Blubber Baby was an extravagantly hurtful name, but for that reason I could marshal a few defenses against it. Booger was worse. It was a nickname anyone could have, a child in a book could have and be defined by completely. In fact, my mother had a friend whose name was Boog which made me think this was a name I could carry all my life. Boog was a fat, hairy, peculiar man, a queer (I was told). Long before I knew what this meant I caught an odor of sadness and shame attached to the man. I didn't want his name. Nor did I was the child's version which I yet felt I deserved: it was true that I picked my nose. I enjoyed it.

There was a chair in the library where I liked to sit. It was a big cool armchair of caramel-brown leather and I would curl up in the center of its vastness with a book.

The library was a grown-up room, but you could sit there if you were reading. And so I read; I read all day. I read while the other children played outside and it didn't matter if they hated me if I was plunged in a story. Reading, I spread out, as endless as the waves of the sea. I fell into myself and the further I fell the more shapely the world became.

While reading, I liked to pick my nose. I pulled out what I found there and wiped it on the bottom of the chair. I knew I shouldn't, always meant to never do it again, but once ensconced in the big cool chair, book open in my lap—the smell of the paper and the binding, the slight jaggedness of the printed text, how the words started halfway down the page at the beginning of a chapter, white space like a room in which I could make my bed—all of that called for a physical response. Picking my nose hooked me to the words. It completed the mood.

When my siblings found my cache of effluvia, the humiliation was instant and total. Everything that went into the experience—my sensual pleasure in the chair, my loving complicity with books, most of all my terrified and arrogant decision to escape the world and get away with it, still according myself the privileges of a human child in the house while I secretly believed myself something like a trapped angel—where scalded with shame. I was Booger, as Charlotte had said. I could see myself, a child, a big, walking nose-picking, viscous and trembling, the hard brown parts and pearly yellow parts clinging together.

I CONSOLED MYSELF with turtles, those little ones we bought at Kresge's for a quarter. Their soft little feet brushing against my palm, the baby softness of their shells. Sometimes I put one in front of the cat . . . watched the cat's sudden alertness, lithe shoulders bunching. I always rescued my turtle.

I liked to hold a closed-up turtle. It was like a damp stone in my hand, a round stone found on the beach which in the silence of one's bedroom at midnight awakens.

I would kiss the closed-up turtles. Kiss all along the rims of their shells, even kiss the underneath, which was moist and earthy. I also kissed my cat. I didn't worry about germs. I loved the tenderness of the little turtles and the wild clean smell of a cat's lips. I loved how my cat hated to be kissed but couldn't escape, how his soul sank back into his bones and his body was offered up, proud and helpless. I breathed in his fishy breath, lifted a lip with my finger, admired his scimitar teeth, rough petal tongue.

We had four cats: Fluffy, big black-and white Angora, her tail missing after an accident with a car, Gypsy, handful of mewly long-haired tortoiseshell, Jinx, bullet-shaped gray tabby, and my own tawny tom, King Richard the Lion-Hearted. Ricky was a long, slim cat, the kind of feline who could be stretched to any length you fancy, like a wad of gum. He had six or seven toes on each foot, slanted golden eyes, a speckled nose.

Ricky had been a gift for my seventh birthday. I had asked for an orange male kitten and when one was found, my mother and I went to look at the young litter. I chose my cat, the only male, then we left him there to nurse another two weeks. Ten days later, he and his mother ran away. The woman called, very apologetic, offered me one of the female kittens left behind. I refused.

I waited three months. The waiting was difficult, yet it was an important event; a test of character. The woman called me in early summer to say Ricky had returned. We went to see him. He was almost five months old. A teenager. My mother asked me if I was sure I didn't want a kitten. How could she not know? I felt so honored to be allowed this wild and swanky beast. This run-away-and-come-back cat.

I wore him stretched out on my forearm, then slung over my shoulder, his paws dripping down my chest. He held on serenely.

I pressed his underside to my ear—to hear the purr and the heartbeat, does one ever get enough of the purr and the heartbeat?—manipulated him to feel muscle and bone, stretched his sinews. I only hurt him a little. He didn't mind. He was too silky to complain.

When he got a little older, he started to run away again. Tomcatting, my mother said. He'd be gone two days, sometimes three. After the first few tormented weekends, I fought back. I allowed him one night's absence, then on the second night, after I was supposed to be in bed, I'd sneak out to call him. Barefoot in the dark, poking through the bushes at the front of the house, *kittykittykitty*. This was before the ticky-tacky houses were built and the front acres were still a no-man's-land. Swirls and tufts of grass, hills and hollows, stones and tough twists of shrubbery. I stood in my thin nightgown, house at my back, the chill damp air thick with ghostliness. I used my voice in the manner prescribed in the stories: the crooning tones of mermaid and sirens. Coaxing all sweetness, all trilling power from my throat.

When I sang this way to Ricky, shivering in my nightgown, he would return. He'd appear in the distance, walk toward me very slowly, shoulders pistoning. He'd pause now and then to look back at his girlfriend. Her green eye-flash in the shrubbery, dark evasive shape. His guttural protesting meow. He'd turn to her. I'd croon. Head swinging around again, my cat looked as if I were dragging him, my voice little hooks attached to his front parts. I was sorry but didn't quit. I reeled him in closer. "I love you," I cried at last, scooping up his rigid body. "I love you, love you, love you!"

I thought we had it worked out, but my mother took him to be neutered. That was her decision. "One day he won't come back," she said. There was also something about the furniture.

Ricky came back from the vet and didn't seem angry. He stayed home now and slept all day, surrounded by our own girl cats, who still loved him. I liked seeing that, my sweetheart sprawled out, his handmaidens arranged beside him. Even old Fluffy was in love with him.

Or if he happened to be alone, he'd snag me with a claw when I walked by, then I'd go down on my knees, bury my face in his feathered belly.

OCCASIONALLY, OTHER CHILDREN came to visit with their families. The Plumbs from Brooklyn, our Arnold cousins from Manhattan. They'd stay overnight or for the weekend. The grown-ups provided meals and left us alone.

If I tried to creep into the room where my girl cousins were playing dolls with Charlotte, she'd scream at me, chase me out of the room and down the hall. If she caught me she'd twist, pinch, pull my hair, those attacks known at "fighting like a girl." As I ran, I felt ashamed of my desire. I felt ashamed of the spectacle we made, my cousins' faces bobbing like balloons in the doorway, my unrelenting cowardice. My alarm froze me, shattered me, preserved me in a kind of perpetual panic.

My cousins hung back; as they say now, afraid.

I didn't think they were afraid. I thought they were mortified to be related to such as I, this fetid child clothed in the veils of the body's effluvia.

I wanted to creep into the room where my cousins were playing, not be noticed, slide like a mist along the floor. Simply be there, invisibly, soaking up the essence of girls, their chatter and warmth. Why couldn't I be invisible? Instead I was the most visible; I was reeking with being, my whole body flushed and shining with a fecal light.

That's what books are for. *Lad, a Dog*, *Narnia*, *Oz*. I am Mistress of the Place, or Lucy in the wardrobe, or Dorothy, beloved of

Ozma. The stitches of my soul picked up, carried a little further. Weave me a self, color it with voices. Later, it will be hard to know it is only me in here.

When the children played outside, I could watch. Gaze my fill at those New York cousins like foreign princesses: light-blond-haired Kate, the eldest, so cool and aloof (her white stockings, her black headband, her spring coat with the peter-pan collar), light-brown-haired Roberta, so timid and tender, as if you could stick your hand right through her face. Roberta was Charlotte's age, Kate a little older.

And then there was Faxy, strawberry-blond Fairfax, my age-mate, tomboy. Faxy wasn't a delicate, girly girl. Nor was she nasty-sisterly. She was wild. You could dare Faxy to do anything and she would do it. She was wilder than the boys. She was so much like a boy she was nothing like a boy, she was a thing unto herself. Later, we'd be friends. I knew we should be now. But my sister wanted her, so I had to wait.

Summer twilights, revelry. The grass squeaky clean but for the roses' fragrance, the dog's curled offering. The adults on the flagstone terrace as if on a spaceship somewhere, drinking, smoking cigarettes. How could I go near even my mother? I was not Margaret but an ugliness I didn't want her to see.

As I watched the other kids, I pretended again that I was invisible, that nobody noticed me by myself, that none of their whispers or laughter concerned me. Our yard was so big, our house so big, it was easy to get a distance, to approach from an oblique angle. I told myself stories of solitary heroines who triumph in the end. These stories were continuous, a kind of paste my mind extruded. Yet the voices of the others would rise, mingling, a braided gypsy music. I was here, only here—aflame with solitude. The beauty of children at play. Wanting to douse myself in their faces.

I couldn't stop watching. Yes, I could. I'd go inside to read, lie on my bed for hours. But I came back out. I came out, crept around the edge of the yard, not quite in the bushes. Sniffing paths to the other world.

Sometimes Jimmy would invite me in the game.

In the game! My body so eager, kids all around me. The sun casting clean shadows on the grass. My bare feet alert.

It's Jimmy and Bobby Plumb and Charlotte and Roberta and the four or five of us little ones, divided into teams for Capture the Flag. Jimmy and Bobby are the captains. I love it when my

brother picks me, even if he picks me last. I don't understand how I can not win.

If I'm running and somebody catches me, I'm so surprised. If I'm knocked out of the game, or just straggle behind, it shocks me. My longing is so fierce, my flesh so willing. How can another body outdo my body when the blood courses through my veins like fire, *when I'm in the game*?

There's nothing like being in the game, and I want it to go on forever. The teamwork, the suspense, the excitement, the action. I can't stand it when we have to stop.

I'm greedy. Now that I'm in the game, I want more; I want to be the captain. I'm too young, of course, too much scorned by the kids, but I also know it's hopeless because I'm a girl. Girls can't be captains—even to want to is not feminine. (This is mysterious to me. How can a girl be not feminine?) but I'm aware of the danger here. I need the affection of my brothers. So I follow the rules. Being a girl is not just what I am; it's what I have to pretend to be.

I stick with the easy part: liking boys. I cling to my brother as the game ends, inhaling the smell of his sweaty T-shirt, gazing at the perfect roundness of his shoulders and arms, the clean lines of his shoulderblades, shock of crisp hair over his eye, his panting, laughing breaths, *that confidence*, waiting for what I know won't happen, to be allowed to go up to his room with him and Bobby.

More mysterious, far better, than being allowed in with the girls would be to be allowed in with the boys.

Isn't there something about me that can make this happen? Something that fits between Jimmy and me? He doesn't always laugh at the things I say, when I dare say them. Or he laughs differently from my sister. He laughs like I'm strange but he's proud of it. He's alert to oddity, the value it can have. The trick of cool is to always find new shapes for resistance, and I feel, I sense, that he knows I might have some potential.

I want to go with him, but it won't happen, I know it won't happen. It can't happen, it never has, and even my hanging around makes Johnny angry, makes Charlotte angry. Charlotte has privileges as a big kid, Johnny has rights as a boy—they sometimes get in the room with Jimmy and Bobby, and my presence, my yearning, makes it more likely that they won't. So I retreat, wandering around the darkening hill until we're called for supper, peopling the grass with ghostly children for a ghostly game.

I'm the captain. I win.

I HAD TANTRUMS when I was four and five. My arms and legs would pound the floor, the red blood coursing through: I felt so shockingly alive. For one moment I was in the world of my siblings, those active, aggressive children, I was in their demanding world—then my mother would make me go upstairs.

"Come back when you can behave yourself. If you lie quietly, you will calm down." No irritation in her voice, only a measured knowledge. I climbed the stairs in a rage, vowing to never calm down. I loved my resistance, flames and flickers of me, the fierce sobs beating a rhythm in my chest, yet I despaired. What I would miss, the family talk, that talk like no other (I understood maybe a tenth.) Upstairs in the dark—or halfway down, on the stairs—my siblings' voices whispering up, like flames catching. Like bees threading through a field of clover, pausing here and there, moving on, it's all so mysterious.

Jimmy and Charlotte, so smart, so capable, so knowing. Already in school by the time I could talk. They were the real children. Johnny and I were more like sacred pets. (Even now I find it easier to imagine myself a harem girl or Victorian garden hermit than any kind of responsible grown-up.)

It's all so mysterious and *I have to understand*. I was always astonished as a child that no one seemed to notice how astonishing it was, *to be alive*, how they kept harping on what I could do or not do, the rules, without ever discussing what we were doing here in the first place. What "here" was. Who "we" were.

I couldn't believe it. I thought they talked about the real stuff secretly, Charlotte and Jimmy, my mother and father, they were keeping it away from me on purpose. I was angry at being left out, at their duplicity. At how, whenever I tried to explain what I wanted to know, they misunderstood willfully, or made fun of me for it.

My imagination was a great source of amusement to my older siblings. Yet I knew where power lay—inside thought. My mind was the one place I was always in charge. It had perfect borders though it appeared to have no borders, to sail on into a sky that was practically infinite. In school we learned the poem "There is no frigate like a book," which the teacher seemed to think was a great convincer, though she spent most of her time explaining what a frigate was, and the boys perked up and made jokes I didn't get. I thought the poem left out the half of it. Sitting in class, I was neither confined nor alone; my mind waited for me like a great soft-pawed cat, able to bring me any trophy, any prey. That boy, for example, turned into a pig. How he would squeal. And the classroom swallowed by an earthquake.

I remember when consciousness switched on; I was three or four. I don't know where I was, except that I was inside the house, I was alone; and suddenly knew that I was me. Only me. Margaret distinct and inviolate, bounded by skin and the silence of thought. I ticked away in the bright interior. I was me. Nobody else was me. (I thought that meant, really, nobody else was anything.) I could think whatever I wanted and my thoughts were hidden. I experimented with this, thinking bad thoughts in my mother's presence, watching her face carefully. She didn't have a clue.

After that I tried to remember myself. Who I was last month, last summer, last year. I had a store of memory—new shoes, a snowstorm, when the kittens were born—but the further I went back, the sparser it became. I didn't know myself at fifteen months, or six months. But my mother did. My sister did. They would tell me, occasionally, what I had done, who I had been as a baby, and it filled me with terror. I had been alive without myself.

I won't let it happen again. I am I, the view is clear. Snow, fire, leaves, animals, cake, clean sheets, arithmetic workbooks. My blue cotton dress with the rickrack on it, the mirror at the foot of the stairs.

I am I; and I'm happy alone; but what can you do in your room while everyone is downstairs talking? That talk—I'll never hear it. They'll never say those things again. If you ask them later What did you say? Why did you laugh? they'll shrug, pretend they don't remember. Alone in your room, you can't whine (I loved to whine, the lulling, caught sound of it, as if time were piling up in my body the way cloth can pile up in a sewing machine. Whining and dawdling. "Stop whining. Don't dawdle." There's a high-pitched whine and a train-rumble whine and the whine with little hiccups in it. Those hiccups are seed packets. If you whine long enough you expand the volume of the earth.) You can't whine by yourself: It doesn't work. You can't scream either. All you can do is cry, which makes your eyes hurt and your nose clog, which fills your brain with something like dirty cotton balls. My mother was right, I calmed down. The anger was sucked back into my bones, taken apart, I forgot, the tears quit. I had to be quiet to listen. To catch the high notes of the talk—rising laughter—*I want them.*

I need them. I'd trot back down, feeling intense humiliation. She was right; I was wrong. I'd enter the living room, eyes downcast, and my mother would smile and pat the cushion beside her. Her blouse was trapezoids of color: golden yellow, scarlet, emerald green. Her slimness, and the slim curves of her lipsticked mouth. Night-colored hair.

IT USED TO worry me sometimes, when my mother would get it. When she would stop telling me yes, Charlotte was wrong to tease me, but I shouldn't pay attention, it was just silly, when she would look at me more closely, experience the revelation. *This one I thought was my darling daughter, look at her!* And it was I who would make that revelation occur, if I exposed too much unhappiness. I wanted my mother to know—but how could I let her know?

Anyway, she'd never get it. In her mind I was innocent and good, and so was my sister. Whatever cruel thing Charlotte did—and was often punished for—wasn't really her nature, had no actual meaning. It was my mother's credo that a child cannot be bad in herself. This made no sense. Where does the badness start, then? Does it simply fall upon one at sixteen, with the big ungainly body? If I was angry and told my mother I hated her she said she knew I thought I hated her, but I didn't really.

I did, really.

She reassured me, lovingly, that my anger, my hatred, could not touch her, and I felt dizzy and lost, in an echoing whiteness. If I had no hatred, if it wasn't real, how could I ever fight back? And just as my hatred had no existence in her eyes, neither did my sister's. All was smoothed into something called "sibling rivalry," which was normal, inevitable, without force or terror. What I knew of its terror was my own invention. Charlotte's rage, my grief, our mutual envy, my swiftly accumulating desire for vengeance: All of this started and ended in me, and it made me faint of heart.

Against this faintness: desire. How could I not stay connected to that radiant highway? Kate! Roberta! Faxy! Even Charlotte—or especially Charlotte, my bright-brown-haired, strong, and lively sister. My tough, lean, tireless, hot-breathed, bold sister, her wit a constant surprise in her face.

Charlotte was the garden in the fairy tale, the one nobody is allowed into. There a plant grows called rampion, which can heal an ailing woman. In the story, you remember, the husband climbs the wall, steals the plant, is caught by the witch and tricked into handing over his firstborn, a long-haired girl called Rapunzel.

Charlotte was the garden, the leafy plant, also the girl in her tower.

A prince can climb those braids, as can the witch, but there's no room in the story for another little girl.

My sister says now she remembers loving me. Remembers having all the good older-sisterly feelings: pride, protectiveness, affection. I believe her because there is a photograph, Charlotte leaning into me, her tall self dominating mine but at an angle of desire, while I twist coyly away. And I also remember, though for years I would have said, *I imagine*, a kind of sweetness beneath our enmity. I see it as a river of flowers of gold, not gold metal but fragrant blossoms. If your toes just touched that stream, you were in bliss.

Charlotte's heart. Yet whenever I became aware of this, I thought I was crazy.

There is another photograph, one I used to look at as a child. This was a picture in the family album, circa 1958. My three siblings are tucked into one sleeping bag, their little flower faces upturned for the camera. I am crouched, half-naked, several feet away. I couldn't regard this image without feeling overwhelming disgust at my nakedness, a shocked reverberation of my experience of exclusion. Yet I would find myself going into the library, taking down the album from the shelf, over and over. Each time it was like being thrown in an outhouse called Margaret. I would suffer it—flinch away—bob up to the surface of my being again, trailing hopelessness, as if trying to train myself.

I would look at the photograph, the facts. My face burned. My belly curled. I became aware of its plumpness and its depths. My sex turned on, that moist embery slit that wasn't supposed to even exist. I thought I was unique, among girls, for being sexual. At night I touched the ruffled lips between my legs, rubbed up and down. I didn't find my clitoris at first: the whole thing unfolded over years. Secret life. That part of me turned on when I gazed at the terrible picture, drew me into its velvet.

Sometimes I wanted to destroy the picture but my mother wouldn't let me. "You're so cute," she said.

Three

My PARENTS WERE both beautiful, and sexually charismatic. This last I knew without words, by comparison: All the other adults seemed to be missing something, the pretty women appearing lifeless, the handsome men without force. Force, intensity, and sheer sensual overflow: For a long time I thought of it as their southernness—and that may have had something to do with it.

Daddy was fair-skinned with blue eyes and black hair. Mommy's hair and eyes were dark, her skin olive. Daddy wasn't tall but dense-bodied, big-headed. His features were small and delicate, his wrists and legs slender. He didn't look like anybody else. Mommy looked like the queens in fairy-tale illustrations and also, not in detail but overall type, her tallness, elegance, and aristocratic bearing, like Jackie Kennedy. For a while I thought my parents were the Kennedys. When I was five they attended the inaugural ball (due to her uncle's patronage of Lyndon Johnson) and seeing them leave, for days, evening clothes packed, I couldn't believe they weren't the stars. And after that, even though I knew two ruled in Washington, I believed them to be my parents' weaker doubles.

My first knowledge of what the adults called evil was Richard Nixon. Mr. Nixon, a slyness, a shadow falling on our fair land. It made me queasy. One night during the campaign they went out to dinner, left us with a new, old-lady babysitter. This stumpy arthritic person wedged herself in a chair, demanding service; my siblings absconded. Only I was left, curious, amenable. She told me to make her a cup of tea, I made tea. I wasn't supposed to use the stove, being only five, but stood on a stool, lifted the heavy kettle, poured the boiling water. I walked slowly, carrying the cup in its saucer, to the living room where I found the old woman on her knees, rear end protruding, scuffed heels up, kissing the television screen. Fuzz and crackle of her lips meeting Richard Nixon's. Moving as his moved. It was so interesting.

My parents went out often. I became used to the sight of them dressed up fancy, her high heels, red lipstick, and rhinestone earrings, his gleaming dark suit as he stands, holding open her coat. Her little head like a lollipop on a stick, her willowy thinness and nyloned legs. Daddy's solid vibrancy, his happiness in leaving. My father didn't want a family life. He didn't marry in order to get that started. He married because he adored her, she bewitched him, and then we came along and spoiled it all.

My father wanted my mother to himself and he succeeded a fair percentage of the time. He took her out, dinners at French restaurants, drinks at the Algonquin, publishing parties (which disappointed her, she had thought people would talk about the meaning of novels), dancing. Ballet, theater, jazz. My father would drive home at the end of a workday, shower and dress, drive her back to the city. I would follow them to the front door, barefoot in the yellow light of the front hall, watch them leave. I wanted them to stay home, shed that grown-up glamor, *be with us,* yet at the same time I pitied those whose parents weren't beautiful. Whose mothers didn't dress well, couldn't flirt, whose fathers were spindly, colorless, or just ugly.

I knew—after awhile—that we weren't royalty or millionaires, that my father didn't have scores of employees doing his will, nobody treated us specially; but then there was their beauty. How they gleamed on the terrace at summer cocktail parties. His white shirt, square upper torso, close-cropped dark curly hair. Her very slim body in a Pucci dress, bare long brown arms, her big teeth and nose and eyes. She smelled of a thousand creams and perfumes but mostly of lemon; he smelled of alcohol. I thought all men did. I thought it was a marker of their separate existence, a spicy, medicinal imprint of otherness.

I USED TO sit on the stairs at night, watching my father come home from work. This would be about seven o'clock. My mother was in the kitchen cooking dinner, my siblings upstairs.

Perched just above the landing, I was in my territory, knees pressed between the slender posts of the banister. All below me was clean and shining: golden wood and white walls, the two small, fringed Orientals by the front door and the library door, then the long runner, leading to the back of the house. The hall from end to end was sixty feet.

The front door was massive, dwarfing my father as he came in. This happened to everybody but I mostly noticed it happening to him.

When he entered the house he was vibrating. His broad shoulders, big boxy head, the whole square picture of him, enhanced by square black glasses, square briefcase, and coat and hat, was in jerky motion beyond what was necessary to cover ground. He used too much force shutting the door, called out loudly for my mother, set down his briefcase, and let his hands free to shake for awhile.

Those hands! Thrust out in front of him as if he were desperate to get rid of them, two inches of slender wrist exposed. This was not a tremble. This was like something out of the movies, like propeller blades, back and forth, churning the air. I didn't think of them as signaling an illness. What I thought was that they were bewitched, they had a power.

When he could manage it, he lit a cigarette, a Lucky Strike, from the red-and-white package. After a few inhales, he'd look through his mail. Mostly long white envelopes addressed to A. C. Diehl. I had already investigated them. Bills. It surprised me that the world was not afraid of him.

I was always moved by the sight of my father alone. I also noticed that he was never really alone. He had the cigarette, the drink. While my mother consumed alcohol and tobacco in much the same way as she ate dinner—with pleasure, in moderation, so it never occurred to you that she needed these things—my father's relationship was clearly different. His fingers fumbling with the cellophane on his cigarette package, the rattle of ice in his drink, or the hand, dangling out the car window, with its white cylinder sheared and glowing in the wind; these were signs of a complicated intimacy. The red-and-white cigarette package—LS/MFT, Lucky Strike Means Fine Tobacco, the cool beaded can of Miller High Life, pierced twice by the tooth of the opener—weren't they akin to my dolls and stuffed animals? I would say I knew my father could love by the tenderness with which he treated his familiar vices.

He spent most of the weekend days on his bed, dressed in white boxer shorts and T-shirt, reading. A beer open in his hand, a cigarette lit. In his dresser drawer, under his socks, lay a cache of Milky Ways. He was not a man to mow the lawn or fix the toaster or play ball. He was a person like myself, addicted to books and slothful pleasures, romance and hiding.

I watched, invisible unless he happened to glance up, which he never did. I thought about my siblings, who had better things to do. They were upstairs, having spent all afternoon with their friends. All three doors shut. I didn't have friends, to speak of. One or two girls I hung around with occasionally on a Saturday, but not *friends*. It was my great and persistent embarrassment, how my siblings would all charge off on the weekend and I had to hide the fact that I had nothing to do.

The magazines said: Be yourself. I read this advice over and over. It was cruel—didn't they know there were some of us, or at least one of us, without a self? The honeycomb of my inner world, the sinewy power of consciousness, I didn't think of as a self. That was the universe, what must be kept hidden. I wouldn't have known, in any case, how to begin to communicate it. It receded in public, swathed in a luminous fog.

Watching Daddy. Pleasure and terror; never a moment in his presence free of either one. The trembling in his hands was how he was in me, a constant quaking which trapped energies too exalted to live without. Daddy's arrival set the house into a glassy panic, which lasted all evening—yet the roar of his car, the shaking of his hands! Of course I can't speak for the others, but I know they felt it. The engine of his sensual life. The fury and sobbing of a machine that is not being used properly, whose wheels will mount the curb as in all your favorite movies. What if he caught me spying? Would he kill me? Sometimes he chased us, enraged, bellowing—took off his belt to whip us.

He didn't hit me with his belt, he hit the boys, and even them not often, or as hard as he threatened.

What actually happened, if he saw me on the stairs, was that he paid no attention. His eyes on us, most evenings, were blind.

Worse than that blindness was an occasional look of violation resulting from the fact that we existed at all. It was as if he tried all day to forget us and succeeded until we forced his awareness. My mother says he asked her to put us to bed before he got home, even Charlotte and Jimmy at twelve and thirteen.

My sister liked to test this blindness. Once she dressed Johnny in my Sunday dress, pinned her cut-off braids to the back of his head. She led him into the room where Daddy was reading, introduced him as a neighbor child. (Charlotte was the only one of us four who would approach Daddy. I remember going along with the whole thing not for the joke but for the chance to participate in any sort of encounter with my father.)

Johnny wore no makeup, no funny glasses. He didn't disguise his face at all, that bright-brown-eyed little face, with its missing front teeth and tiny nose, its high bony forehead and the train-track scars from when I fell on top of him while he was lapping water from a glass bowl, pretending to be my dog.

That one-of-a-kind face was right there, on top of my dress, a couple of braids dangling behind. Daddy looked up from his book politely, stuck out his hand. "How do you do, Janet?"

Johnny whirled around, ripping off braids and dress as he hurtled down the hall. Charlotte stayed behind to explain the joke, while I walked slowly away, picking up my dress from the floor.

Daddy didn't recognize my Sunday dress. He was so polite to that supposed Janet. I'm bad to think this is about me.

After Daddy read his mail, smoked his cigarette, he would go into the kitchen to talk to my mother. His voice was urgent and quick, continuous; I would creep down the stairs and stand outside the door, listening. City stories. Names I didn't know. What so-and-so did, that bastard.

I was just so offended. I refused to make sense of what I heard. The anxiety in his voice, the concern: I blocked that out, too. What I paid attention to was the rhythm of their sentences, the rise and fall, the counterpoint. Mommy and Daddy together. Simply the sound of his voice, bleached of all meaning, just the sound—and her musical response, those soothing tones.

I was impressed by how they could keep it up. It was like something in nature: crickets or frogs. I didn't need the words. Words were for books. There they were honest, sacred, and friendly. They lived on the page and deep below the page. Sometimes if you stared at one you could see it vibrate as if the letters were about to open. Even a small word like *the*.

After his torrent of conversation, Daddy would take his drink into the library to read until dinner. As soon as the door shut behind him, I'd run into the kitchen. I'd stand next to my mother as she worked at the stove. I measured my height to her body; I brushed against her clothes—the slickness of silk, the lighter gauzy rayon, or the special, fine cotton she wore, cut wide at the shoulders so her bra strap showed.

She never minded my closeness. She accepted devotion mildly, not drawn out of herself by it but pleased, as if things were in order. She went on like smooth clockwork, making the dinner. "You can set the table," she'd say.

I stood a moment longer, watching. What I wanted to do was cook. I was fascinated with the meat browning in the pan, throwing off little pieces of itself, pancakes of scum, by the fiercely boiling water that melted the frozen peas. I loved how the rice drank all the water and puffed up. This, too, was transformation. I would get lost in it, knew I could, but my mother was cautious, and wouldn't let me use the stove. Besides, she was getting lost in it herself.

"Set the table," she repeated.

I gathered the spoons, forks, and knives, the plates and glasses. What I liked to do was carry too much at once. My mother told me not to. "You'll drop something." I knew that could happen, and I hated it when it did: Breaking a plate or glass sparked in me a quite disproportionate sorrow, as if I had killed something. Yet I had to be reckless with the dishes. Carrying too much, balancing dangerously, righted something in my body. Something that had been askew was corrected.

My indifference to her warning irritated my mother and she would scold me. That high tone in her voice, as if my actions had no meaning. Even then, I knew they had meaning and was stubbornly interested in what that meaning might be. The change in my body that was effected when I carried too much was so powerful, like anger. Was it anger, a longing to smash all the dishes? I think it was simply action. Something physically difficult to focus my awareness, secure my spirit to earth.

I wanted to explain this, I knew it was important, but didn't know how. I had the feeling, in all its shapeliness, but not yet the words. But even if I had had the words, I wouldn't have spoken. My mother seemed to imagine that everything I knew or felt, she, too, had known or felt at my age, and yet that couldn't be true, because she didn't get it. The manner in which she scolded me: as if I needed instruction in the precariousness of things.

By the time I finished setting the table, my siblings would have come downstairs and the four of us would be in the kitchen, milling and jostling. Talking, snitching bits of food, drinking milk, talking louder to drown out each other. This didn't ruffle our mother. She moved calmly through her edgy, hyped-up kids—more edgy and hyped up than she would ever be, yet attached to her by radiant, unbreakable leashes.

"We're ready to eat; go call your father."

Jimmy was suddenly busy finishing his math homework; Johnny simply refused. Charlotte or I would go. If it was my turn, I'd run to the library door, legs twinkling as if I were on a mission, and shout the information through. Then I'd leap away as if he were coming fast, though of course he was in his chair and had to creak up slowly, as grown-ups did.

It half surprised me that he came. That I could say a thing, he could hear it, and hearing, obey. I scampered back across the hall with the message: He's coming.

And then it began: where to sit? We all wanted to sit next to Mommy where it was safe, but Mommy didn't have a particular seat. Our parents sat at either end of the table but not at the same end every night. It depended on our father, whether he needed to go to the freezer for more ice or not. Mommy was always standing, serving the food, until we were seated. Still, we tried to guess.

We tried to coax her. "Where are you sitting? Why don't you sit here? Let me take your drink to the table, save you a place."

She pretended she didn't know what our maneuverings were about. She kept her drink by her, told us to sit down. "Sit down *now*."

We hovered. We poured ourselves glasses of milk as an excuse to stay up, or sat down and quickly rose again, claiming we hadn't chosen. We ignored our mother's scolding and waited for Daddy.

Finally he came and then it was quick. He was there in the doorway, exuding that bewildered fury that was his most characteristic response to us. What was it like to be him, coming blinking into the room where his children saw him as the enemy? In my case, an enemy I secretly loved, felt so tender toward, protective, yet no less scared or angry. I wanted him there but at a distance, not right next to me. I couldn't stand it. His force field, the inverted nine-tenths of his rage, melted me inside, my ordered self fusing so I could barely think or know, so that I would be, for the length of the dinner, insane.

Daddy sat down, and Charlotte and Jimmy dove for their chairs. It seemed they always got to sit next to our mother, able to converse with her all through dinner while Johnny and I were left alone.

It helped to have Johnny there. Sitting across from me, his face both still and wild, his eyes not focusing except occasionally on me. If Daddy got up for another drink, I could shoot a pea across the table to Johnny. The danger was if I made him laugh and he couldn't stop laughing.

Daddy didn't merely criticize or scold us. He didn't only yell or hit. The words he spoke were vicious—suffused with an endless rage. As if he hated us. As if he had hated us from the beginning of the world, for the best of reasons. Chaotic unfocused fury pulsing through his body, clearly unbearable. He couldn't help himself, he was being shredded—I could feel it, though I didn't know

I could feel it. I thought the conventions were correct, we were all separate beings. But his panic was a madness in my flesh.

We, his children, were so disgusting, so cretinous. It was a quality of hatred for which there are no words; a hatred that did not, I'm sure, really depend on us, we were merely in the way, but which paralyzed us like a nerve toxin. To shake and tremble in the gale of that hatred—I've known it from the other end as an adult—is to realize it lies beyond human relationship. But what could we know then? Only fear, only stillness. Any mistake of table manners, any opinion voiced drew the fury. I said nothing but in my anxiety lost track of things, knocked over my glass of milk. It seemed to happen of its own accord. He screamed at me, he slapped my face. Terror like a drug: I can't move, I've gone crazy. Frozen in the cage of the room, clinging to my consciousness of the present moment yet as if stretched on a rack, vertical slices of pain as his voice goes on.

What happens if your mind *just comes apart?*

If I could be an animal, I thought, put my snout down on the table, weep pig tears, trot outside to live—that would be okay. I'd go. But Mommy won't let me. She makes me stay here, pretending to be a girl. It's so important to her that her children be people. That her husband be a father, the six of us a family. She doesn't understand that it's impossible.

My mother sends rays of scornful anger at my father, says low rebuking things. Her disapproving force makes his hands twitch, his ice rattle, makes him angrier and more frightened. She sits upright, her back straightening and straightening. Never more queenly. I don't know how to get under her armor. I sense that she wants me to, that I should be able to, but how is it done?

I concentrated on the food. Juicy meat, buttery soft potato. The crystal edges of salt, cold lake of milk. I was engaged in a project. I had noticed that pleasure provides relief from tension, that a moment of flavor unknots wrongness. Flavor righted me but it didn't work entirely, and it occurred to me that if I could speed up and intensify the experience it might effect a more powerful release.

What Johnny would do when he was attacked was to run out of the room, knocking his chair backward. Charlotte would cry, hunched over her plate, as Daddy humiliated her for the tears and snot on her face. Her face would seem to come apart, like a book underwater. Jimmy would argue back, then walk away, slowly, with dignity. I couldn't do any of these things. I didn't want to leave, nor make myself ugly. I wanted to be like Mommy, the perfectly-in-control, the always-desired. But that's not true exactly. I did want to be like her, but also to be myself, and for this reason, precisely for this reason, in terror of any success in becoming her, I fell in love with my defenses. I didn't know they were defenses, of course. I thought of them as games, projects, elaborate structures. I was proud of this mental stuff, Margaret in more and more fantastic packages. This idea, for example, that the pleasure of eating reach an apotheosis: I was proud of it. I loved how I could think to bend my perceptions, to twist and shape them. What a world I made. It was so interesting . . .

I concluded that dessert was most likely to render the desired transformation. When I ate sugar there was a change in my mood, something subtle but promising. If the sweetness were climbed like the rungs of a ladder, I thought, one bite, another, faster and faster, and I concentrated and didn't allow the outside world to enter my consciousness at all—the pleasure of that, of *focus*, tongue and taste buds learning the pleasure of pleasure, or the pleasure of the pleasure of pleasure—

"Look at that disgusting pig."

I was never the least bit prepared for the attack. It seemed that everything I did by way of escape only made me the more exposed and vulnerable. That's what I remember being ashamed of. Taking a third piece of cake in front of Daddy, so stupid, and the fact that I had done so *in order to* hide from him. It made no sense; I deserved what I got.

I sat very still. He was shouting; I shuttered my senses. I had simply not done it enough, that was all. Hadn't focused enough. Don't pay any, not a scintilla, of attention, don't speak or move—

Creating great oceans of blankness within myself. Oceans that would rise and fall with their own gravity, which I would drag with me for years and drown in again and again. Yet in the blankness somebody was noticing. His eyes on me: Brobdinagian disgust. The love of cake which I yet declared innocent and folded back in myself never to let go of became in another aspect a blue-violet cable running from his eyes to mind. My desire. My visibility. The energy running up and down his arms, his baffled ferocity crackling and lunging toward this thing called Margaret who dangled in his space. I kept still, holding my other selves, the good girl and the secret me, securely behind; I waited on my father.

Daddy in his square white shirt, hand trembling toward his drink, was waiting, too. His taunts were a kind of hunger. He needed something. But what could I possibly give? I sat still.

The connection faded. He drank. He didn't escalate as he did with my siblings; I was only hit once; my stillness defeated him. And when it was me he attacked, nobody left the table. Not Jimmy, coolly rising; not Johnny, speeding off; not Daddy himself, shaken by my sister's tears or my mother's fury.

Nobody. I sat still.

I believed it was me who was always supposed to be attacked, that his attacks on my siblings were mistakes for which I was guilty. I was the one who was trying to steal power. The power of Daddy's emotions, of Mommy's control, of my siblings' very beings. I wanted it all. And for a moment I had it, I was God—I created a hallucination to console myself with, brilliant colors swirling on the white wall of the kitchen. Nobody but God can make colors where there are none. And while I looked at them—the red, blood-orange, indigo blue—while I assured myself of their distinct reality, my family bent over their plates like robots. I choreographed each move. At least, I assumed I did, since I could predict, in this state, every gesture a few seconds before it happened.

THE PROBLEM HAD always been: Which story was the true one? The modern stories, where you could feel the crackle of the man's pen on the page, were reassuring because of the promise of an abundance of tales, invention never running out. As in the Narnia book where the children put on the magic rings and fall into the wood between the worlds, a twilit place where nothing happens or has ever happened but from which you can go everywhere. Shadowy wood of big trees with still pools of water, each of which was the entry to a world. I could easily live in a wood like that; drowse beneath the trees, stepping forth into a world now and then. . . .

Of course the Narnia books as a whole were the opposite of that halfway place, aiming toward completion. Lewis even, in the end, brings death into the story. All the children and the creatures, the talking animals, the giants, choose death: walk through an open door to a second Narnia, heaven. I didn't like that at all.

He was swallowing up his story. He had them all on his tongue—down they went—

Death. It would happen to me when I was seventy years old. As if I were to say now: seven times seventy.

One day the window would blow open, the boy step through. Or in the woods, a fairy would appear in colors like music. An animal or a bird would begin to speak, or the wall of my bedroom give way to moonlight, an utterly strange landscape, winter to our summer, or vice versa. Or I would dawdle behind my siblings and

when I came to the bend in the road, I would turn another way. Or swimming in the ocean, be pulled under by a bare-breasted girl. Or I'd discover a hollow in a tree I could climb inside, then down the long corridor to a little round chamber with a hearth, table set with pink cakes for tea. Anywhere, anytime, it could happen, was waiting to happen. I went on, school, home, dinner, bedtime—learning to skate, to ride a bike—sort of interested in these things, and in my mother's promise of the future, "When you have your own children," but never more than half present, half concerned, if that much (except, perhaps, when I was listening to Jimmy). This was the world for other people.

They could have it.

I used to sit on a stone in the middle of the path through the little wood behind the old house. Waiting all afternoon for the fairies to take me while my siblings played with their friends in the distance. Are they coming? Are they coming now? Each moment of beauty, the pointed red leaves, the gray flank of stone, leaf pattern, branch pattern against the sky, each sight brought messages from the unseen. I felt presences as one does a cat in the room, or a person staring at you from behind. I tried to deepen this awareness, fall into the exquisite. Here I am. Like a pie on a windowsill.

Four

ONCE UPON A time, my father had come home with gifts in his pockets, bright whirring toys from a place called Times Square. Daddy, that fresh-air-smelling man in a hat and overcoat, so pleased with himself as the charmer of little children. We'd run up to him at the front door, yelling "Daddy, Daddy!" And then he'd pull the surprises from his pocket as if surprised himself, but given away by that delight—like the wagging body of a dog—in his grinning face. He was the one loved. He was the abundance. It lit him up entirely, but he was not *light*. He was dense. He was squarish, and roundish, with a hard, round belly. We skittered around him like dogs ourselves.

A few years later, on weekend afternoons, I would check his overcoat hanging in the closet. Sometimes a handkerchief, a quarter. Lint. Where were the toys? I could see so clearly the brightly colored metal parts, the sparks that flew when you pushed a lever, or the pink paper umbrellas, size of a toothpick, with writing on them, or soft cloth dolls with black hair. . . .

I wasn't able to think *the past*. I thought they were still here somewhere, I had just misplaced them, forgotten what was the thread of my life. I would stand among the coats in the coat closet, my hand in his pocket, aware of an emptiness that had no name. It settled in my body, as if my chest were an empty envelope, a letter arrived with nothing in it.

My mother says that what happened happened fairly quickly, when I was about four. "He began to snarl at you-all. He pushed you away when you ran up to him—pushed you so hard you fell down. I didn't know what to do. I told him every night, 'You can't do this to the children' but he snarled at me, too. I said, 'You don't want them bothering you now, but one day you'll miss them and it will be too late.' He just brushed me aside. He didn't think he was doing anything wrong."

(I wonder about that—that he didn't think he was doing anything wrong. Sometimes, later, when we were so afraid, I saw something in his eyes, a kind of bewilderment or regret. It pulled me toward him. Poor Daddy—an almost unknowable feeling, unheard music, but there.)

Yet that violent rejection, half remembered—even now, a seizing up of my mind so that there is no fluidity, no one to speak or sing. Affection stops and whitens, freezing like a river, and the whole world has then a glow, as of dense, impacted matter.

Inside the green moss grows, that which is damp and clings to the rock, which is soft and invites your cheek. Come, says the moss, here, here. The velvet under the trees in the middle of the wood.

When I was a newborn, according to my mother, I was Daddy's favorite. He liked babies and toddlers. Jimmy and Charlotte were just losing that status as I gained it. I don't remember being Daddy's favorite but I remember remembering it. Sitting at the dinner table while he was being vicious to us all, thinking: He loves me best. It kept me isolated and hopeful, this belief. A singing in my heart—he loves me best—but a faraway and eerie song. He loves me best. Doesn't he? It was my only weapon against the fact that I didn't believe he loved me at all.

All of this was going on when my father finally had a job he loved, after unhappy years in the insurance business. He was the director of subsidiary rights at Putnam's, had clinched a deal so spectacular it made the front page of *The New York Times*: the most money ever paid for paperback rights. (My sister remembers his wild grin that night, face unable to stop smiling.) He was a success.

Easy to imagine. He could be so charming, so funny and earthy, when he wasn't angry. And he behaved so much better around grown-ups.

Was his triumph not enough? Or was it simply the case that no success could touch him inside? My mother remembers him looking at himself in the mirror one night as he was dressing for a party, exclaiming in shock, "My head is too big for my body! I never noticed before. My god, people have been laughing at me all the time. *All the time.* I never knew." She had to coax him into going to the party.

My father was a man who made fun of everyone for their bodily imperfections; who was shocked when the conversation turned to sex; yet whose copy of Krafft-Ebing is underlined everywhere, who negotiated for the rights to *Lolita* when no other company would touch it, whose favorite scene in literature was the one in *Ulysses* when Bloom is sitting on the toilet. As my mother tells it, Joyce's realism was something he was powerfully struck by, grateful for.

I knew this as a vibration. Daddy and sex, Daddy and bodies. He had a sexual charge that was pure gleeful energy, that could make you want to jump out of your skin. It sparked in me a daring that I adored and was ashamed of. Once he threatened to take off his belt and whip me for some misdeed and I said, "But, Daddy, then your pants will fall down." He laughed, blushed, turned away. I hopped around wildly, proud of my wit—was he proud of my wit?—embarrassed.

As time passed, more embarrassed.

I don't remember ever having a private conversation with my father, or one that lasted longer than a couple of exchanges. He never taught me anything, took me anywhere alone, or gave me advice. On the other hand, he did bring me home boxes of books. These were the titles his company published, the random harvest of a season. Unlike the books my mother chose for us—fairy tales or classic imaginative literature—these books could be about anything. Some of them were nonfiction. And even when purportedly magical they often lacked conviction or were not well written. I would plunge in, expecting to be transported, and plot lines would go nowhere, characters remain opaque.

I didn't dislike these books. Their odd, dry, modern flavor was an astringent pleasure; the nonfiction enjoyably outlandish. As for the badly written books—it never occurred to me they were badly written. I thought they were doing it on purpose, and I felt respect. If I could read a whole novel without losing consciousness of the chair I sat in, I regarded that as a new and superior trick. The important thing was Daddy, bringing home boxes of books. Coming home one evening, looking for me specially. He says offhandly, "There's something in the backseat of the car." He speaks to me but doesn't use my name. I run barefoot across the driveway in the dark, lugging in the heavy box. Daddy grins his wide grin as he stands in the hall with a drink and a cigarette, not too close to me.

I kneel on the rug, face down among the books. I may be forgiven for thinking he brought these books home just for me. My siblings might browse through the box at their leisure, read one or two; but none of them read one or two a day, staggering palely out of their bedroom for dinner.

I feel my father's dense, highly colored soul disturbing mine. I listen to the rattle of ice in his glass. Everything about my intelligence—high scores on tests, facility with numbers—pleases him; but nothing so much as the hunger with which I read. He's in the business, of course. He's in the business! As if he runs the Bronx Zoo and the Museum of Natural History, as if he is, not the president, but more important than that.

He makes books. I don't know how exactly, yet I'm terribly impressed. He's in the business. He gets up every morning, goes to New York City. Look what he brings home.

I admire the weight of the books, the bulk of them. How they've been tossed in every which-way, sharp new corners sticking up. I admire their glue-and-paper smell. Mommy says something cautioning—don't tear the jackets, look at them one at a time—but Daddy's grin widens. He knows excess. Certain excesses are permitted.

Sometimes Daddy took us all out for ice cream on summer evenings, four kids crammed into his VW Beetle. He'd drive too fast, whipping up our excitement, run red lights. He'd jolt over the railroad tracks, turn sharply, throwing us from side to side, warning us, with his manic buoyancy, not to tell our mother. I wasn't as much in favor of this as the others were—I've always been physically timid—but I was excited by their excitement, and most of all by his.

He drove with one hand, his elbow out the window, a Lucky between his teeth. That hot, jerky rhythm of his, the wide grin on a face, when I see it now in my mind's eye, I can only call cute—sweet blue eyes, snub nose, the odd juxtaposition, in structure, of the chunky and the elegant—all of it won me soon enough, I was his, flying around screaming in the backseat.

At any excuse my father would sound his horn, yell out the window at the other drivers, "Sonofabitch! Shmuck!"

Nobody ever yelled back. They looked startled. They were all driving big cars and his little car would wiggle through, the curses still warming his lips.

I loved that word *shmuck*. Nobody used it but my father. Its first letters crowded together so closely, holding the sneer on your lips. It was a New York word. "Shmuck! Shmuck!" we'd all yell, then slide down the car door in helpless giggles.

Another joke had to do with nuns. Daddy hated nuns, having been raised Catholic and escaped; we knew nothing about them. When we went to church, it was the Unitarian, which was a bland religion mostly affecting us with boredom. Sometimes we went to church, sometimes my parents slept late. When they slept late we fed ourselves quietly, watched cartoons in the basement.

Yet Johnny was afraid of nuns. He thought they were witches. My father loved this, what he considered to be Johnny's rightful instinct. Whenever we passed a group of those black-clad gliders—their big white faces like dough protruding from the napkin of their wimples—Daddy would point them out and roar with laughter at my brother's response. "Nuns, Johnny, nuns!" Johnny would go under the seat. "Nuns! Shall we run them over, what do you say, get right up on the sidewalk, scare them a little?"

We pressed our feet on Johnny hiding, drumming on his bones; we said we were protecting him. The car jigged and jagged, Daddy's joy sparking in the air. What delight, to hate a nun! To run one over! We understood, we approved, though we'd never met a nun.

Charlotte wanted to discuss the question seriously. "Why do you hate nuns?" Daddy wouldn't answer that, but he told us how, when his mother visited and he had to drive her to church, he made sure to wear only an undershirt and pants. Then she couldn't try to entice him inside. He wouldn't even shave. He was proud of this strategem, told us about it several times—how he escaped going to Mass by the skin of his teeth.

But mostly my father was angry, or I was afraid he would be angry; I stayed away from him. I knew where he was likely to be and I was somewhere else. I was in the Long Grass behind the house, on the third floor, or on the porch—a room I favored for its distance from the rest of the downstairs. The porch had French doors leading to the garden on two sides, a back wall with a fireplace, a black-and-white checkerboard marble floor, wicker chairs. There were plants in pots along the perimeter of the room, and sometimes the cats would chew the leaves. The cats closed their eyes when they chewed. They tilted their heads sideways and I could hear their teeth. Otherwise it was very quiet. I would spend hours in there reading.

I remember particularly one Saturday afternoon in May, 1963 or 1964, I was deeply engrossed in the last third of a book, occasionally listening to the rustle of leaves outside, the distant sound of children playing. I was in the web of my solitude, its sticky filaments reaching out into the air. The air, the world. As the book's pages lapped against my face, the world was becoming mine.

Crack of footsteps on the marble floor. I looked up; it was such a shock: Daddy. Just to see him like that, unexpectedly, overwhelmed me with a shyness that was like being sick, a whiteness stitched into every cell of my being. My father said nothing. He moved slowly, drifting around the room. He gazed out the French doors, smoking.

I had thought it was safe here. He never entered this room except in the evenings when they had parties. I had uncurled like a hedgehog, exposed my soft parts to the wave of the story. I had no idea if he knew I was in the room. He didn't speak or look at me. I sat utterly still, holding my book. I should speak, I thought. Courtesy required it; also I didn't want him to know I was afraid.

He didn't speak. The ash on his cigarette grew longer and he knocked it into his cupped palm. This, I thought, so he didn't have to turn, walk the few steps to the ashtray on the coffee table, acknowledge me? No, I wasn't able to even think that. It was my fault nothing was being said. He didn't even know I was present.

My shyness the barrier to all that is sweet in life. My sister would say, "You have to assert yourself. Nobody likes people who are shy." But if I should speak, what could I say? I had no script for talking to my father. It never happened that I was alone with him.

I thought longingly of my mother. When Mommy was alone she talked to herself. She did this all day, a mild running list of what she had to do next so if you passed a room where she was, you heard that sweet, self-contented murmur. It was easy to say something to her because you knew what she was thinking, the curtains, the groceries, the dog, and you could answer as if she were speaking to you, and she would jump. "I was just talking to myself," she would say each time innocently, and you could pretend you were really bothered about this, that you thought she was crazy. And she would reassure you so kindly that no, she wasn't crazy, don't worry, you don't have a crazy mother, how terrible that would be. Mommy never knew when she was being teased. You could smile, wander away, hear that low murmur pick up again.

I never had any idea what my father was thinking. I didn't let myself wonder, his image in my mind was walled off and shining: I have a father, everyone is supposed to have one, he's Daddy—and then nothing. A very full nothing. It was like the place in fairy tales where the treasure is kept, guarded by flashing swords, a mountain of ice, the whole made invisible, or almost invisible. To think about Daddy, my father, not in the grounding details (Remember when the kittens were born in his sock drawer? Making the socks all bloody? We thought He'll kill them, but he didn't? He turned it into a funny story?) but in terms of love—the thought would barely come to mind when it would slide away as if on oiled casters and there would be something like music, like the theme song of *The Twilight Zone*. A feeling, not quite shame, not quite fear. Grief, I suppose, but I didn't know what that was.

I was awed by it though. Its strangeness.

But here he was, just a man in a room, smoking, and here I was, uncurled. I couldn't avoid the fact of him, and his quietness, his gazing, made me anxious. As he moved from one glass door to another, right to left, I thought he would have to continue that way, making smaller and smaller circles, gazing at the plants, the couch, me.

Feet tucked under, bare-legged, in shorts, book in my lap. Glancing up secretly. I thought, trying to get it straight: I am good. Well-behaved, smart, clean. I am reading and reading is good. I am good.

But something was wrong. The silence was my fault. I was the girl without personality. Was it too late to change? *Change.* But my white shyness would not let me speak. I threw my will against it repeatedly; it held firm. It stitched shut my lips. Daddy finished his cigarette. He stood still for a moment and left the room.

I read my book.

Five

I USED TO serve hors d'oeuvres at my parents' cocktail parties, held on the terrace, in the garden, in the summer. The men were in suits, holding cigarettes, the women in necklaces, patterned dresses, and pointy shoes.

I would wind my way through the party, offering the tray. I was bare-armed and -legged, and of course barefoot. The sun low, its long gold rays lighting up stone and flowers, glasses full of ice cubes, rustling leaves. The warmth was like a hand on my skin. I twisted this way and that, letting the sun have me, each bare part. I silently drank in the gold, experimenting. Is it lovelier if I keep my eyes open a full minute? If I open and shut them rapidly? Or if I shut them a long time, then open to a dazzle?

At the back of the garden, across from the house, was a little stone pool of which I was fond, believing it gave to our property an antique grace. Our house had been built in the twenties; it was a place where flappers had danced and slick-haired men drank gin. I had absorbed something of that era from old children's stories and was not surprised to find the echo of it here, in New Jersey in the 1960s.

I anticipated all sorts of things emerging from that stone pool. A bad-tempered fairy in the shape of a fish, a frog-prince, a white-throated lily whose heavy odor would gradually dull all of us to sleep. But there was only scum, cool and slimy to the touch.

I wandered through, offering my tray. I knew adults mostly cared about drinking and talking, but they did eat. I could make them stop talking by standing in front of them. I loved that moment. Their hesitation—maybe a remark to me!—the odd, long adult fingers picking up a morsel of party food. How they ate it so carefully, wiping their mouths. I mostly watched the men. I mostly served the men, at least in this conscious excited way, imagining myself a forest girl who brings delicacies out of the woods, things I had cooked up over a little fire. I was a runaway girl who lived in the forest, sewing her clothes from leaves. No, I was Margaret, daughter of the house. Offering food, I participated in my mother's power, participated so swooningly it was like being drugged. Perhaps because of that altered state the gleams of my perception were so vivid. The men, for example. What intrigued me was the evidence of their yieldingness. Of how they looked at a girl demanding something—take a canapé, stop talking—and felt obliged to respond. It thrilled me, the merest glance, a courtesy . . .

The gentlest ones got seconds and thirds. The jovial, joking fellows were also favored. They were given first pick if something was hot, or lingered by so they could munch at their leisure. Certain other people were never gone near. I remember that so clearly, deciding who did, who didn't get fed. And if I ever noticed—did I ever notice?—that any grown-up had become aware of how I detoured around him, if he displayed even the slightest of frowns or a moment of confusion, this was not a pleasure to be thought about. It simply beat into my body like the sun.

When my tray was empty, I would wander through the party a little longer, my bare feet exchanging messages with the grass. Children and grass are brothers, I said to myself. I didn't think about the fact that only boys can be brothers; I preferred that locution. The wind lifted my hair, the night was breathing on my arms. I was in a sort of trance, abetted by the dancing motions of my feet, certain regular steps I took following patterns I could feel on the ground. This way, around here, there. Tree, stone, grass. To do it properly brought joy to the inner column of my body.

I didn't hear the adult words at all now; their voices were like the thrum of bees. I threaded in and out, in and out. Beyond the fringes, into the real dark, back to the body-heated silky colored throng. Of course they barely spoke to me. They were grown-ups. I was alone, seeking and binding pleasure, hoarding it. Oh, let me stay awake a little longer. The grass faded to a silvery gray, the bushes turned dark. Mommy would notice me soon, send me to sleep. I had to steal more of the savor of being. It was only me; I was the only one like this.

I WAS OFTEN in love. Mr. Angstrom was the architect who helped my mother design the renovations to our house when I was seven. He was a tall, fair, shy man. I'd run up to him when he came over, fling myself forward, throw my arms around his legs. He suffered my attentions mildly. I appreciated that mildness, how I could twine my beaming self around his passive knees. Because of his light hair I saw him as golden, as something like a woods where sun filters through leaves. His tallness, his stillness. Perhaps he was like a giraffe, munching on the high shrubbery. He stood quietly while I embraced him. I was allowed one moment. Then Mommy would lead him off to the living room, shut the door.

I skulked in the hall, listening to the murmur of voices, rustle of blueprints, snicker of ice in their glasses. I wandered into the kitchen, not going too far. They must have stayed in there an hour, which felt like three. I held a vigil. When Mr. Angstrom emerged from the living room, portfolio in hand, I'd embrace him again, refuse to let go. I thought I deserved a portion of his time.

My mother said he had children of his own to get home to. I thought it was cruel of her to mention it. With a flick of my secret powers I turned those privileged children into wraiths in the wood, calling "Daddy, daddy," as he drove by, oblivious, in his car.

His blond, or strawberry-blond, hair. Mildness, quietness, kindness, tranquility.

My mother showed Mr. Angstrom out. "Margaret, you stay here," she said, then would stand in the driveway with him, talking a little longer. She had rights she didn't even care about.

I fell in love at school. I went to a small private school called Brookside in Upper Montclair. It was a comfortable place, the teachers mostly kind, the work not at all difficult. I was usually ahead in reading and math and spent a lot of time waiting for the class to catch up. I loved to learn but was disappointed with school in this regard. Books, for example. We didn't read real books but absurd things written just for schools where there were words and sentences, paragraphs, but no story. Or else we read little chunks of stories or essays, selections in a series of colored pamphlets with questions on the back page. This made me think that teachers, principals, authorities in general, were much stupider than my mother, with her whole library of books; were in some basic way, like their "books," not to be taken seriously.

I didn't know my place in the social arena. I was never teased at school, yet I was not one of the popular girls either. I was in between. I went back and forth between hanging around with the cool kids as a kind of mascot and befriending one or two of the others. This is a place, of course, a role, and not a bad one, but I thought I had no distinction. I wasn't really anybody, so couldn't be liked too much or disliked too much. And the fear of suddenly becoming someone—the outcast—as if that name *Booger* would shoot through the open window and land on me, like a boomerang finally returning to its owner, wove a soft blanket of terror around me. Soft because it didn't happen—day after day, didn't—and that not-happening, over years, began to register. Also soft because my terror was erotic, it was about being noticed, it was about my sister's wild longing turned to self-hatred turned to hatred of me, about my wild longing turned to self-hatred, and then back, into a secret self-love. I knew, I think, that terror was love, without knowing a thing about it. Only that it was somehow a barrier not to be crossed; a blankness I must sit inside, endlessly berating myself for shyness.

A long time ago, in kindergarten, my classmates had all played together, nobody was popular or unpopular; and Chris Schultz and I would kiss, every day at recess, in the playground tunnel. Soft dry lips touching soft dry lips. Leaning against the cool slidy wall of the tunnel, breathing in its metallic smell—it smelled like a nickel—doing what the grown-ups did, as the other kids climbed on top of the tunnel, feet thumping above us, occasionally a red-cheeked face hanging upside down looking in. Smiling.

Sitting quietly with Chris. His thin shoulders, face turned to mind. His wide-set brown eyes—brown, brown, brown—and the brownish color of his skin beneath dusty freckles. That moment when our lips touched. I expected something which didn't happen, but another thing happened. A thing with no color, no sparkle, almost nothing, but which was good.

Kissing was good. I didn't know why.

Kindergarten ended, and I missed Chris fiercely for three months. In September I was so excited, saw him in the schoolyard—and waited for him to say hello. He didn't say hello. Not on the first day or the second. The reason for this, I assumed, was that I had been diagnosed with a lazy eye over the summer and was wearing an eye patch over my right eye, the strong one. An oblong, flesh-colored patch that Johnny assured me made me ugly. Chris didn't speak to me. He was hanging around the boys.

On the third day he said hello and I said hello, but then we didn't know what to say.

Was it my patch that scared him? That he thought was gross? The teacher had explained it to the class first thing, and they all nodded solemnly, nobody teased me . . . I didn't quite understand this lack of teasing. Even Jimmy had said I looked like a pirate and then laughed at the incongruity of that, so my soft scared plumpness came vividly to mind.

Chris started spending all his time with the boys, who had decided, at some point over the summer, that girls were cooties. From then on, they'd band together and jeer at us, or run away from us when we wanted to play, or flip our skirts up. Chris didn't do anything mean, but he clung to the other boys, still quiet as ever but in a different way, like a Chris-shadow. I didn't understand. What had we done that the boys should hate us? We hadn't done anything, we were the same. It wasn't fair. Once I got so angry I tried to fight back in the same spirit—to pull down a boy's pants in retaliation for my skirt being flipped up. I couldn't quite manage the zipper. But even the attempt shocked that boy so much—he squawked like a chicken for months, his flinty little face bright red. For almost a year he swaggered, boy the size of a burnt match, telling this story, hitching his pants up. Other boys guffawed at his description of what I had dared to do—I kept trying to explain that it was *only fair*—and the girls listened in a deep silence, as if they were dead. It seemed to me it was in all of us girls, this liking of boys, the not understanding and the sadness.

In first grade I had to wear an eye patch every day; in second grade I got glasses. The day I was scheduled to pick them up, I wept hopelessly in bed. My mother was cajoling me, telling me I had to get dressed. I knew I had to—had to obey her because she was the mother, had to wear glasses so I could see—I wasn't defiant. I understood. I simply had no motive to do anything anymore. Or only cry: how much I had wanted to be loved by a boy and never would be. Crying like one of those weekends when rain lashes against the house, pauses, then beats down with a greater fury. It bent my body, exhausted me, but I couldn't stop.

My mother said, "If you get up, I'll make you pancakes for breakfast." I went still then, profoundly embarrassed. I stopped crying. I got dressed as she smiled, ate like the little pig she must assume I was, filling my mouth with syrup. Sitting at the table in a strange, in-folded tranquility, my remaining tears a shimmer beneath my skin.

When I was in first or second grade, my sister was sick for awhile, maybe a week, though in my memory it seems a month or more, Johnny had not yet started school. Jimmy and I rode the schoolbus alone. We were at the beginning of the route and he'd let me sit next to him until his best friend Michael's stop.

We'd walk down the hill, wait for the bus, five minutes, in our zipped jackets, carrying books. Jimmy had lots of books, I had only my blue binder and a softcover math workbook. He wore khakis or corduroy pants, I wore a skirt, ankle socks, and oxfords. I was with Jimmy, just the two of us. Boy, girl, brother, sister: It was his job to look out for me. Mommy wouldn't have let me walk down the hill alone. We talked. What we talked about I have no idea. Just the tone of his voice, conversational, normal.

Then the bus came, empty but for one lone boy in neither of our classes, and the driver. We climbed into the warm, vibrating tunnel, took our seats, me beside Jimmy. Nobody else. (Not Charlotte! Charlotte home in bed as we move farther and farther away.) Ten minutes. When I picture it now I see us as orphans, riding a bus to some unknown destination. The tall boy by the window, his small sister beside. The two look alike, their upturned noses, lightly freckled (he has more freckles than she), generous lips, and blue eyes.

The boy studies his homework. Maybe they're going away to school, to a boarding school in the English countryside. The girl likes school. She likes to learn, it fills her up, and she loves to lean against his shoulder, read a few sentences from his difficult book.

He understands that difficult book. He says that she's too young to understand it, and his voice glides with happiness because he is older and wiser. She's happy for the same reason.

When Michael got on the bus—tall lumbering boy, ducking his head as he climbed on—the first pleasure was over. I'd move one seat back. Jimmy and Michael would put their heads together, and I'd turn my attention to the green metal of the bus wall, the high stiff green foam seats. There was a hump on the floor in front of my feet on which I could slide my shoes, making a scratchy noise that was awful and wonderful. It went up my legs, into my crotch, like a buzz. I'd savor that, and lean my cheek against the vibrating window.

The bus had its own smell, not like a car. The driver was way ahead and had nothing to do with me. I was given this long emptiness, rows and rows of seats. Filling up now but there were still pockets of emptiness. I could float out of my own body, sit in all those places—this was such a prickly pleasure, like running my hand gently over a dress pattern glinting with pins. Then gradually settling. Yes, I was there, rows ahead—I could almost see myself. Feel that other seat, other window. I liked it, being here and there. Like two feet on either side of a stream. (The kind of streams you get in fields after a rain, swift channels of water.) It was disconcerting, however, to have to move quickly when some physical body plopped into the seat.

Dry, dusty green of the bus interior. Camp green, camouflage green. Outside, the moister green of the trees. The trees with their tall branches that I often imagined cutting down—I had a long, invisible knife that could shoot out the window of any vehicle I traveled in—to feed my dependents who lived underground. These creatures had no name, were more primitive than trolls or gnomes, and utterly helpless; they lived in caves and would die without the bounty of these trees, rolling down chutes from the unknowable upper world. It soothed me to feed them the thick white pith of the trees, the tender, candylike twigs. I cut down wood after wood; there could never be too much. If I sliced through a few houses along the way, that was unfortunate.

Jimmy and Michael whispered in the seat in front of me. I couldn't hear the words. I watched their heads tipped together. Pieces of their hair mingled, a straight hank of Michael's lying on Jimmy's darker curl—funny how they couldn't feel it. Sometimes separate vertical strands met in a shaft of sun.

More boys got on the bus. One, two, then several at a time. The boys clustered in the seats around my brother: in front of him, to the side of him, beside me. He was the magnet for all the bigger boys. They wanted my seat, and they didn't want me listening. They told Jimmy to make me move but he wouldn't. "As long as you don't bother us," he said.

I knew I had no right to be sitting among the big boys, no matter how quietly, absorbing their laughter and breath. I didn't belong, but there I was. Jimmy allowed me. (I barely even glanced at the kids in my class. I assumed they must envy me.)

I took it all in—the jokes, the insults, the opinions. Boys hanging over seat backs, leaning into the aisle, arguing over placement, pushing each other. The swirling forces around the calm boy in the center, my brother, with his low-voiced ironic wit, his floating grin. They vied for his attention, whole torsos leaning over the seat, as if about to topple down headfirst in his lap, words flying out of their faces. He mediated quarrels. He let them all talk, and then he talked, and what he said was the authoritative thing. Sitting down low in his seat, his smallish head cocked. He liked to add an exotic twist to each piece of gossip offered, something more far out or subtly dirty than they had thought of. I usually didn't get it and lots of the other boys didn't either. They would kick their seats restlessly, faces eager. Jimmy and Michael, or Jimmy and Smitty, laughing.

I FELL IN love with Michael. For awhile I spent my allowance buying him Ring Dings, that chocolate-covered, cream-filled cake he had a passion for. On Saturday afternoons I'd present the Ring Ding to him unwrapped on a plate, its aroma teasing my nostrils, in full view of the other boys, Jimmy's gang in the basement.

Jimmy liked to watch me offer the Ring Ding. His eyes cool and luminous: Was he sympathetic? Amused? It was impossible to tell.

Michael would blush. He would mumble a thank you, eat the cake head down as we watched, the other boys—not Jimmy—snickering. My mood was something like exaltation. Jimmy's eyes and silence protected me. I didn't mind the snickers, nor believe that Michael's embarrassment was greater than what must be pleasure, to be thus singled out. I was giving him a *good* thing. I looked at the cream on Michael's slightly protruding upper lip, the crumbs of chocolate on his shirt collar. He was a handsome, high-colored, well-taken-care-of boy. Not slender and limber like my brother but large, a little awkward. Yet it was an awkwardness contained within the look he had of being loved. You could almost see his mother hovering over him, combing his shiny brown hair—it fell in a flap over his high forehead, his large, soft eyes—buying him a fine wool jacket. It gave me a curious satisfaction to watch him eat.

Six

EVERY NIGHT THE year I was seven and eight, I would climb out of bed after I was supposed to be asleep and creep down the hall to Jimmy's room. I crept the way he had taught me: Indian walking, on the sides of my feet. It made me feel strangely unbalanced yet interestingly aware of my body, my plump torso and nimble legs, rounded slim arms inside a short pink nylon nightie.

Long lit-up hall: occasional sounds of grownups below me. My parents were drinking scotch and reading, or quietly talking. Lots of space between us; the ceilings were twenty feet downstairs. Yet they don't seem too far away. My mother is listening—she'll come upstairs if we're not quiet—or my father will come, threatening to take off his belt. Mostly he doesn't bother. The downstairs is his territory.

I would meet Johnny in the hall outside Jimmy's door; Charlotte was already inside. Johnny—fox or monkey, anything that darts or scampers, that dives for cover or leaps away—was, in regard to our brother, also a petitioner.

Sometimes Jimmy wouldn't let us in. He and Charlotte wanted to be big kids together, performing their mystery cult of what we would never know. Johnny would look at me as if it was my fault we were exiled. We'd shuffle away, Indian-walk back. We'd park ourselves in front of our brother's door and eavesdrop. All we could hear was the tinny sound of the radio, the rise and fall of their voices. Johnny was worried that I had tempted him into something that would make Jimmy displeased with us; I didn't think he understood the rights of vassals. "We are guarding his door," I'd say. "We're protecting him from assassins."

"There aren't any assassins," replied Johnny, who at all times strenuously resisted my fancies. "We live in New Jersey, they don't do that here. Anyway, Jimmy's just a kid in school."

I'd smirk in the dark, sure of my ground. "Assassins can be anywhere, and what do you know about it?" He didn't know. He didn't read. Against his will he suspected I might have superior information, but he never surrendered. He devoted himself to rejecting my every statement, and for some reason this made me bold and I invented more freely. "There are more assassins in New Jersey than anywhere in the world. Sometimes they kill an innocent person just for practice."

We were making too much noise. The door opened—he was slim and stern—"Hit the road, Jack."

We'd get up and slouch to our rooms. Perhaps our mother would call up the stairs, "You-all go to sleep now," and then we were relieved, saved by the adventure of having to hurry. I'd dive under my covers, close my eyes, breathe evenly. My mother might come upstairs, her tread slow and calm, pausing in my doorway. "Are you asleep, Margaret?" That's the question you can't answer yes to without lying—which for some reason delighted me. I wanted to laugh but I didn't, I lay there still, pretending it mattered more than it did if she found me awake. Her lemony tall shape in the doorway smoothed the tensions of the night; with her, in her, I was placid, relieved of awareness.

She'd leave, moving down the hall. I was satisfied when she doused the light in Jimmy's room, driving Charlotte out of there like a cat.

But sometimes Jimmy would let us into his room. The door swung open and he stepped back; we trotted in without a word. Jimmy lounged against his pillows, Charlotte beside him; Johnny and I curled at the bottom of the bed. I was afraid of my sister yet I wanted her there. It had to be the four of us. Two boys, two girls. That was the proper number. Jimmy was our leader, Johnny and I the subjects, Charlotte . . .

I see her lying there like a smoldering log, fiery beauty, painful beauty, yet in a way I don't see her at all. I shut her off, I make her less than human. A two-dimensional character while the rest of us are three dimensional. It's the only way to feel safe, and yet I wanted her with us, absolutely. One thing I knew was that the only possibility of things being put right lay in this magical number: four. The four children at the beginning of the story. I could relax in the perfection of the figure we made, everything accounted for; the beginning of a journey.

Jimmy's bed was our vessel. It had a high headboard and footboard of brittle dark wood. It was like the three-masted ships that discovered America: the *Niña*, the *Pinta*, the *Santa Maria*. In the lower right-hand corner of the headboard he had carved his name with a penknife, the *y* of Jimmy curling around to cradle the other letters. I was impressed that he had dared to mark the furniture this way, as if it were completely his, and not on loan from the grown-ups.

His signature was neat and unmistakable, like the alligator on a shirt. He put it in the corner of his drawings, on the flyleaf of a book, here. It floated, exactly the same each time.

Jimmy also wrote his name in the air with his finger. He drew pictures in the air, and this was something I could imitate. "It saves paper," he said, and, "Nobody knows what you're drawing." I liked that and the give of the air and the trails of my fingers which I saw as fire. I would write my name and any interesting words I had heard and draw pictures of faces; it soothed me. Watching his fingers was soothing in a different way, like being conducted.

Secretly I thought I had him beat in the area of signatures because my name was longer and so contained more power. I had the other longest name in the family and I believed this was because there was more of me. For this reason, I never shortened it.

We listened to the black clock radio by Jimmy's bed. "The Little Old Lady from Pasadena," and "The Lion Sleeps Tonight," were two of my favorites as well as a gooey love song called "Norman." Jimmy explained to us why certain songs were cool. All that I remember on the subject is that songs that weren't about love were cool and that some songs about love managed to be cool. The Beach Boys and the Beau Brummels were especially cool. The Beatles were okay for girls.

Jimmy knew many things, not only about rock-and-roll. He would expound on the fantastic tracking abilities of African Bushmen, or the fact that in the South people ate fried rattlesnake for dinner, or how our mother's silk dresses came from thread spun from a worm's ass. Johnny denied that our mother could possibly traffic in worms' asses. Jimmy said how interesting it was, listen, the worms fed on the leaves of mulberry trees like the one in our garden, spun cocoons, and then a human worker collected the cocoons, which were made of silk.

"How could they be?" You bought silk in stores.

"Because that's where silk comes from. That's what it is. I told you."

"Mom doesn't know," Johnny insisted.

"She knows." And then, he went on to say, the cocoons were

unraveled carefully for thread. Spun into cloth. (I knew about spinning: poor princesses forced to spin cloth day and night.) All of this far away, in China, though we had a little mulberry tree in our own garden where Jimmy and Charlotte would sit, dropping mulberries on our heads. Though our mother wore silk nearly always when she went out.

I always believed my brother. He was so smart; he read nonfiction. Someday, Jimmy said, he was going to canoe down the Amazon, collecting specimens. There were thousands of kinds of animals, and plants, too, that nobody had ever seen. He was going to go to Australia and to Greenland, which was really white. To China, which was called Red China and was our enemy though we were not at war.

"It's a cold war. That means they can't fight us because we have the hydrogen bomb, the H bomb which is a hundred times bigger than the A bomb." I was impressed with both these bombs—O America!—and couldn't fathom either one.

"Where is it?" asked Johnny.

"What?"

"The bomb."

"In the White House. Under the president's bed." Jimmy smirked. "I hope he doesn't have a dog."

"Not really?"

"Who knows? They don't tell anybody where they keep it. But the president has a box with a button, and if he pushes the button KABOOM!"

"What if he leaves the box on the bed and somebody sits on it?"

"No, I'm kidding, it's in a locked suitcase. There's this Secret Service guy, see, who has it locked to his wrist at all times. Even when he's on the crapper."

My brothers were fond of the subject of war, and I enjoyed it, too. Switchblades and pistols, machine gun nests. My brothers had toy machine guns, Tommy guns, and camo suits that I longed for. My mother said, "If you don't want dolls for Christmas, of course you can get a gun like the boys." I didn't dare, it would make my brothers too angry. Besides, I wanted dolls, I had to have dolls, with their pale, odd-smelling limbs, curled hair, and long dresses, their sweet faces and eyes that blinked. Dolls were the most powerful of toys, incarnating the invisible dimension. But I did have a hankering for a weapon of mass destruction.

Most of all I loved listening to Jimmy describe strategy. His slim body would lean forward as he explained flanking, pincer movements, ambush. He was very pleased with the concept of ambush—both boys were—though Jimmy said that Johnny didn't have the patience for it. He had the patience for things done entirely alone, but conflict made him too excitable; he couldn't fight by waiting. Jimmy said this not particularly as an insult, and Johnny listened. It pleased us when our brother noticed things about our characters.

I had my fantasies about war. About crisp, decisive action, heroics, the intense dreamy glare of the moments when you cross a minefield, each foot laid down in slow motion. I had heard about what people felt at times of extreme peril—their senses heightened radically, the meaning of life become clear—and this fascinated me. To risk death and live. Forever after holding that memory like a jewel. *To have been brave.* Or to kill somebody; what was that like? To blow some bastard's head off so the brains fell out and, as Jimmy said, maybe a pig would come out of the woods and eat them. "That's gross," Charlotte said.

"You're gross," I told her. She pinched me. I kicked her. Jimmy told us to stop. I made faces at her.

Jimmy reminded us that this guy wasn't even your enemy, just some shmuck from the other side. "I hate all the Japs and Jerries," Johnny exclaimed, his little bony face alight with ferocity; but I understood. The exquisite irony of war against someone you weren't even mad at.

Lying on Jimmy's bed, listening as he whistles to the songs on the radio. Breath made music. I couldn't whistle.

In the jungle/The mighty jungle/The lion sleeps tonight . . .

It was Jimmy who decided when it was time to move. Lying on his bed, utterly limp, only the whistle between his teeth and the faint rise of his chest betraying life, it seemed that he would never want to do anything more strenuous than dismiss us with a wave of his slender-wristed right hand. If his bed were a ship or a car, if he could steer it lying down, he'd roll us off of it, he'd be out of here . . .

Then he'd sit up abruptly. "H.R.," he said. Relief loosened me to a prancing feline state. Or rather I felt as I had when I wore my black cat costume on Halloween—perked ears, tail, soft feet with the claws painted on, and me.

H.R. was House-Roaming, a game we began when the house was still new, its wonderful hugeness needing to be conquered by darkness. H.R. was obvious—sneaking, spying, stealing—but it was also subtle. You had to be of the house. You had to know certain things which were never spoken of and feel the bond of blood as an unbreakable cord. Whenever my siblings seemed in danger of forgetting this, I would remind them.

Jimmy was out of the room already, crouching at the top of the formal front staircase. "Stay back," he said. "I'm going to reconnoiter."

I tried to obey but my siblings didn't; they flowed behind him so I did, too, sliding down each wide, polished step. Too quickly. I stayed close to the banister.

The big gleaming hall beckoned—Jimmy was almost there. On the far wall the tall mirror reflected the chandelier above the first landing of the stairs, the yellow glow of the kitchen behind us, and the dimmer silvery light from the living room to the left.

Our crouched bodies in that landscape were tiny yet powerful; we were the only things moving.

Jimmy crept across the wide expanse, his grin when he turned around to us—his stuck-out butt and dramatic gestures—a pantomime of what he was doing. I followed him, a little quicker now and more careless. Hugging the wall, I peered over his shoulder to where our parents sat side by side on the living-room couch, reading or chatting, drinks and cigarettes at hand.

Mommy and Daddy. Like painted statues, of a height, both fully dressed. Daddy in a suit. The warm pinks, aquas, and ice blues of my mother's clothes, her bright lipstick. They contain so much of power, glamor, and charm, yet how constrained they are in their shoes and wristwatches. How thin my mother, how bitter the smoke of her cigarette. Adults like everything bitter—black coffee, whiskey, bitter vegetables. They don't move much. They drive cars but can't climb trees or skateboard. They never run around or play. At the ocean they merely wet themselves up to the hips, then come back to lie like reptiles in the sun.

It's a kind of mummified life they lead. I could never get anyone to tell me exactly when one crosses over.

After we looked at them, we'd creep up the stairs again, sit on the top steps. The steps were so broad and smooth, stained such a welcoming golden-brown, the risers painted white, that I could imagine living my whole life on them, sleeping and eating and conducting all my business.

Each step was different. Each had a personality, a social status and private life. It would never have occurred to me that someday I would forget even their most obvious characteristics, that the whole mythology would be swept away and only this dull grown-up remain, fumblingly describing a flight of stairs.

You, reader, if you can, remember. The parents are below; we are above; here are the stairs. The parents grow tired climbing them while we do it effortlessly and slide down on our bottoms.

We sense the living tree. We lie on our bellies, communing with wood, while looking down through the banister at the dog crossing the hall or Daddy, his routine mission for ice. Even when the hall was empty it wasn't empty—the big mirror gleamed, reflecting another staircase.

The top stair, the second, the third. Territories, alliances. Royal beings who lived inside the wood. When we were present they had to hide, but sent messages up through our skin. Was this my own fantasy, or shared? It seems to me it belonged to my elder siblings, elaborated in the old house before I could talk, which is why it was so precious, and probably I seized on it when they were getting bored. It lodged in me, not reworked as were my own stories, but left alone like a ship submerged in water. Do you remember, I might ask, about the stairs? Even then—a year or two later—they didn't.

Up one stair, down one stair. Such a difference in perspective, never enough time to think it through. My siblings would become impatient. They always wanted to be doing something active while I only wanted them with me while I did things in my mind. There were so many effects of space, of the visual world, and it changed with who you were with so it couldn't all be known by myself. I might want Jimmy and Charlotte—and Johnny, though Johnny was always creeping—to sit still for a half an hour while I felt who I was in their company interact with the rich polished wood of the stairs, the long emptiness of the center of the house. The drama of the four of us! It was exquisite; not just being with the elders, but the way we each had our place in the family, each of us a different age, like a step, connected, and nobody else anywhere related to us as we were to each other. It was a metaphysical pleasure, this number four, a sensual overwhelm, to be thus a part of. The joy of stairs. I could stay there all night. Going up and down, up and down. Rivers of sensation, each degree of upness or downness and where each other sibling was placed—distinct patterns that brought with them pictures, stories . . . (all the while I was trying to fit these pictures and stories into the vaguely remembered fantasy I had inherited, which must be the true story).

Why did nobody else feel it? As we abandoned the stairs, crept down the long upstairs hall, I trailed behind, pausing now and then to absorb the essence of each discrete area. If I half shut my eyes, didn't move for a second, it was easy to tell where the barriers were. The zone of influence in front of each bedroom, for example, had strict borders, and between each zone was a buffer, a couple of feet of no-man's-land, waxed wood floor, creamy-white-shadowed wall, which made me feel specially excited. Imagine an alcove in an old church where a small statue used to stand. Imagine turning a page and finding it blank—a printer's mistake—and not wanting, quite yet, to continue with the novel. But I had nothing to compare this feeling to. No name for it, nor for this place. Nobody ever thought about it—the zone of wall between bedrooms. It was just there, a gap in the fabric of things. If I concentrated, I could feel the wind from the other side; my body, my breathing, loosened.

Mocking remarks, admonitions from the others. "Why are you always behind?" I would trot to catch up. And I see myself, soft-fleshed, in my short nightgown, hurrying, glancing back with desire at some empty stretch of floor, feeling exquisite sensations and knowing there was something ridiculous about this. My siblings laughed if I tried to explain how things looked to me, while everything they said was somehow too sinewy, as if they were jackals chewing on the world.

Our first stop was the blue guest room, where my grandmothers slept. This was a big cold room full of antiques or what I thought were antiques, old-lady furniture with carved legs and feet and tall windows curtained in lace. It was painted French blue, which is to say a spooky gray-blue, and the floorboards creaked. There was a little anteroom, like a parenthesis, before you entered the room proper.

We had grandmothers but no grandfathers. There was something deliberate about this.

Jimmy would enter first and we would follow. There was nothing to do in this room. Sometimes Jimmy rifled through the night-table drawers, finding a pack of matches from a New York restaurant. Charlotte would go to the window, peer outside. My tall sister seemed to grow taller standing by the window, looking out at the tops of trees.

Grandmothers—so remote in age, in their nearly useless bodies. My mother's mother was friendly but excessively elegant and not skilled at talking to children. I liked her rambling house, all on one floor in Houston, her terrace with flowers, her golden retrievers, John-John and Honeybun. Her shy and ladylike gaiety, her vagueness, her big soft old nose.

My father's mother, who lived in Mississippi and visited twice a year, was a different sort of creature altogether. Short and blond, ferociously intent, Nana had once been a beauty. She imagined she was still desirable and behaved with a coyness we found repulsive. As if she thought we were fools.

In the case of our mother's mother we felt sorry for her that she was old. But while Grandmommy wore her age bravely, Nana was made monstrous by hers. She didn't keep secret what one must keep secret: the longing for a second chance, the coveting of young flesh. We didn't know it but saw it, a sickly light coming out of her.

Nana was sly. She was attracted to slyness and malice and looked for it in our play. She would follow us into our rooms and watch us—a peculiar intensity in her gaze, ever-present little smile. Her big pale blue eyes in communication with that twitching mouth, a private conversation we felt but didn't understand.

We wanted to shake her off but had to be polite. "Nana came all this way to see you," our mother said. We knew Mommy didn't like Nana either. Daddy couldn't stand her. Yet she came, and we had to be polite. She would stand in her long dresses and clumpy black shoes—her ankles were weak—holding a cigarette. Her big head and bigger bosom. Her eyes in search. Our play as opaque and innocent as we could make it; we played like children in a how-to-read book. But she always spotted a trace of cruelty. Then she would scold us, her smile triumphant. Our souls fluttering up to the ceiling like birds, or the shadows of birds.

I see us in memory retreating from one room to another, Nana in pursuit. Calling out in that heavy, slow southern voice, that voice like cloth dragged through a swamp, "Where have you children got to? Jimmy? Charlotte? Margaret? Johnny? Nana's here to see you." Why did our parents even tell her we were born? And Johnny's mad hate of her—worse than mine, his whole agitated little brain whirling, you could see it in his eyes, he might fly apart.

At bedtime Nana would insist on being the one to sing to us, sitting on our beds so we had to scrunch over. She sang in her pure soprano, showing off her voice. She liked to tell us which of her grandchildren had inherited her voice: Vicky, Peggy, Bobby . . . I don't remember; only I wasn't one of them, so I didn't care. She seemed to realize that this might be a problem—she'd have me sing and when I revealed my utter lack of tunefulness, she looked confused—but kept on with it, as if I might conveniently turn into Vicky.

I remember the song about Ireland being a little piece of heaven that had fallen into the sea. I liked it—it was sentimental—but Nana was half Irish, and she would tell me, almost weeping, that I was Irish, too, so I had to privately deny it.

Not entirely. I knew I was Irish: I had fairy blood. She was Catholic Irish, which was different, a wickedness. In the fairy tale, the girl who married the merman, the sweet, kind merman, and went to live in the sea, abandoned her mer-family when she heard the churchbell ring. For the sake of her religion she left behind forever her fish-tailed children.

My parents agreed with me about Nana's religion. Daddy hated Catholicism and my mother thought it misguided. My mother would have stayed with her children in the sea. She told me about the Yeats play *The Countess Cathleen*, where the countess sells her soul to feed the poor in Ireland. "What happens?" I asked.

My mother twinkled. "She didn't go to hell."

"So if the women had stayed with her mer-children, she wouldn't have lost her soul after all?"

"I don't know. What do you think?"

"I think mermaids have souls. The stories get it wrong."

My mother nodded, pleased.

The antidote to the blue guest room was the yellow guest room. On the other side of the house, near our parents' room, tucked into a nook by the stairs, it was small, cozy, and warm. It had a fitted, grass-green carpet, the only fitted carpet in the house, and a bed with a dotted-swiss bedspread. The heating system, which scanted the blue guest room, indulged the yellow. And what a yellow it was: eggs sunny-side up, the itsy-bitsy-teeny-weeny-yellow-polka-dot bikini of the popular song.

This was where our babysitters slept, when they spent the night. When our parents stayed in the city too late the girl, Sue, Kathy, Marie, would change into her ribboned nightgown, brush out her thick hair. Charlotte and I would watch, or investigate her beauty products: Noxema cold cream, pale lipsticks. This teenage stuff wasn't as heavily scented as what our mother used, nor so darkly colored. I liked the dry silvery pinks of these semivirginal girls. I liked the cheap plastic cases and the names of the colors.

Sometimes I would knock on the door late at night just to see the babysitter in bed, reading a paperback romance. Her hair would be spread out on the pillow, surrounding her creamy face. There was nothing dangerous about babysitters. They played cards with us, made popcorn, they were cheerful, and even when they kissed their boyfriends in the darkened living room, the boys would eventually leave.

They wore turtlenecks and kilts, loafers and bobby socks, corduroy jackets. Their hair was held back with headbands or gathered in ponytails. They smelled like soaps and shampoo and flowery thin perfumes; one day I would be one of them. Boys would pick me up in cars. Maybe I would even live in a house like they did, a house that fronted directly on the street with a postage-stamp front yard, laundry on the line, a little house . . .

Babysitters were like Betty and Veronica from the comic book, though more sensible and solid. I remember the thickness of their bodies—not fatness but just warmth and smoothness, arms, stomachs. Healthy girls. Babysitters would pull up their shirts to show us tan lines or freckles, they made elaborate pretenses of teaching us to pull taffy because they wanted the sugar, too. They wore long flannel nightgowns and bunny slippers. They were shy of my mother. They told Charlotte more than they told me but were nice to me: I felt cleaner in their gaze. My mother would sometimes say in surprise at my ardor, "Oh, you're going to be much prettier than—" It wasn't prettiness I wanted so much as to be normal, in a headband and white sweater, bouncy limbs and cheerful eyes.

We grew somnolent in the yellow guest room. The warmth was like a drug, the wall-to-wall carpet so soothing. As green as grass—like having a sunny glade inside the house—and the room was taller than it was wide, like a gift box or an elevator. My siblings fell back inside themselves, and I, too, began to drift. This somnolence was magical. Like Sleeping Beauty we'd sleep a hundred years—and then everything would be ours . . . Jimmy's lashes over high cheekbones, his crisp hair. And Charlotte: the great length of her. Her righteous force, like a tree alive, and, as in the stories of trees coming alive, awful. Aweful. But quiet now. Her chestnut-colored smell. Robin Hood and Maid Marian.

I wanted to keep us here in the yellow guest room, no parents, no friends, and if it took a hundred years' sleep to bind us, so be it. I was willing to give up the rest of this century, everyone I knew, my mother. I would do it. Let the door disappear into the wall, even the seam of the door disappearing. Let the room be furred over with the mold of impregnable magic—Jimmy and Charlotte wouldn't know it was my doing. They would think we were in some enchantment together, nobody's fault, it would be an adventure. Then we'd have to depend on each other.

As I daydreamed about this, brooding *go to sleep, go to sleep,* Jimmy would stir restlessly and Charlotte yawn, stretching her jaws. Then they'd be up, just like that, alert and listening, on their aristocratic feet.

Jimmy led the way into our parents' room. He walked calmly, back straight, I noticed a freckle on his neck where the downy hairs curled. We halted on the threshold. This was where Daddy would come if he came upstairs, where I always half expected to find bloody remains.

"I'm going to brain you," our father used to say when he was angry. "Beat the living daylights out of you." He never fulfilled these threats so I never learned what they actually meant. How do you brain a person? Where were my living daylights? There were moments, as I got older, when I liked to hear him threaten, because I knew he wasn't going to follow through. His real fury came in words. To threaten to beat me and then not do it; didn't it mean he loved me?

"He'll do it someday," Jimmy said. "Brain one of us."

"But what does it mean?"

"You'll see."

We filed inside. A wavering, red and black—the colors of the rug—toxic shimmer which was also home, the two bodies we came out of.

The room was dominated by a queen-size bed and the vast Oriental. The walls were painted white, the bedclothes disarranged. Books and papers were strewn about, as were articles of clothing, packs of cigarettes and ashtrays. It was not that the room was dirty, or even as messy as I now keep my own, but that it startled me, how richly and carelessly they lived. Nobody to tell them to make their bed. Her silky dresses and flimsy stockings draped over chairs. Magazines. I hated the titles of their magazines—*Vogue* because I didn't know what it meant, *Esquire* because it reminded me of my southern relatives who sent birthday cards to my brothers with *esquire* written after their names. But mostly, in that room, I was affected by the smell.

It was the smell of sensual indulgence, by which I mean not sex (though maybe sex, too) but smoking and the adornment of cosmetics. Tobacco, perfume—those were the pleasures of the grown-ups, and they were pleasures enjoyed every day, continuously. Her dressing table was crammed with bottles, its drawers were full, and cigarette cartons were piled up on the bureau, more than they would need in a week. It was like Halloween or Christmas, that surfeit, and we moved through it as if through a bewitching fog.

Jimmy sat down on the bed. He lounged back on the pillows, pretended to snore, then lit one of Daddy's cigarettes, blew smoke rings. Johnny would slide out of the clothes then, demanding a puff, so I would, too, playing the game, and Jimmy warned us mockingly about stunting our growth—this was mostly aimed at

Johnny, whom he called the Runt—he would dole out the cigarettes, one for him, one for us to share (Charlotte didn't want any) as if everything were just as usual, but I never failed to notice. Crossing the threshold of this room, Jimmy transformed. His posture changed, his bones became lighter. He began to resemble the boys at school, the clowns always grabbing attention, or more oddly, a grasshopper. A slightly built boy with a reedy neck, holding a cigarette, sharp elbows sticking out; his big eyes, agitation, which he tried to hide, pawing through our father's stuff.

I didn't want this vision, it was like the end of everything. If he was merely a nervous, clever boy, if boys were only boys—I looked away. I sank down to the magical level, concerned myself with the dangerous energies.

These were obvious in my parents room. The furniture was hostile to us because we had the power of motion, violence lurked by the window our father longed to throw us out of, there were reptiles under the bed. Their bed was so big, and there was a moistness to it, like a swamp. I hated finding my mother in it. Daddy I didn't mind, he liked to be in bed, all tucked up in his suit of white underwear, he looked at home, but my mother . . .

In the big bed she looked so small. Face on the pillow like a cupcake. A tiny mommy. It was upsetting.

I set my mind to defuse the danger, gathering the scary places—door, window, bed, under the bed—sucking them into myself, surrounding them with coils of thought, sticky and luminous strands. I barely knew what I was doing, only that I was doing something. Margareting the room. I was used to it. It wasn't pleasant or unpleasant; it was a job. Complicated, fairly arduous, removing me from where I was. I was accustomed to my dislocation, how I would glance around having coated every threat with glistening thought only to find that things were different now, time had gone by. It was only then that I would feel confused.

My sister was investigating our mother's jewelry box. I joined her, unable to stay away once she opened the lid. This jewelry box was a three-tiered affair of smooth black leather containing pearls and rhinestones, glass beads, silver bracelets: Mommy's plunder. Every time I looked in I wanted to upend the box, scatter the snarls of jewels on the bed, on the floor. I discreetly tried on a necklace.

And so did my sister, a lovely garnet one I hadn't noticed. Elegant. We looked at ourselves in the mirror. She was tall and queenly. Her face was big, her eyes were big and bright with a confident shine. I was small and blobby. My cat's-eye glasses, chosen by my mother, made me resemble, in my opinion, a retard.

Charlotte stood too close to me. I wanted her, didn't want her. Even the cells of her body were dominant; I felt the edges of my flesh crest, harden where she nearly touched me. We took turns palming the silver dollar, minted in the year of her birth, that my mother kept in a slot on the top tier of the jewelry box. This was a sort of amulet; if it disappeared, who knew what would happen to Mommy? If Charlotte kept it too long, what would happen? I, on the other hand, needed it, deserved it . . . wouldn't let go . . . my sister sneered, said I'd spend it on candy if I thought I could get away with it. I snatched the garnet necklace off of her, looped it around my own neck, my first choice discarded. I was ready for a fight. But Charlotte didn't fight. She put on the necklace I'd let go.

Immediately that became the beautiful one, the only beautiful one. Green glass beads. I didn't understand. I stared at her, stricken, and she smiled.

Jimmy was going through Daddy's pockets, stealing quarters, counting dollar bills. Johnny was in Mommy's closet, plunging into her clothes. I could hear his rustling passage, see him peering from between the silks. He might emerge wearing high heels, a long, drapey dress, a fox stole. The bright glass eyes of the fox rhymed with his own as he promenaded, and whatever he was—the funny splendor of his soul—provoked in me a new desire. For a moment I was free of my vassalage to Jimmy and Charlotte, my absorption with the invisible world: I wanted something else. What?

Seven

MY FAVORITE BOOKS were the Narnia series, in which four children enter the magic country. Lucy, the youngest girl, goes first, through the coats in the wardrobe where she is hiding because her siblings have teased her, the coats gradually giving way to a snowy wood. She has tea with a talking badger in his den, but when she gets back no one believes her—she's only been gone a second. Peter, her eldest brother, wants to believe her but is too rational to make the leap. Then Edmund goes, is seduced by the White Witch with Turkish Delight, and later lies about it. Eventually all four children are in Narnia and the girls, Susan and Lucy, ride on the back of Aslan, the god-lion, which is a joy they can never quite remember, never forget.

There were four children, and they became kings and queens, ruled for hundreds of years (Narnia time.) Peter was the eldest, the high king, and he was good and noble; Susan was strong, the best hunter of them all. But it was Lucy who was the heart of the story. Aslan made her a gift of a little diamond bottle filled with an elixir that could cure any disease, heal any wound. She kept it hanging from her belt as she ruled with her siblings in the castle of Cair Paravel.

It disturbed me that in the story Lucy was the youngest, younger than Edmund. I wanted the characters to match my family exactly so that I'd be sure I was Lucy. I was afraid I might be Edmund—the one who betrays (though only briefly) due to the seductions of sweets and a flattering woman. The one who is self-serving, jealous.

Jealous of Johnny, who seems to never be afraid. Who used to take off his clothes at any excuse, run through the house naked, presenting himself like a devil to my parents' guests. Our father called him Nature Boy. Jealous of Charlotte, who had Jimmy's ear. Who was like his twin, yet still leaned on him, who had an intimacy I would never have. Jealous of Jimmy, who was my mother's favorite.

You had only to see her look at him when he was talking, his slender wrists and speaking hands in the air. They'd sit at the kitchen table talking about politics, civil rights, Vietnam. "Mom, why . . ."

I'd lurk in the background, wondering: What's Vietnam? If I ask she'll tell me she'll explain it to me later. "Jimmy and I are talking now." She adored his curiosity, concern, his reaching that age when he could be intelligently talked to. What is more charming than a smart thirteen-year-old considering the world? I saw it, too—how he straddled the two realities of childhood and grown-up, how he made adulthood seem something possible, desirable. "Mom, why . . ." Probably nobody listened to her views so carefully; I'm sure my father didn't. Jimmy did, and not only because he was a boy. He was like that, curious about the other person, he was good at listening and watching, then leaning forward with his own bright thought. With us he was the leader; with his friends as well. With my mother he was all there, young and old at once. In that sunlight of thirteen, limber, beginning to taste his inheritance.

They sit at the table talking; I open the refrigerator, pour a glass of milk. She says something to him, he responds, she listens. Their small faces so alike, even her temples, the hollows of her cheeks are listening. *I shouldn't be in the room, she wishes I wasn't here, she is carefully not noticing me, not letting me see how much she wishes I would leave already* as she watches him with a half smile, her eyes like melted jewels.

Jimmy is Mommy's favorite. How can I blame her, he's my favorite, too. He's clearly the best, smarter, older than Johnny, nicer than Charlotte, braver than me. Jimmy was more like my mother than my father. He had a calm temperament, poise, deft hands and a good eye, a wide-ranging curiosity. He had confidence in his own body and tastes; you would never find him in front of a mirror, descending into shame. (It is I who do that.) Jimmy was like my mother, and he resembled her physically as well, but he had Daddy's wit. He was prankish, clownish; riding his bike outside the window of the kitchen, as my mother talked to one of her friends, he did the sequence in reverse, like a movie rewinding, and kept it up, inventing more and more elaborate mime, until she noticed.

He delights me, why shouldn't he delight her? It's natural, there's nothing I can do about it, though it makes me sick with longing. What I don't understand is: Why are boys better than girls?

Why? Even the question was risky. You'd never ask it around boys, for example; in class you'd never ask it. I ask my mother and she is passionate about how terrible it is that society values boys more, that our own private school has trouble enrolling enough girls. "People think that because boys will get jobs, they need a better education," she says, and then asks me: Doesn't a mother need to know things? Don't I like it that she's read a lot, has ideas and opinions?

Why does it matter what I think? Either boys are better than girls or they are not. I have to assume these things have been settled by now. Whenever my mother hints the opposite—about this, or about civil rights, "Maybe your generation will change things," I become angry. I don't want to change the world, I want her to have already done it. Besides, it seems to me a lie—she can't really want things changed. Look at our house, how we live.

She seems to be happy staying home, being a mother. The house, the garden, the children, the nights out.

There's a disturbance, like a waviness in the air, around my thoughts of Jimmy's place in the family. I know she loves me, but there is some part of me she'll never love—the part where my jealousy is a continual burning. *Everybody loves her. She loves Jimmy best.* I stand in the hallway watching my parents leave to go out to dinner; I stand in the kitchen holding a glass of milk.

This is the real me, the one she doesn't know, the one that is ambitious and cold, *a traitor.* What made me a traitor was that I wanted to one day compete against my brother and win. He had more all-around good qualities, I knew that, but I suspected my talent went deeper. And I had the will. Jimmy could take things easy. I would dig my way out with a spoon. I could feel the power of this will, I trusted it but knew it wasn't loveable.

If I made reference to the fact that Jimmy was her favorite, my mother denied it; she said she loved us all the same. She explained how it had hurt her, as a child, when her aunts played favorites. Stories about this aunt, that aunt, her sister's blond sporty charm while Mommy was the bookworm.

I understood from what my mother said that she wanted to love us all the same, this was her idea, *she tried;* which meant she loved us truly. She just couldn't help it, loving Jimmy best. I believed I was willing to forgive this if only she'd admit it. But she couldn't admit it. The disturbance in the air was too great. Into it were sucked her unspoken protest—this is what I feel, what can I do?—and my unspoken violence: I'd give anything to have his powers. To be able to turn her eyes into melted jewels, to draw her to me, soft of face, even her temples, the hollows of her cheeks listening. What if I, Margaret, were Jimmy?

There were so many *places* in that house, so many arenas of solitude. Twenty-two rooms. We liked to play soccer in the upstairs hall, kicking a tennis ball from our parents' bedroom to the blue guest room. Or to run from the front door to the back of the house, to the marble-floored, fire-placed room called the porch, reaching our full speed by the time we passed the staircase. To skateboard in the big basement room with its wood-paneled walls; to explore the dungeons and the attic.

I especially liked the wine cellar, long narrow room like a big closet with its six-inch-thick door. Every so often a cat got locked in the wine cellar. You could hear it meowing from the kitchen. I'd have to go down and rescue, my bare feet cool on the dim stones, opening the door that creaked on its hinges, and find the cat just standing there, shoulders a slim writhe. Meowing and meowing, pink throat exposed.

I'd hold the door open and rest my eyes on the dusty bottles in their slots against the wall. I didn't want to drink one—not yet; I'd tasted wine at dinner and one swallow was always enough—just look at them. Sometimes pull one out by the neck, its wadded gray tissue falling to the floor, cradle it in my arms, try to read the French script. I knew each bottle cost a lot of money, even five or six dollars, knew it got better as it got older, which was so peculiar. Sometimes, my mother said, wine stayed in wine cellars for a hundred years.

A cat locked in a wine cellar. Would it eventually—left alone—break open the bottles, lap up the wine? And then become human, a fluffy gentleman from the nineteenth century in a waistcoat, padded slippers? No, it would starve to death, Jimmy said, and talked about cat skeletons found in old houses—cats bricked up in the walls. Why? For sacrifice.

Johnny had the bushes. These densely curling shrubs covered the back hill to the right of the garage, and were generally impassable to any save he. Tiny, nimble, and slippery, my little

brother had seeded them with a dozen forts, stocked with rope, knives, crackers, peanut butter, and army canteens of stale water. I investigated the ones nearest the driveway but he had a half a dozen or more, and I got tired of crawling on my belly. I preferred to imagine them anyway: the water, the rope, the knife. Caches of stolen goods. Matches.

He'd stay in there all day, come out a uniform dusty brown. Clothes, face, hair, all mixed with the sandy earth and that defiant expression, as if he were doing something illegal. Johnny was the dismantler of civilization. He crawled out, only the whites of his eyes not colored, and Sue would wriggle out after him, round snout caked up with dirt. Charlotte and Jimmy liked to surprise him with the hose, thick jet of water melting his disguise. He'd shout and disappear into the bushes again.

Jimmy's places to be alone were the rec room in the basement, the dungeons in the basement where he built his haunted houses, and the top of the garage where he'd sit with a half a dozen friends like a line of crows. That wasn't really alone of course but alone from me—I'd watch from the kitchen, boy boy boy, the sticks they whittled, stones they threw. Legs dangling. Why was I a girl? I wanted to be a mother, that was one reason; wanted to wear a wedding dress. To be a queen would be all right. Boys made fun of girls, Jimmy and his friends as much as anyone. Two girls in his yearbook had their faces scratched out. "It" he had written on one girl's face. "It no. 2" on the other. But he liked other girls, Sandy and Rae and Colleen, he talked to them on the phone at night, nor did he mind when the neighborhood girls fell in love with him.

Jimmy also had a chemistry lab in a closet on the third floor: racks of test tubes, vials of colored powders, a Bunsen burner. Open the door, there he was, slim-wristed, barefoot boy in a white shirt, standing at a plank counter. He told me he could make people invisible, turn them into dogs.

On the first day he set up his lab I hid fifteen feet away to await the results of his experiments. Charlotte and Johnny crowded in next to him, eager as dogs already. Why was it that I knew fear, and they didn't? I was the one who lingered in the bathtub, pouring potions of warm water and prayer over the cuts on my knee, who mixed all the liquid ingredients in the refrigerator to make the elixir of eternal life, which I fed to Johnny; I was the one who knew, if not what chemistry was exactly, what alchemy was. I should be in the forefront here. I moved a little closer.

I told Jimmy I wanted to be a black dog. He produced smoke and odors, told me I was one, but just didn't know it. "All dogs think they're people," he said. I shook my head. My arm was not a paw. I waited. He laughed and began to explain chemistry. Not only chemistry, but science in general, the scientific method, how it differed from magic, which happened not to exist.

I sat on the floor to listen. He argued with such clarity and fresh enthusiasm, and he let me answer back, which I couldn't do at school. In the classroom, magic and myth were described as belonging to the childhood of the race, an insult so poisonously tangled it silenced me. Jimmy spoke the words of the world—*Science, Progress*—but his heart was pure. It gave me an uncommon delight. Representing reason, he struck me as entirely magical.

My places were the garden, the side yard under the mulberry

tree, the branches of the mulberry tree with its soft, red fruit, and the little rooms on the third floor. It was very quiet on the third floor, in the afternoons. Sunlight came in the big front room where our dolls were kept—why were dolls all female, so they had to marry each other and have Amazon wars?—a sun that dimmed to twilight in the little rooms.

So many. How many? A half a dozen? You couldn't keep count, they melted into each other, mazy and indistinguishable, burrows. Servants' rooms. When we first discovered the little rooms, the day we moved in, Jimmy led us through with his master-of-ceremonies timing, flourish of his wrist: "Do you know where you are yet? Could you find your way out?" I was seven, Johnny not quite six. Johnny so anxious to prove he could find his way, I more interested in proving the opposite, wandering and wandering until the floor became turf, the ceiling a canopy of interlacing branches. Beings come out of the shadows then, servants who were really princesses, with long uncombed hair. I would suffer some exquisite punishment for being one of the masters—something painful but not too painful, which would leave me clean (you must have the courage, when they ask, to step into the tub of boiling water and let your old skin slough off); then I would be initiated.

That was a while ago. My hopes had diminished. I made do with less, tuned my mood to get the most from suggestive atmosphere. I was beginning to feel a certain anxiety about this: how much was up to me. Something like sadness, which I would ignore to enter the magic. I did it with my head—getting in position to catch the light just right, settling my brain like a bowl of liquid you carry carefully so the surface only barely shimmers. Another way was to select one chamber to decorate. I decorated as my mother did, with a passion bordering on ritual. That is to say, her passion bordered on ritual, but mine was ritual.

A chair in the middle of the room. A scarf hanging from a

hook. One of her silver spoons or odd ornaments (a bowl with legs and feet) her tarot cards. I wasn't allowed to touch her tarot cards. She said it dispersed the power, but I did it anyway. I sneaked into the little drawer of the spindly, highly varnished side cabinet in the living room and removed the Magician, the Hanged Man, the Star, and the Fool. On my way upstairs I would press the tall, stiff cards to my cheek. Delicious coolness, an exotic swirl of mood as if my insides were being rearranged.

I set the cards against the wall, lay on my stomach, and looked at them. The bright afternoon was far away. Each little room fed power to the next. Concentrated here. I prepared myself. Smoothed and polished, hollowed out and festooned, mostly just inhabited with excited breath myself.

Only rarely did my mother come upstairs. Then she would say, "What is this? What's it doing here? Margaret, this is not your toy." I paid no attention. Of course it wasn't a toy. A scarf hanging from a hook, a silver fork climbing a wall. Be still, something is about to happen.

I've been dreaming, lately, about the little rooms. Now there are even more of them, they take up a whole wing of the house. Crumbling, dilapidated, yet with a haunting charm; rose-beige, like the ruins of Italy. In the dream there are other wanderers like myself, coming in with a chair and a pillow, a book or a glass. No longer the entrance to anything, the little rooms are like a wayfarer's hotel, a bohemian palace buttressed by the presence, somewhere in the house, of my mother and sister. The women remain concerned about daily life. There are tasks, anxieties, children to feed, bills due. That is their province, and I feel guilty and grateful as I abscond, sneaking away to that unchanging emptiness.

Eight

IT WAS THE last Saturday in February 1965; a light snow was falling. I was nine years old, almost ten, my birthday in two and a half weeks. I sat at the kitchen table dressed in a pink velvet dress that had been my sister's, and patent leather shoes. Grandmommy was visiting, and we were all going out to dinner.

Johnny and I had been ready first. Our mother, who didn't understand that we could clothe ourselves in two minutes, had insisted we begin almost an hour ago: bathe, dress, brush our hair. Then we were too fancy to play so we sat at the table waiting.

Charlotte came down, wearing one of Mommy's tortoiseshell combs and a necklace, two-inch heels. A blouse and skirt, beige and off white. I had seen her in my mother's room, asking for something special, my mother fussing, her olive-dark fingers in my sister's light brown hair.

We heard the grown-ups minutes before they appeared. The clank and rattle of jewelry, the tap of high heels. When my parents came downstairs, on any evening, dressed to go out, they reminded me of circus animals: the gaudy trappings, the ceremony, the caution with which they moved. It was as if they were on stage, in a performance where my father knew his moves—coat held, chair pulled out—and my mother added weight with her perfume, like the noble elephant (though she was so slim.) That night she wore a red satin full-skirted dress, a heavy rhinestone necklace, dangly rhinestone earrings. Daddy wore his dark suit and polished shoes.

All of the pomp of going out to dinner was heightened because of my grandmother's presence. Tall, plump Grandmommy, easy, friendly, mild-mannered, ready to declare herself content with any offering, had her requirements. Her life was social life—martinis, luncheons, dinner parties. Sardi's and the theater, bridge. She drank a bit too much, was fond of little jokes, and was much loved. In her sixties, she was still called Baby by her peers. It was important to show her a good time.

My parents were on their best behavior; they'd had a party for her the night before, tonight she was treating us to dinner. Which meant we had to be twice as polite. We didn't object. We liked her. She brought us gifts from her trips to Mexico: jumping beans, piñatas. She was kind and had a festive spirit which, while it didn't quite include us—she didn't know how to include children, she stood awkwardly to the side when we opened her presents, as if she weren't the real giver—was appealing.

Her body was appealing too. Big-bellied, bosomy, coaxed into her dress. She carried herself with great dignity, stood up straight on slim legs, so she didn't seem fat exactly, though she was fat. In her house in Houston she had a weight-loss machine, a platform you stood on with a strap that went around the stomach. You turned the thing on and the strap vibrated, shaking your fat. We played on it until we were dizzy and had red marks on our stomachs; she didn't mind. I loved that she had it, right out there in the open, would tell you what it was for.

It was easy to behave, to be good around Grandmommy. She

was the opposite of Nana in that she made a point of not noticing if we did anything wrong. Our mother told us this was true courtesy, so we asked why she, Mommy, didn't not-notice, too? Because I am your mother and have to teach you things, she said with that earnestness that always provoked us to make fun.

I was willing to be good in my own way. I surrounded myself with a beam of kind feeling to offer my grandmother. Vague inklings of maybe talking to her like a person, not just a grown-up. We could discuss the food; we both liked reading a menu. I had confided to her once that whatever you ordered in a restaurant, when it came you wanted something else; and she said Yes, exactly, that always happens to me.

I could behave but I couldn't control the others. We had a particular problem tonight—our reservation was for seven, and Jimmy wasn't home yet.

My brother had spent the day at the house of his new friend, Spike, who lived across town. He had ridden his bike over in the morning with another boy, his best friend, Grant. He had promised to be home by five, then had called at five thirty to ask for a ride; it was dark. My parents said no. It was his responsibility to have left earlier; he had promised; and anyway two bicycles wouldn't fit in the car trunk.

It was a special thing, them letting Jimmy ride so far. He had turned fourteen on February first, and his green bicycle was his birthday present.

Johnny and I were so admiring of that bicycle. Johnny was fascinated by the five gears, I by the color. I wouldn't have thought of green. I had suggested red when he'd asked me what color he should get, but green, this cool, mid-range green, halfway between leaf and acid—once you saw it, you knew it was perfect. It was what it meant to be as old as fourteen, to be a boy.

* * *

It was almost seven. We were all in the kitchen waiting. My father checked his watch, remarked in anger that we'd certainly lost the reservation. Grandmommy said soothingly, "Oh, I'm sure they'll find us a table," and I liked how she did that, not reacting to him but rather as if flowing around. I thought maybe they would find *her* a table, this lady with her ruby clip earrings, her gray-and-chestnut hair. Daddy paced, shoes tapping the floor. He wouldn't exhibit his real anger in front of her.

Grandmommy made things safe; my mother didn't have that power. She couldn't stop his rages, especially, lately, against Jimmy. As my brother moved through eighth grade, turned fourteen, his obvious growing-up set my father against him. Whenever Jimmy had an opinion, Daddy said it was stupid. Jimmy would try to explain, our father wouldn't listen. Then he'd get angry at Jimmy for not listening to him. His whole body shaking with that raw Daddyness, that snarled-up energy like bees in your hair.

Jimmy's taste in music, clothes—which was, to us, of course, exciting, our brother so generous, bringing us this news from the frontier—disgusted Daddy. He said rock-and-roll was crap, nothing but crap. His voice getting louder. As if he could knock over this straight-backed boy, erase him from the world of opinion. Jimmy said finally, "Your music is crap." Then Daddy sneered at him, puffing like a snake, sneered and frothed, as if his rage were a liquid rising in his chest; how stupid, ignorant could a person be, to think classical music crap?

Jimmy shrugged.

I shrugged too, invisibly.

Jimmy left the room. He looked small, exiting. Surely he knew he was right, Daddy was wrong?

How strange that was to know—Daddy was wrong. *An asshole.* We all looked at him and knew it. He knew we knew it. We were quiet so he had nothing to attack. Rattle of ice and whiskey.

Jimmy told us he actually thought classical music was okay. He liked some of it. But he liked rock-and-roll better. Who wouldn't? My favorite—"I Saw Her Standing There," with Paul singing: His voice sounded like the velvet of the dress I was wearing but with a breeze coming through to touch my skin. Rock-and-Roll was everything I didn't know, wanted to know, couldn't find anywhere else. This Christmas Jimmy had given Charlotte and me both copies of *Beatles 65*. Not only this expensive record but the same thing for each of us, as if Charlotte and I were just the same. Two sisters, two girls who would grow up to be girls like Jane Asher and Marianne Faithfull.

Last Christmas he had given me a half-pound box of candy. This was the first time any of us sibling had spent real money on each other. Usually we wrapped up pencils, or nothing at all. We didn't even spend money on our parents. We didn't have much and weren't encouraged to anyway. Our mother always said she wanted something we had made, and though she didn't use what we made—the sewn change purse, the ceramic ashtray going in a dresser drawer—some two-dollar store item would be even less appreciated. So when Jimmy made the leap, gave us real presents, I was overwhelmed. This whole box of candy!

It must be a joke. Was he making fun of my sweet tooth? Was he waiting to see how much I would eat, was it a trap?

I looked at him; he was grinning. I thought he was grinning in pleasure at having been so generous, but I couldn't be sure. Also, this was strange candy. Jellied fruit slices—nothing I'd ever buy. It was old-lady candy. Was the point that Blubber Baby would eat anything at all?

I held the box in front of me awkwardly. My mother was annoyed that I'd been given candy, she liked to control our sugar intake, so I couldn't expect any help from her. Jimmy was still smiling. He might mean it kindly, and if he meant it kindly I had to respond. I started eating the candy. I started eating it and couldn't stop, though it made me feel sick, orange and pink and green sparkly sugared jelly on an empty stomach. I wouldn't know until the candy was gone if he was going to mock. (Amy Plumb's brother Bobby once gave her a sponge dipped in shoe polish and said it was chocolate cake. The story went that she'd taken a bite.)

After a while Jimmy asked me for a piece of candy. I was at the far end of the living room, hiding from the others opening their presents, my gaze fixed on the emptying, sugar-littered box. My brother hooked his chin over my shoulder, the sharp point of it digging into my flesh. "Give me a piece?"

This was how he was with Charlotte, casual, cajoling. Prancing, presenting himself in need. He had never been like this with me before.

I had two pieces left. I gave him one—not the flavor he liked best. He preferred the green, and they were all gone. He seemed a little wistful that his gift disappeared so soon. "You must have really liked it," he said; I heard the wistfulness and it pierced me. If only I could make it full again, all the jewel colors of the fruit slices laid, one over the other in their sugar crusts, heaviness of the box in my hand. I could keep it on the bureau in my room, barely touch it. Feed Jimmy as many pieces as he wanted because I realized now, it was obvious, he didn't think of this as old-lady candy, he liked it. It was his favorite kind. And I had eaten it all, not even wanting it . . .

What a relief it was the next year to receive that record album. Nothing to interpret or be scared of. So grateful to be seen as a girl just like my sister.

We were changing. Jimmy changed first, becoming more generous and expansive, and I was going to change too, become feminine and wonderful. Smooth, beautiful, under the music's transforming cloak. Date my brother's friends, learn about everything that was out there, a world I imagined made, in its best parts, in Jimmy's image. It was as if we were insects coming out of our cocoons, our mother was the cocoon—the silk of her silk dresses, the silk of her cheek—she had no idea what we would be. *She had no idea.* She talked about when she was young, but this was not that. Nothing like. As we changed so would reality. My brother's laughter, his excitement, was a promise of that.

I knew Jimmy didn't know everything. There were kids even older than he who really knew. He told us about counselor Mike at the camp he'd gone to last summer, who seemed to be Jimmy's Jimmy. The concept awed me—a ladder of boys, reaching up to the stars.

But Jimmy was the focal point. What came before him prepared the way—he would be the heart of the change, the blossoming. I didn't know it was odd, to think this about a brother. It seemed to follow naturally on the idea that boys were better than girls—which I thought the world agreed on. I didn't quite agree, actually; at least, not in regard to myself. I had ambitions, but I kept them private. They were like fish that dive deep where the water is so heavy and so cold. . . .

I didn't need to think about my ambitions yet. The miraculous thing was, I was beginning to believe I'd grow up. There might be no such thing as fairyland—and maybe it didn't matter.

Wasn't Daddy pitiful? Still powerful, scary, but I'd put my bets on Jimmy. It was mythic what was happening. Daddy was the tyrant, Jimmy the avenging hero. An old story. Jimmy was doing it perfectly. There was a new pride to my brother these days, a consciousness of his rights, that was thrilling to watch. If Daddy was like a bull, Jimmy was becoming matadorial: slim, dark, swift, piercing. He answered back with cool wit while our father raved and frothed.

I knew how it had to go, but I was nervous.

I was anxious particularly about what would happen tonight. Long term, we would win, but I didn't want a battle tonight. Daddy's rage and insults, my brother's refusal to take it. Jimmy going upstairs, back stiff with dignity, into his room, shutting the door. That teenage thing—shutting the door so we little ones lost his presence too. I wanted him at the restaurant. At the table, doing things with a toothpick or a matchbook, finding stuff on the menu to laugh at, making faces the grown-ups wouldn't see. Or just the tilt of his body lounging in the chair.

For a moment I was angry at him for being late and how he would answer back when Daddy yelled, provoking more yelling so he'd have to stay home. The inevitability of it. If he was soft and agreeable, like me, he could come with us. If he cared about the fact that I couldn't stand him staying behind, that I needed him there; but this thought embarrassed me. You weren't supposed to need your siblings that way.

I was wrong to worry so much about myself when it was Jimmy who'd get yelled at, Jimmy the target of Daddy's wrath. It awed me a little: How could he bear it? I couldn't imagine doing things to bring that fury on myself: poor Jimmy. He had to fight Daddy all alone, we didn't help him. I should help him. I wanted to, the wanting swelled in my chest. *To be brave.* But I wasn't brave, not enough to say or do anything. I could only work on the invisible plane.

Wasn't that worth something? Our mother always said, when things were wrong, "I love you, I *love* you," even if that wasn't the problem. So love had some invisible influence. Also, of course, I believed in imagination. So I sat quietly, focused on becoming my brother's ally. Surrounding the thought of him with lines of force—I saw them as arrows of light, myself as a quiver of light. By summoning that power, feeding it my being—which made me feel swoony and dizzy—I was weighting the room for him, holding his ground. I was constraining my father from taking advantage of Jimmy's absence, adding to Daddy's natural frustration and confusion. Opposition, steady opposition, was what our father couldn't take. Jimmy offered it; I was offering it now.

Suddenly I noticed my father wasn't angry anymore.

I had missed the moment things changed. We were just there, in another place. Daddy standing at the counter, swiftly making drinks. He made one for my grandmother, one for my mother, one for himself. I listened to the crack of the ice tray, cubes shaken out into the glass, watched the liquor poured. I noticed how the ice cubes responded to the alcohol, snapping and jumping, then, as the level went higher, settling into a simmer of pleasantries.

Daddy wasn't angry. Something else? What? I didn't know, only watched them drink. Him especially, the glass at his lips. Always that tender moment, the glass at his lips.

Mommy picked up the phone, dialed, spoke for a moment, hung up the phone. She told us she had called Spike, that he said Jimmy had left over an hour ago. I didn't know what this could mean except he'd be home soon. The grown-ups were being strange. I was hungry.

Then something came off my mother like a great wind. Not as clean as wind. It was more like water, rolling, greasy gray water, and I had to look at the adults through it, as if through an aquarium.

The air was moving like greasy water but the walls weren't moving. Usually walls do—they rise and fall, breathing—but so subtly you don't notice unless you become very still, go into a kind of trance. It's one of the things that made me happy, the secret springiness of walls. If things got too bad I could just walk inside one, into the foamy plaster. But now they were hard.

I glanced at Charlotte. Her face had gone white, her eyes fixed on Mommy.

I glanced at Johnny, who was kicking the chair leg. He didn't know.

I knew; but I didn't know what I knew.

A few things were said. The ice cracked in my father's drink. He lit a cigarette, looked at his watch. I looked at the clock on the oven. A lot of time had passed suddenly. I wondered if the clock hated us.

My father said, "I'm going to look for him."

He left quickly, grabbing his keys. I was startled by the speed of his departure; then I understood. They feared an accident. A car accident, a car running over Jimmy on his bike; Jimmy hurt. An idea immediately offensive to me—anger at them for even imagining it.

The house was silent but for the odd whirs and clicking of the kitchen appliances. My mother and her mother stood across the room, several feet from each other, perched on their high heels. Mommy was clinging to the counter, her little face white, motionless, and distorted. Her head and shoulders were tilted toward the door, as if she were being sucked out. The slightest angle of tilt—and yet the power enormous. Her long-fingered hands spread on the countertop.

It was as if there were only one moment, or one second, and we were all trapped inside it. Time making a loop, over and over, as when you spin around in a circle and get sick. All of us inside it, but mostly her—

Then we were all speaking, we were saying things like, "He's almost here, Mom, I'm sure of it, he's coming."

"He's riding up the driveway right now."

"He's wheeling his bike—he's going slow because he's tired."

"Maybe he's late because he had to stop and help someone."

"Yeah like an old man with a flat tire who's really a millionaire so he gave Jimmy a hundred bucks."

"Or a thousand."

"It's just the snow. It's hard to ride a bike in snow."

"He's probably hungry."

"I heard something—did you hear something!?"

Johnny was at the door. "It's Sue," he said, his voice falling. He let the dog in. We stared at her and she cringed. "Go back out, Sue," said Johnny. "Go look for Jimmy." She cringed some more, our young boxer bitch, glancing out of her brown pop-eyes at all the weird human faces. She tried to slink past us, out of the room, but Johnny wouldn't let her. "Go outside!" He pushed on her hindquarters.

"Leave her alone," said our mother.

I was thinking about exactly how Jimmy would come home. He'd wheel his bike up the driveway through the snow, which wouldn't make any noise, to the kitchen door, then drop the bike. He probably wouldn't bother walking it into the garage, even though it was brand new, because he was tired. He'd come inside first.

He'd wheel the bike up the steep part of the driveway (dark, cold, snow falling, gusted in his face) then across the straight front section past the terrace and through the porte cochere, between the cement posts, up the hill to this door.

He could be on the driveway now, and we wouldn't know. I strained to hear even those tiny sounds. The snick of bicycle tires going around, soft whoosh of footsteps. I imagined his face flushed from the cold, his whole body aching. It was almost eight. These last moments. Nobody knowing he was here, just about to open the door—

Suddenly, terribly, I didn't want him to come in. My desire pulling, hand over hand, something out of the dark night, snapped and switched, I was pushing now, pushing him away. Don't come in.

Don't.

I didn't understand. It was as if I had turned against myself. I tried to switch back but all I was saying, sending, like a thunderbolt, was: *Don't.* Go away.

Silence. My mind emptied. I was hungry.

* * *

The phone rang. My mother picked up the phone immediately, yet didn't grasp it firmly, didn't hold it to her ear. I heard my father's voice—not the words but the buzz of it, as if he were being chewed by insects. Then she hung up. "There's been an accident," she said. "We don't know how bad yet. I'm going to the hospital now."

She was already halfway out the door. Charlotte yelled, "Mom! I want to come too!"

"Get your coat, then."

Johnny and I, startled, yelled: "Me too!"

But it was too late. "I can't take you all. You stay here with Grandmommy. She'll make you dinner." They were already outside; we had to run to follow. Bare-armed in the cold, in the night air, Mommy backing the station wagon out of the garage until it was parallel to the side of the house, Charlotte climbing in, then starting forward, the yellow lights sweeping downhill. I wanted to run after the moving car, yapping at its wheels like a dog.

We went back inside, where things were immediately calmer. Grandmommy was talking about eggs. "Would you like some eggs? Eggs and toast? Nice scrambled eggs?" She said this three or four times, her voice singsong and choppy, like a small boat in water.

"We don't eat eggs," I replied politely. "We're not really hungry." She took the eggs out of the refrigerator and cracked them into a bowl.

Johnny said, "What if he broke his leg?"

I considered. "He'll have to be in the hospital for a long time, maybe a month. He won't be able to go to school."

"He's lucky—except he likes school now."

"His friends would bring his homework over." That happened sometimes when you were sick. I had even done it once or twice. The teacher gives you a folder and you stop at the person's house on the way home, or ride your bike over later. Jimmy's friends would fight over the privilege.

"He's going to get the guy who did it," Johnny said.

"No, he won't. Unless it was on purpose, and I'm sure it wasn't on purpose."

"Why would anyone hit him on purpose?"

"That's what I mean. They wouldn't. So he'll forgive the guy."

"I think he should at least punch him in the nose."

My grandmother was standing at the stove, cooking. She had put on an apron and it surprised me to see her like that. She wasn't the kind of grandmother to fix us dinner. At home in Houston, she had two black servants to take care of her, one handsome young bachelor named Jewel and an older woman, Lucille. When Johnny and I visited, Lucille made us biscuits for breakfast, we lunched at the country club, and dined either at our uncle's white-columned mansion or at the drive-in with Jewel and his girlfriend. Naturally we preferred the latter. The best things about Grandmommy's house were Jewel's sly talk, Lucille's biscuits, the two golden retrievers, and the possibility of snakes at the creek—cottonmouths—which we were warned about but could never find.

I thought maybe eggs were all Grandmommy knew how to cook. She put the plates in front of us, and we tried to eat. "A broken leg isn't so bad," I said.

"He could have two broken legs."

"Or just a broken arm."

"If he has just a broken arm, maybe he could come home tonight."

We finished most of our eggs. They were tasty though usually eggs made me sick: those bright yellow lumps, sometimes with a bit of white showing, stiff and lacy like the foam on a dog's mouth. Our grandmother asked if we wanted more to eat. "Some buttered toast? Nice buttered toast?"

"Can we go upstairs?" I asked. "We could fix up Jimmy's room in case he comes home tonight."

"That's a grand idea. A grand idea. What sweet children you are. Not all children are as sweet as you. Yes, a grand idea."

"She's being weird," said Johnny as we left the room.

"She can't help it."

"I know—I don't mind."

We took the extra pillows from our bedrooms into Jimmy's room and arranged them, then turned down the bed as we'd seen on TV. "We should have one of those little TVs for in here," said Johnny. We moved the clock-radio so it was easier to reach, moved it again, then roamed around, looking for something else to do. I wanted to put a book on his nightstand but didn't know which of the several on his desk he was currently reading.

I thought about putting flowers by his bed, red roses, but it was snowing outside, there weren't any flowers. No banners to hang in his room either, no time to hook up the kind of system I once read about, and ferociously coveted, wires and pulleys and relay switches so a person could do everything from bed. All his books on shelves that slid, toppled into baskets on a rope, a robot hook that grasped things, opened and shut windows.

Yet if he had a broken leg, there'd be time for that. Lots of time, weeks. I began to get excited, thinking about the opportunities for service. Long afternoons of running his errands, bringing his meals—how captive he would be, here in his room. Never out with friends (though his friends would come over). Never at football practice. Just here with us, lonely, bored.

Maybe months. Jimmy in bed.

In the afternoons, sometimes (more often last year) Jimmy would let Johnny and me roughhouse in his room while he did his homework in bed. We'd take turns walking the narrow plank of his footboard, small bare feet carefully placed, arms swaying, often losing our balance. He told us we had to bail out on the floor when that happened, and we did, mostly, enduring the long fall down, thump, breath knocked out of us. But sometimes we fell on him, on his warm limber body, his books, and then we'd giggle, we'd roll around clutching our knees, we'd say, "Sorry, sorry, sorry! I won't do it again!"

We'd try not to but we'd do it again. He'd kick us out. Or not. That tolerance he had—not always, but often, like swimming into a warm place in the ocean. You just hang there when you find it, it's so delightful.

Jimmy's convalescence. Sickroom full of friends, full of us. It startled me to notice the fantasy was gone. Johnny was too silent and the room was empty, empty in a strange way, like cellophane pulled off a package, left clinging to itself. The whole house was quiet. Grandmommy was keeping mum, downstairs with the eggs.

We wandered out into the hall, then into our parents' room to stand guard at the window that overlooked the front driveway. We stood for ages watching, silent, light off, and I tried to get Johnny worried about Daddy catching us in here—would he throw us out the window, brain us?—but he shrugged me off. "It doesn't matter tonight."

I knew that.

Finally we went into our rooms and played quietly until we heard the car door slam. By the time we were on our feet, into the hall, at the top of the stairs, our mother was coming up, tall and regal in her red dress like the Queen of Night. Her face still, waved dark hair like carved wood, eyes cold and burning. Charlotte was beside her, then ahead of her, her body twisted to one side; she was scrabbling at the banister and crying. "Jimmy's dead!" she called to us. "Jimmy's dead!"

How dare she? Say such a thing. Our mother was silent. "He's dead," our sister sobbed again, level with us now, legs pumping, cheeks plastered with her snarled hair.

"Mom!" we shouted. "Mom! It's not true, is it? Is it?"

She was taking one step at a time. Her red dress burning. For a moment her jewel-cold eyes rested on us. "Yes. Jimmy is dead." We didn't believe her; we were angry.

"Did you see him?"

Yes, she saw him.

Yes, he was dead.

No, we couldn't see him.

There was nothing anyone could do.

As she spoke, she moved smoothly up the stairs, down the hall, into her room, rigid yet not mechanical, a willed queenliness. We followed, we asked more questions (accident, a car hit the two bikes, Jimmy and his friend Grant, from behind, head wound, killed instantly), the words breaking against our minds, no reality, only the repetition convincing us, nobody would make this up—then flung ourselves on her bed, sobbing. Warm tears, the shaking of our bodies, the shift and give of the mattress. Charlotte and Johnny and me.

Charlotte and Johnny and me—three of us. Only three. Today, tomorrow, next year. Jimmy is dead. Where is he?

I knew he was dead because this was happening, and he wasn't here. If something like this happened, and he were alive, he'd be here, because it was happening to us all as a family, because no one could not be part of this great ripping and tearing. We couldn't be other than in the same room, the same picture, as if our life were a painting and someone had slit it. Cut out the figure of Jimmy so the cold beyond the canvas came in, we were so bereft, so afraid.

I said to myself: there are four children in my family, two boys and two girls, Jimmy Charlotte Margaret Johnny. There are four. That is the right number, the correct number. It is what is.

Sobbing. Thumping the mattress. Where is he? Where is our

brother? Rolling in the pain that cleaved us in two, made us forever three. Charlotte crying as if she, too, had just found out, she is one of us now, down with us, the little kids, our sister—

Charlotte and Johnny and me. Where's Mommy? She should be here. *Our mother, who made us all.* Her long body curved across the bed, mother of tears.

Mother of all the griefs of the world, her body a river.

Mother of Jimmy and Charlotte, Margaret and Johnny. We would press our heads into her belly, her belly that would open up as in the fairy tale when they open the wolf's belly, take out the seven little kids and replace them with stones. Her belly would open like that, without blood, she would be dry and calm inside like a cave with leaves on the floor. Just for a while, a secret magic, nobody would see. A magic without consequence, Jimmy was dead forever. Still . . .

My mother was sitting at the far end of the bed, by the nightstand. I heard her voice; she was making phone calls. Her address book was open, she was dialing the phone, she was speaking, hanging up, dialing again.

"Jimmy died tonight," she said. "He died instantly."

How could one die other than instantly? Why did she say it again and again?

"Jimmy died tonight."

I looked around and saw that the world was different than it had been. Here was an alien planet, every molecule changed. The colors of the room throbbed and shimmered; I saw red and black lift themselves out of the rug, the clothing and magazines, and hang in the air, striped and wavy, like veils. Real color, free of its stuff, inhabiting the air. Sinuous lozenges, geometric shapes. What it meant was not-life. Not-life, not-home. I had thought our family was somehow of a piece with reality, but I was wrong.

I was wrong, this wasn't our world, we were just here. Were the rest of us in danger? Not immediately—probably not. Death could happen at any moment but probably not right here, right now.

My parents' bedroom was a kind of safe haven, simply by virtue of its walls, its floor. Yet we were not home. There was no knowledge of us in this room, no welcome or protective regard. Such did not exist anywhere in the physical world.

Lying still, breathing shallowly—*I can breathe here.* I can breathe here, I am here. Where am I?

I am in my body. I glanced down the length of this peculiarly massive object. Down my leg to my foot, still shod in its patent-leather shoe. The buckle buckled. Curve of my ankle in white textured cotton, leading up to the knob of my knee, hem of my dress. My gaze went back to my foot again. Hanging off the bed, gleaming blackly. Was my foot part of me, or of the alien world? I could imagine it both ways. It was me, I felt its pain when I stubbed my toe; it wasn't me, I could cut it off. It could kick me.

Don't think. Just know—was my body me or not me? But I saw after a minute that it was good to think. That activity seemed to make the horror fade, the violent danger draw back.

Mommy was still making calls. Over and over. Lifting up the receiver, putting it down.

Nine

I HALF-EXPECTED SOMEONE to stop me. Walking past my father, my grandmother—who were hovering by the door, helplessly, Daddy holding a drink—as if they were furniture. Outside the room, the room where everybody was, traveling the length of the hall. Acutely aware of the distance, of myself walking. Crossing space. The empty hall: Why is air empty? Nobody speaks, stops me, runs after me. It's my own choice. I am Margaret, doing this.

I am Margaret; this is my room. This is where I live with the door shut, the raised white bumps of my bedspread familiar on the back of my neck, the backs of my knees. White ceiling.

What is death? Jimmy is dead now, I have to know. *Dead.* The word seemed to have no reference. I couldn't fit it in my mind. When I tried to stuff it down, it bounced out. If I thought *Jimmy*, he was here, strolling across the stage, that stage behind my eyes where people lived when I wasn't seeing them. He was perfectly alive, vivid and chatty, talking with his hands. What could it mean, dead?

Not here? He bounced back, flowering.

I watched my mind accelerate, working on this problem. Death, what is it, how it is; is it this, is it that? Chattering almost, turning itself inside out to find the angle—I was astonished by the clank and whir, the mechanical inadequacy of the operations.

This awareness was in contrast to all previous self-consciousness. Before, my mind seemed infinite in its velvety depths and powers; and it was not the same thing as me. Me was a nervous light or a striving wrongness, it was confusion and the longing for pleasure, excitement, sleep. But my mind was a working god, a cornucopia. I could never get to the end of it or see into its structure. It was a theater I never grew tired of.

But this, death, made my mind a bad machine. It made it grind against itself, go out of gear . . . which I had to admit was fascinating . . . I could actually glimpse the operations of memory, of logic, how makeshift they were, hurried, anxious, like stagehands changing the scenery with the curtain open—

My mind is not seamless. It can be seen into.

Yet I am here, seeing. What does this mean?

Then I was not thinking, *Death, what is it?* but rather seeing my brother rise off his bicycle, into the air.

Did he hear the car coming? Did he turn around to look? How surprised he must have been to know that he, Jimmy, was about to be hit, to feel that rise, body still intact, in motion, to imagine—what?

I tried to be there in that split-second helplessness—to find, taste those last thoughts, as if my knowing about his knowing could matter, could wrap around him, enfold the nugget self, snatch it out of time—but all I saw was Jimmy flying off his bicycle, plummeting down against the street. Off his bicycle, knocked off. The picture kept coming. I didn't want it, I wanted to think of him but not that, just him; *Jimmy.* Yet his body in the dark air like an arrow coming down. The great sky all around him, above and below, not holding him but letting him fall. The clouds and the snow and the dark and the wind. Not holding him. Not waiting for me to catch him, not calling us to say *I have this boy falling, come quick,* not giving us time to be there, lay down softness.

And then he was hurt. My mother said he died instantly, but I knew he was hurt. Body on the cold street, not getting up again; still there. I knew it wasn't—not his body—but he was. Still there. Wasn't he?

I tried to imagine him falling on a dozen mattresses, or mounds of autumn leaves. I raked the leaves, I carried them to the highway, laid them out in beds. If I could see him fall upon the beds, he would have. But each time he fell off his bicycle, nothing was there.

This went on for a long time. You know what it's like, the same picture over and over. I didn't know what it was like. I thought it meant I was supposed to do something, not that this was what I was doing. I was supposed to change it, that's why I kept getting the same picture, like a problem, something unfinished; and I couldn't.

I couldn't. Not once did the car miss Jimmy or did he fall so he wasn't killed. I had to look at the known scene, over and over: snowy night, green bicycle, boy rising, boy falling.

Exhausted, I picked up the paperback I had been reading earlier: Alfred Hitchcock's *Mystery Magazine.* This was a monthly periodical, costing fifty cents, with a photo of the master in profile on the cover. It contained six or seven stories, printed on cheap paper, about men killing their wives for the insurance money or wives killing their husbands. Occasionally a man killed his mother or a wife her husband's mistress, or a husband his own mistress, to shut her up. Sometimes a thief killed his partner so he could keep all the loot.

My eyes forced my mind to the page. Scent of the paper, leaf-mulch, its yellowish tinge, uneven margins. I liked both the unevenness of those margins and the order they aspired to, marching down the page. I admired the titles of the stories—bold black letters: the effort made to lure me in.

I would rest for while between title and first sentence. My head on the pillow. My room, my book. Then let go—impossible indulgence—into beginning, middle, end. Who is Margaret who descends into the story. A being of a piece with the white (the yellowish) paper, inky twigs of words. Left to right.

After reading for a few minutes, I recognized what I had not known before: the fraudulence of these stories. People were being killed—by accident, murder, suicide—but there was nothing about death on the page. None of it, not one sentence, was about death.

And that is why, I said to myself, this magazine is comforting me now. I was immediately terrified by the high irony of the thought. How did I dare think such a thing? (To think is pleasure.) Jimmy was dead. He would never read, never lie with his head on the pillow. And as if waiting for this moment, all my knowledge of my privilege—our wealth, my room to myself, my four limbs, five senses intact—reproached me; I lay like a glutted worm, the edges of my vision black.

Jimmy was dead. The pain of it already hauled off center stage. Not far off—just a little— It aroused a deep anxiety that someone would see me, see me here in bed, lolling, reading. See what I was reading. What I was thinking, the very fact that I was thinking: this newborn (death-generated) intelligence itself a perversity. Such as I did not deserve comfort, the right to be a part of the sensual heap, children on their mother's bed. Maybe she was on the bed with them now, telephoning stopped, her long body bent around. Maybe she was wondering where I was.

I had to remain alert, ready to slide the book under my pillow if anyone opened the door.

* * *

I couldn't stop reading. Never has that activity so consoled me. Fiction; there is fiction! Pages and pages of wrong stories about death. Gangsters, murderers, thieves. Stories like railroad trains, on track. No alien peculiar universe. No boy falling out of the sky. You didn't have to remain in the agony, his body slammed against the ground, every second. You could turn your mind to a tale, a tale that skimmed along the surface, you could hang on to the sentences like the tow rope when water-skiing.

Still, it hurt me to abandon him. How alone he was, had been, in that moment when nobody knew— Did he know? For how long? Shock of his body leaving the bicycle, scramble of mind to catch up. *I'm dying; am I dying; it's me, Jimmy, stop it; it's me!* Wanting to cover that moment, interpose myself cell by cell, in his body, the sky, the street, pulse of blanketing light, wanting—

Things were moving again in the house. Nicky, our neighbor from across the street, came over; I heard her squeaky kitten voice in the hall. I heard my sister's voice and my father's. Daddy's heavy tread as he went downstairs, came up again. What were they doing; what was there to do? I wanted to go out into their company, in the lit hall. Yet experiencing such powerful anxiety about what I had done.

What had I done? Thought about myself. Wanted my mother.

I read another story. A man kills his wife because she nags too much; tries to hide the body. A police detective relentlessly questions. Nonpeople. In the woods, under the floorboards, in the river. He hides her in pieces. It is a task.

At some point Nicky led my mother down the hall to the blue guest room. I heard the slow passage, heard Nicky say something about rest, and my mother's hoarse threads of speech in return. I didn't understand why Mommy was being taken to the blue guest room. She wasn't a guest here. That twilit chamber with its white muslin curtains—little foyer like a parenthesis. That room that had never belonged, that could so easily detach, drift off into the night sky.

I was angry at Nicky. I was still waiting for my moment on the bed, Mommy's body coiling down like unpinned hair. I thought of the way a dog or cat becomes a mother, lies stretched on her side so relaxedly, the tiny bundles snapped on.

The blue guest room meant too late. I wanted to shout; I saw my arms wheeling. I didn't move.

The door to the guest room shut behind my mother.

I wasn't anywhere in this story. I was only reading it.

Nicky met my father in the hall: murmured voices. The phone was ringing.

I DON'T MISS Jimmy yet, not really. He's been gone this long before, been gone longer. He was gone for two weeks last summer. If I don't miss him, I'm okay, aren't I? Why don't we all just say that—he's gone to camp, or away to school, he'll be back later. We can get away with it for months probably.

But you know he's dead. Dead, he's dead—get it?

His face, that sweetness, in the snow. The body, flung high, lies still. There would be blood. (Of his blood I imagined only the color, poppy-red. A splash or a stain on the snow. Terrible, yet with a pure severity, like my mother's red dress as she walked up the stairs.)

Jimmy without face or blood floats high above the street. Suspended there, in a whirlpool of darkness, his awareness never quite catching up with events. What I was imagining, or trying to, was the nakedness of being without a body. Snatched out of life, consciousness not extinguished; I couldn't conceive of that extinction. Jimmy alone, understanding nothing. Not knowing what had happened or even his own name. His the unimaginable loneliness.

I don't really miss him yet. Not really.

After awhile—a long while, I'd finished reading, was wondering if I was supposed to just go to sleep—the door opened and Charlotte and Johnny came into my room. At the sight of them, I felt immediately shy. A visit from Charlotte never happened.

They sat down on the bed; I moved over. My whole body was quivering with the desire to please, and what amazed me was that my sister seemed to be in the same condition. How had she managed to get so much smaller, so much softer in a few hours? Her face was pale, her eyes rabbity, her voice tentative and questing.

She was anxious to talk. She told us some of the details of her time at the hospital. She and Mommy had driven there in silence—"really fast"—and met Daddy in the parking lot. They all went into the lobby together, and then the doctor came out and told them Jimmy was dead.

"How did he say it?"

"He just said he was sorry, he had bad news; Jimmy didn't make it."

"Did Mommy cry?"

"No."

Mommy went in to see Jimmy. Dr. Delorenzo had thought Grant was Jimmy because their faces were so damaged and so our mother had gone in to the room where the body was and then come out and said, no, that's Grant. (We paused to feel sad about Grant. Charlotte said it was awful but still, in a way, you know, she was glad Jimmy had his best friend with him. I tried to picture the boys together in the whirlpool of darkness, that bodiless place, but couldn't do it. Jimmy was alone.)

Then Mom had gone in to see Jimmy and said This is Jimmy (though his face was so damaged) and Dr. Delorenzo had asked her if she was certain of her identification. We thought about that. How certain she must have been. How certain we would have been.

Charlotte remarked somberly, "Half his face is gone."

"Which half?"

"I don't know. What does it matter which half?" she snapped.

I was stung. I didn't know why it mattered. It didn't matter a lot. Yet it seemed a reasonable question. Which half? They were different, each eye was a little different and his smile was lopsided. I imagined him coming back, living here with one rounded cheek—faint downy hair on it lately—one blue eye, one ear. I would settle for that, I thought. There was no reason to keep him dead because he had only half a face. He could go to school with the other half all bloody and if people didn't like it, too bad.

I imagined myself calmly talking to my brother, treating him in every way exactly the same, as he went through life with mangled meat for a face. I could do it.

Charlotte said that several of our relatives were arriving the next day. Our other grandmother, our mother's sister, cousins, some people we'd never met. Already they were calling back with airplane arrival times. Johnny and I were shocked. Why were they coming now?

"It's what people do when somebody dies," said Charlotte. "They come to the house to help."

"It won't help us. We don't want them here."

"It'll help Mom. You think she wants to deal with feeding us, and taking care of stuff?"

"She doesn't have to feed us. We can eat cereal or call Chicken Delight."

"There's a lot to do when somebody dies. You guys are too young to understand. Anyway, Mom wants them here."

We couldn't argue with that. We'd seen her make the calls.

Charlotte kept talking, telling us the mechanics of death and funerals, every word distressing me, though still I wanted her here. What mattered was the raw softness of her voice, the skinny bumps of her shoulders, her pink-edged nose. Her body leaning toward mine on the bed, as if Jimmy's power to separate us had instantly vanished, gap closed over, healed, and I was able to feel that and be grateful, now worrying how it had come about. It seemed natural, *we are all so sad Jimmy has died, we are all the same now,* though I couldn't have predicted it. But when she said, speaking intently, "It's worse for Mom, you know, because Jimmy was her son," when she said that to us with her open sisterly face looking at me, beaming it toward me, I recoiled, as if from an electric shock. She elaborated—what mothers feel, how they feel more than we do, how we can't imagine it. I couldn't stand it.

Johnny and I started mimicking our relatives, the old southern folk with their wavery, quavery voices, and Charlotte became upset. "Jimmy's dead," she cried. "They're sorry, too. They loved him."

"No, they didn't," said Johnny.

I agreed with him. I thought of our relatives, on both sides of the family, not as people but as powers to be appeased. When they visited us we had to especially polite, keep our faces washed and our shoes on. We had to make meaningless conversation, inhabit robot selves. Our shyness was instinctive, we didn't question what it told us. Old people of all kinds were not like us—though Grandmommy was okay. Burbling about eggs. I loved Grandmommy. But not any others. We had so much to do, wasn't that obvious? Charlotte said they were coming to help, but it seemed to me just the opposite, that they were coming to prevent us from mending ourselves at all.

Our conversation broke down over this question of the relatives. Charlotte felt herself outnumbered and left the room, then Johnny did, too. I didn't know how to keep them with me.

I lay on my bed reading, but not really paying attention. My glittery solitude was gone. Meanwhile—constantly—Jimmy was coming home, wheeling his bike into the garage, putting down the kickstand, walking across the driveway. Jimmy was at the kitchen table, talking to our mother. Jimmy was on the phone. Jimmy in every possible pose, all ages and places, every memory I could find.

I got out of bed and left my room. The hall was empty—the door to the blue guest room shut. I walked the familiar route to Jimmy's room, my feet tingling. My knees softening. The door was ajar. I was quickly inside. Johnny was there. "What are you doing?" he asked.

"What are you doing?"

"Nothing. I'm not messing up his stuff."

I was silent. He said. "I thought he might come in here."

"Yeah, I know. This is where he would come."

We discussed how foolish our parents were, not to keep a vigil. It was almost midnight.

The big bed like a ship, his name carved on the headboard, his cocoa-brown-and-red fringed rug, his desk. The painted paddle on the wall from his Canadian canoeing trip last summer. "It's a good room," said Johnny.

We stood in the middle of the floor, looking around us. Seeing it all, glances resting lightly.

"Should we say anything?"

My task. I considered. "Please come back, Jimmy. We want to see you. We won't be scared."

"I'm scared."

"We're scared but not too scared." And then I remembered the moment in the kitchen when I had not wanted him to come in. He must have been dead then, I thought. He was coming to say good-bye and I wouldn't let him in. I was scared of a ghost. I'm sorry, I said silently. I didn't know you were dead.

"What if he really comes?" asked Johnny.
"It's Jimmy."

As we drifted around the room, touching things but not grabbing or rooting through, just running our fingers over or lifting up a book, I remembered something about Johnny. How once, a couple of years ago, we were all talking about death. Jimmy had set before us the most famous possibilities: nothingness, reincarnation, heaven and hell. In keeping with his scientific stance he had stressed the one sure fact: Nobody really knows. Some of the grown-ups pretended to know but they didn't. None of them.

Johnny insisted that when he died, he'd come back and tell people. He'd find a way. Jimmy repeated calmly, maddeningly, "How do you know you'll be able to to come back? *You don't know what it's like.*" Johnny became more and more agitated. He said he'd jump off the roof right now and find out—and come back. His wiry little body tensed as if to scramble out the window.

We all laughed.

I felt bad now about laughing. I also remembered how easy it had been to imagine Johnny stepping off the roof. Not dying, not like this, but vanishing.

After a half an hour, we decided Jimmy wasn't coming. But maybe he could hear us, so we talked a little bit. We told him how sad we were, told him he could come back anytime. (And say hi to Grant.) Johnny asked for a sign that there was life after death. Anything weird that happened—we would know.

I wondered about that.

We said good-night.

Ten

I WOKE UP the next morning in a dazzle of pink and gold. Sunlight on my pink walls, on the ceiling and moldings, on my butterscotch-colored rug. Such clean and delicious sunlight, the rays coming through the glass in perfect cones, diffusing on the bed, warming my arms, the softness, the courtesy of light! Is there anything milder and more pleasing than winter sun? Playing over me like the gaze of a perfect animal, my room lit to the exact right degree of revealing.

My books lined up on the bookshelves, how pretty their jackets were, I loved them; and I loved my companionable china cats and dogs. Also my white wood jewelry box with the hinged lid; gold fleur-de-lis on the domed top.

I lay between my covers, happy. For a minute I savored it, such dancing gratitude, then needed to know why. Had something wonderful happened?

And realized at the instant it was gone: I was happy because I had forgotten that Jimmy was dead.

Jimmy was dead! My mind narrowed under the assault, the unbelievable theft. And just as quickly remembered all my strategies of the night before, shuffled through them: trying to refuse, to get around the fact, trying to re-create him from the stuff of memory. Memory—on whose every page my brother moved, spoke, in vivid color. Last night it had seemed, for a little while, that memory *was* Jimmy; and to some extent I would keep thinking so for awhile. Still, it was different today. Jimmy had died, we had gone to sleep, and now it was the morning of the day after he died.

When the agony started up—the moment of impact, did he know he was dying? How could *my brother be dead*—I turned it off. It shocked me that I was able to. Last night my mind had been out of control, but sleep had restored my powers of discrimination. I could not-think about it.

I climbed out of bed. There was a power in my arms and legs, an eagerness or indifference, that was so surprising. I walked across the warm rug, through bands of sunlight, to the mirror that hung on my closet door. I looked at Margaret, a rounded, pretty, nine-year-old girl, pink and gold herself. My hair was cut short with bangs, honey-colored. My eyes were big and luminous and blue, my face untouched.

Untouched. Quiet, calm, the blood moving in its steady loops. As if there could be no ingress, no egress. The utter smoothness of the skin, the discreet curl of my ears. How well-made and pleasing I was. My arms, my legs, my lips. The inside and outside were one.

I saw the presence of something I had never noticed before. An all-over subtly irregular glow, a shimmer like the sun through leaves. What was it? My eye followed, tried to locate, the sparkle: There was no focal point.

It was everywhere the same, pulsing and strong. As if just under the skin, yet it was skin, too. It stopped my mind from analysis, like a warm hand over my inner eye. I fell into the dream-trance, yet kept wanting to know more. What was it?

I thought I knew. I thought I had glimpsed immortality: the difference between my brother and me, why I could not have been, never would be, killed.

Jimmy. I loved him. Yet a steady wind moved me away from thoughts of him. Bliss allowed no company. Rise and fall of my chest, felicities of my inner workings. Gaze in the mirror. What was coiled deep in my cells, the very stuff of the universe which could never be taken.

All I had to do was stand here forever.

But then I got lonely and went out into the hall. It was empty and quiet, every door shut. Charlotte's door, Johnny's door, my parents'. All the doors cool and dim, only a faint light coming up from downstairs, and through the windows of my room and open door. The panels of the doors, hung neatly in their hinges, under the molding, the brass doorknobs, round and blank. Anything could be behind them.

I couldn't believe I was the first one awake. That never happened. I paused just past the threshold of my room, the smooth carpet stretched out in both directions, the bigs staircase empty as a school building in summer. I listened, heard nothing. I wanted to go see—in their rooms—but was afraid to knock. I imagined the rooms stripped and bare. I imagined the outer walls gone, like pictures of houses after bombs have hit, only it wouldn't be the garden or front yard revealed but another place, unimaginable. I knew this was foolish yet I couldn't knock on the doors. I stood for a long moment in the silence, then walked slowly down the stairs. I ran my hand along the banister and made myself think reasonably. *Everyone is asleep or downstairs. Probably downstairs. They knew when to get up, what to do. What to do? This is the morning of the day after Jimmy died.* How does one act on such a morning?

The length of that staircase. It was three times as long as usual, and I walked three times more slowly. Paying close attention to my bare feet padding across the broad steps, the warm whisper-sound. Thinking, as always, how I loved the house; preparing my-self to be Crusoe here. *It's okay if they're all gone, it doesn't matter, I am in my house. My house, my house.*

Not, like Crusoe, needing to build shelter—*I'm lucky*—but rather to fashion companions. More life into the dolls, the ornaments, the silver forks and spoons. More responsibility to the animals. Were the animals still here?

It went without saying no one from outside would come in.

When I reached the first floor, having lived, it seemed, a whole other life—the shock, the stoicism, the work, the loneliness—I heard voices from the kitchen. Strangers' voices. Even so, it didn't occur to me there would be only strangers in that mother-room.

Soul shriveling to prepare for human contact, I saw three ladies I'd never seen before. They were standing, all drably dressed, fussing at the counters. They turned when I came in and the tallest said, "Good morning, dear."

It was a voice like the blender going. I mumbled good morning. The three ladies introduced themselves and claimed to be neighbors. I didn't believe this. I'd never laid eyes on them. They must live very far away, blocks and blocks. They didn't have to come here.

They were witches. Pretending to be nice, offering to cook me breakfast. I refused their offers, pouring myself a glass of milk. My mother didn't like women in her kitchen. When she had guests she wanted them to stay in the living room while she did the work, alone among her things. Her good china and crystal: Only she could handle them safely. These witches were taking advantage of my mother's sorrow to invade, Mommy was powerless to stop them, and what could I do? I didn't know how to be other than polite to grown-ups.

Here were three women, *drab and ugly*, making coffee, opening drawers, cabinets, lifting the kettle of boiling water. I averted my eyes.

Where was my mother? As if the air had closed around her, taken her—not dead but hidden—sewn into a pocket of the sky. If Jimmy's absence was unbelievable this morning, far away, (maybe I never had an older brother; maybe he was a dream) my mother's absence was all around me, a high-pitched wail.

My gaze, avoiding the women, rested on counters piled high with boxes, tins, and covered platters. What was this? Our counters, especially the island counter where the eye went, were always clean, cleared off. The blender and Mixmaster, glass canisters, a green-and-white bowl of fruit, perhaps a copy of *Gourmet*, or my mother's sunglasses—and plenty of white Formica gleaming. Not these stacks of stuff.

I got up to investigate. Lifted tinfoil, opened boxes. Platters on top of platters, nobody taking care. Just piled haphazardly, cakes, casseroles, side dishes—I knew what this was. I had heard of it, people bringing things after a death, though the image I had was from a storybook: foxes and monkeys in aprons, carrying pies. The reality surprised me. So much food. What did they think, we were hungry?

I wasn't hungry. But you didn't need to be hungry to appreciate such a variety of things to eat. Cookies in several flavors. Oatmeal, peanut butter, chocolate chip, molasses. Brownies with nuts and brownies without nuts. Also cheesecake, poundcake, crumb coffeecake which my mother never bought, she thought it was boring, but which I liked with its buttery brown-sugar topping. Casseroles.

The array made my mind race. How to get as much as possible. What sleight of hand was needed, where to hide it. Could I just grab it? Mommy probably didn't even know what was here yet.

I knew what the women were thinking: I was a disgusting

child who cared more about sweets than her own brother, who could enjoy cookies when Jimmy lay stiff and dead. Who might even be glad Jimmy was dead if it meant cookies! The fact that my heart soared at the idea of food on a morning like this was shameful. Everyone knew that grief made you unable to eat, that people wasted away with sorrow.

It never occurred to me that these foods were intended to help me. That this was solace, and I was welcome to it. I thought they were meant, first of all, for the grown-ups; more insidiously as a temptation.

The women were ignoring me now, standing in a clump by the stove, drinking coffee. I knew they would remember my greed all their lives. I grabbed a handful of cookies and left the room.

I headed for the most distant part of the house, the porch. Carrying the cookies down low, in a rage, and ashamed of this, too, what was wrong with me? And so frightened by the lack of people in my family, empty stairs, no sounds from the second floor. Would the witches have said if my family was gone? Maybe they were going to say but when I refused breakfast they decided to punish me. Let me find out by myself. Maybe tell me in a day or two, "Oh, girl—you, piggy girl; they left. They all drove away in the car early."

Johnny was on the porch. He was kneeling on the rug just inside the door, talking to Sue. He was trying to explain to her what had happened.

"Otherwise she'll keep waiting for Jimmy, running to the front door whenever anyone comes home." He was very distressed over the fact that she couldn't understand, that all she understood was his distress, which made her whine softly. She put her paw on his arm, scrabbling at his sleeve with her blunt claws as he kept speaking, saying Jimmy's name, then lying down flat and closing his eyes. Sue whined more loudly. I told him it's a well-known fact that dogs can see ghosts. I mentioned, offhandedly, that I thought Jimmy had been at the door the night before, right after he died; I had sensed him—and if I had sensed him, I said, Sue must have, too.

Then Johnny asked Sue if she had seen Jimmy's ghost. His serious face—big forehead, tiny nose, eyes as brown as chestnuts. All his teeth in, finally, fair skin with its ornament of scars. The dog seemed worn out by his emotion—she wasn't very smart, hadn't much tolerance for frustration—and only stared, her pop-eyes bulging. I thought she must hate being as stupid as she was. She wasn't like the TV Lassie, or Lad from the Terhune books. Johnny and I were constantly trying to improve her intelligence, to teach her subtle tricks that she never got. Our only success was a backward one—Charlotte had been giving Sue obedience training, and Johnny and I would take her up the hill, out of sight of the house, and go through the same practice in reverse. Praising her disobedience. "We're teaching her to resist," Johnny had said. "She's a dog, she should be free."

"It's okay, Sue," I said now. I gave her a cookie.

"Where did you get those?"

"In the kitchen. There are about a hundred boxes of all kinds of desserts."

"Yeah? I couldn't go in the kitchen. Those ladies are there."

Johnny wanted cookies! He was more afraid than I was! I ran down the hall on my toes, swooped into the kitchen, cast one cool glance at the witches, *dirty witches*, opened the boxes, and loaded up. Why should I care what they thought? I carried the provisions back down the long hall stowed in two napkins, handed them to my brother.

We began to eat.

I watched him eat.

It seemed to me that a long time passed as we sat there with

Sue. I had no idea how long. I wasn't even sure what day it was—Sunday? Yesterday had been Saturday so it should be Sunday, but maybe nothing was the same. The day was a gelid block of light we were stuck in, the sugar in our systems making us dreamy. Maybe we were stowaways in a time ship.

I did know we couldn't go back in time, though we talked about it. But neither could we go forward in the regular way. We had to be going sideways.

We talked about what if we'd had a premonition. Last week, for example, if we'd had a clear dream or just knowledge coming into our heads. ("It hits you like a lightning bolt.") This hadn't happened to either of us, but what if it had? You can't change the future but what if we had *known*? Would Jimmy have believed us?

Telling him *you're going to die*, not being believed. We'd tell him over and over, he'd scoff. Jimmy in his red pullover cotton shirt with the pink shiny synthetic sleeves that he bought at the thrift shop, that shirt our mother hated, it was so cool; it brought out the color in his cheeks. Red and pink, like a valentine. It was big on him. The pink made his hair look darker. It was hard to talk to him lately he was so busy, always studying or at football or wrestling practice or with his friends. Make him listen. *You're going to die—really.* His ear like mine, small, curled, the warm lobe and the ridges and the inside. If he had known. Could he have stopped it?

Johnny said Jimmy wouldn't have believed me, since I was always making stuff up, I was famous for it, but he might have believed him.

I thought but did not say that if anybody had gotten a premonition it would have been me. There are rules, after all, about the one who is chosen. You can't just be like Johnny, making forts in the bushes, playing army games, and expect to be visited by the gods of prophecy. I didn't say it because I felt guilty for not getting such a visit. What was the use of believing in magic, of spending shivery twilights in the garden, attuned to the unseen forces—reading all the books—if I couldn't do an obvious thing like foresee my own brother's death?

We were alone for a long time. We finished the cookies; we ran out of things to say. (We talked a little while about how we would kill him, the boy who ran over Jimmy.) Johnny wanted a glass of milk, but I wasn't ready to go back to the kitchen for that.

Then we heard their voices; we got up and peered around the door to see our father, grandmother, and sister on the stairs. They were all dressed up, Daddy in a suit, Charlotte in a blouse, skirt, and heels. Talking as if they'd all been somewhere together, were returning from a party. I quivered with loneliness which immediately turned into a profound desire not to put on a dress. I mentioned to Johnny that we might be expected to get fancy.

His face shut down. He wouldn't go anywhere near them now. It was like a shell forming—I watched in fascination, also feeling a little guilty. Maybe he wouldn't have had to dress up.

They went into the kitchen and we sat down again, moving a little farther into the room, to the green-and-white rug in front of the fireplace. I liked how this room was both winter and summer, the furniture and French doors summer but the fireplace—small, white marble, discreet—snug against the back wall. It was lit during parties, or on Sunday afternoons. Our parents would sit here, by the fire, reading the paper, having drinks; when Mommy moved into the kitchen to cook and Daddy went upstairs, we'd crowd in, sniffing the melted ice and whiskey, palming a half-smoked cigarette, looking fruitlessly through the *Times* for comics. In novels, newspapers always had funny pages, and I couldn't believe, refused to learn from experience, that in the paper my parents read this was not the case.

I was waiting for Charlotte to find us. I wanted to hear what she had learned, what that conversation on the stairs was about.

Were there plans for us; what were they; and where was our mother?

Many minutes passed, and my sister didn't come. It made me angry. Didn't she know we couldn't go to her, couldn't be around those grown-ups?

The doorbell rang. We could see, down the sixty feet of the hall, our father and grandmother answer it. Grandmommy's long, pretty legs below the plumpness of her torso, her slim ankles and high-heeled shoes. The shining elegance of Daddy in his suit. The two of them standing there, greeting people, Grandmommy an inch or so taller.

I couldn't see who it was who'd come, and then when I did see, it didn't matter. Grandmommy led them into the living room. Daddy went to the kitchen, emerging in a moment with cups of coffee, Charlotte beside him. They both went into the living room. Johnny and I fell silent.

It was shocking to us, this social ritual. Our own sister, our father and grandmother, willingly letting strangers into our house still echoing with the news. The house where the car and the blood, his body flung into the air, were still happening; where the body had not yet reached the ground. The house needed to be swathed, like a wound, in bandages. It was so obvious to me, and I think to Johnny, that we couldn't comprehend this other way of handling things.

As if these strangers—or half strangers, everyone outside the family was at least half a stranger—were so important. Everything made easy for them: coffee, cakes, Daddy and Grandmommy host and hostess. Why would you do that while a body was still in midair?

The doorbell rang again, and then again. Slowly our big rooms filled up with people. They went in the kitchen or the living room, or they stood in the hall holding cups of coffee, smoking cigarettes. Two, four, eight, sixteen. Johnny and I got up once or twice to spy on them—who is it now? Why them? remembering this or that adult at a barbecue in pink plaid shorts—venturing a few feet down the hall, then retreating, waiting for them to leave. We wanted to see our mother, our sister. To go upstairs or outside, eat. But instead more people arrived and we kept hiding.

By the time we realized it was a party, a real party, wave upon wave of guests who would stay for hours, it was too late. Bodies were everywhere, holding glasses and plates of food. They had dispersed into all the rooms, their voices were a continuous murmur, the whole house was like an ocean, the water deep.

We had never had such a party as this, filling all the rooms. Filling the hall as if the hall was a room—I thought it was, of course, but that had been a secret—filling the corners and edges and even the air above. Smoke rising, a blue haze. Ripples of movement through the crowd of packed bodies, cloth swishing, ice rattling. The doorbell. Someone opening the door. The doorbell again. The hum and energy of it getting louder and louder, my own family swallowed up—

What could this be but pollution? They were erasing Jimmy's imprint on the air, stealing from us the time to collect his last traces. I didn't know, Johnny didn't know, what rooms he had been in last. Neither of us could reconstruct the events of yesterday morning. I had seen him at breakfast, Johnny had seen him leave the house, but what had he done, where had he been for the two hours in between? We knew a few places he had been the day before that—in the basement, skateboarding, in the living room after dinner, and Johnny said he had come into his room and they talked. I believed that if we could walk around the house (the properly empty house) we would be able to find his impressions. If he had sat in the red Eames chair in the living room, if he had stood by the window, I would know. Even his footsteps down the hall could be followed. I thought of these traces as warmth, a trail of warmth throughout the house, like summer.

People came into the porch. They came to get away from the others, sat on the couch. We were tucked behind it. This was the Danish couch, blue cushion and teak frame, open space beneath it, like a table. They could easily see us, but they didn't see us because they weren't paying attention. Adults were like that, walking in straight lines, keeping their gazes fixed. Of course they were looking at each other, though I didn't see why they bothered, they were mostly ugly and their expressions were fake.

The men who came in here talked too loud, and the women listened, moving their lacquered heads. The women leaned down to tap the ashes off their cigarettes and made idle remarks about our house. I was so angry. *My brother is dead*; they swung their legs and chattered. In relief at not having to talk anymore about what they were supposed to be here talking about, *Jimmy is dead*, they chattered and flirted. The women languorously tapped their cigarettes.

Imagine knives up through the cushion of the couch. Imagine South American poison blow darts; we could aim for the back of their necks.

Sue, who had left us, now returned—looked at us from the doorway; we mouthed commands. "Get 'em!" Grimacing, eyes signaling wildly, hopelessly—she'd never learned that command, she was utterly placid, though if one of us sat on Johnny, even in play, she'd growl—and the dog sighed and looked abashed and went to the strangers for a pat. They ignored her. She came around the back of the couch. "Get 'em!" She trembled. She hated this, being confused.She left the room again, toes clicking. The adults noticed nothing.

In a pause between infestations—these flirting scum left, later others came, lots of people liked this room where nobody else was. *Why don't you just go home.* Johnny said if Jimmy were here, he'd know how to get rid of them. He reminded me that Jimmy had been reading up on Vietcong guerrilla fighters: how a few wily men can defeat a superior force. They hide in the bushes and the trees, blend into a landscape they knew well. They pick off our blundering soldiers one by one.

I remembered Jimmy talking about his: my amazement. Vietcong beating American soldiers? Jimmy had admired them; he said our men should learn the same tricks. My mind had wheeled slowly, receiving the new gestalt. There was a darkness to it, a rushing riverine thrill; this was a real war out there we were talking about. Killing American soldiers. Grown-ups.

Johnny said Jimmy would think up a strategy like that. Create a diversion to lure the people outside—maybe say the house was on fire—then shoot them from the bushes. Since they would be panicked and unprepared, we wouldn't need many guns.

We gazed out the window at the crusted snow of the garden, at the evergreen shrubbery. Guerrillas. Jimmy out there, fighting, a rebel force in the hills. It filled me with a longing I didn't understand, more piercing than just wanting him alive. It was strange—how could anything be more piercing than that?

I thought I saw the bushes move. *Outside.* Maybe death took you *Outside.* I didn't know what that meant, but there was something . . . I lost it.

"If Jimmy was here . . ." Johnny said.

"If Jimmy was here, this wouldn't be happening."

"I know. It's weird—but if he *was*—"

We fell silent. Of course we needed him to make things happen. There was nothing we could do by ourselves. I don't know how Johnny felt about this—I suspect he was already gathering himself to be the boy—but I grabbed at the chance to turn my longing into an engagement with the paradox: Only Jimmy can help us handle Jimmy's death.

My mind in a shiver, pondering. Spooked by, hurt by, yet clinging to the knot, the chewy almost-yield of it. Like a problem in arithmetic, one just a little too hard. Only Jimmy can help us deal with this that is happening.

Did I imagine, then, that he somehow would?

Johnny grew tired of waiting for the people to go away and decided to run upstairs. This made sense, I should go, too, but I found myself unable to leave the spectacle. I was ashamed of this—didn't I want to be alone—but I was held by the crowd as if by gravity. The size of it, the buzzing hive. The novelty. My hate was beginning to bore me, though I didn't think of it quite that way. I thought I was weak, lacking in conviction.

I said I wanted to find Charlotte. Johnny said he wouldn't mind seeing her, if she came upstairs. So we parted, his fluid sprint down the hall and up the staircase anguishing me. How could he be left alone?

I was alone. Careful, now. I moved slowly-quickly through the throng of guests, advancing as in that game Simon Says. Keeping my head down, looking for my sister. I wanted to find her but not my grandmother, who'd tell me to put a dress on, or my Aunt June, who'd look at me with her cool sharp gaze.

I needed my sister. I had had enough of Johnny for now; I needed my sister. She could be a liaison, she could tell me what I was supposed to be doing without having the power to make me do it. And her pink eyes and the story she told last night, how she couldn't cry at the hospital but twisted up Kleenex so the nurses would think she did. Then she did cry on the bed with us.

I expected the grown-ups to all be like the witches in the kitchen, saying, Good Morning, Dear, Can I Get You Anything, but they weren't like that. Most of them didn't notice me, or they looked away, or waited to see if I would hold their gaze. I didn't. I edged through. It was affecting me, this press of bodies. I hardly knew how, but it was dizzying, so much flesh and soul—pieces of cheek, clumps of hair, shoulders, people kept apart by the length of cigarettes, mosaic of people, a mouth, a wrist—it was transporting me who had already been transported, who didn't know where she was, it was losing me, finding me, multiplying me, and all I could hold on to was my fear that in the multitude Jimmy would be swept away forever.

Charlotte was talking to my cousins in the hall near the kitchen. All the girls were dressed up: party dresses, white stockings, patent-leather shoes. Their attire made me feel self-conscious. My shorts and T-shirt were like the cookies, meant I didn't care. And once that idea started, panic set in. What if they teased me, if Charlotte tried to push me away and my cousins acquiesced with their blank faces. If Charlotte didn't think anymore that Jimmy being dead made any difference, if I was still Booger, and what are you doing here, you think we want *you* around? They would see as soon as I walked up to them that I wanted to be with people, I had never known how to manage it, to join people without having them know I wanted to.

As soon as they saw that, of course, I was dead.

Barefoot, circling behind, I came close, hidden behind some slab of a man. I heard one of my cousins ask, "Where's Margaret? I haven't seen her at all." I liked that, yes, I caressed it in my mind: Where's Margaret? *(I'm here.)* Where is she, whom we so much want to see, whom we miss, our own darling Margaret?

It was good, the tone of my cousin's voice, clear, fresh, sincere; I savored it. But I couldn't risk showing myself. Even now, on this august occasion. Especially now.

I couldn't risk it, though I feared they'd all be mad at me later. *Where were you, why were you hiding? Jimmy's dead, you know. We're supposed to be together.*

Later I saw Charlotte by herself in the dining room. She was arranging something, or gathering up plates. I let her see me—she wouldn't attack me if nobody was around—and she said, "Where have you been?"

"Around."

"Grandmommy was looking for you, and the Arnolds were, too."

"What for?"

She shrugged. I hovered. "They just wanted to see you," she said at last, plaintively. I took that in and could think of nothing to say. I asked her where my mother was.

She said Mommy was sleeping. Still sleeping? It was past noon. Then Charlotte said she wasn't actually sleeping but resting. I'll go up and see her, I said, but my sister said no, I wasn't allowed.

Not allowed?

No. "She's resting."

I roamed, one of the Vietcong, moving not through jungle but a mass of thick bodies, always one or another stranger I could hide behind. The adults who didn't know me didn't speak to me, so I could treat them as trees or inanimate masses, and they didn't know this either, having no sense of their own impersonal presence. The men were easiest. They were the most unconscious as well as the biggest; their suited backs made walls. But some of the women were also impervious, their rear ends like shrubbery. I could keep a few feet to the left or right of one person crossing a room and so escape Grandmommy's glance. Once or twice she did see me but couldn't do more than motion with her eyebrows; she was in a conversation, caught, I could safely ignore her. And I could hide from Nana and my aunts.

I went in and out of the kitchen, taking cookies and slices of cake. I sat on the back stairs eavesdropping. I checked on the yellow telegrams piling up on the hall table. So many. The doorbell ringing with a new one every fifteen minutes. I spied on my cousins—if I could catch Faxy alone . . . But she was never alone. Charlotte was with her or my Aunt June.

Johnny came back downstairs. I got him a plate of food; then we hid in the coat closet, going through the pockets. We waited for our mother.

When she finally appeared, late in the afternoon, down the stairs, she walked very slowly, leaning on her friend Nicky's arm. She wore a short black dress, black shoes and stockings. When I saw her I thought her loneliness was my loneliness. I couldn't tell them apart.

She went immediately into the living room, stood in the middle, by the piano. The living room was a long, airy room, French doors to the terrace, the Danish Modern furniture somehow too insubstantial. The colors were blue and gray, cream, and the reds in the rug. All the shadows were blue. We dove toward our mother, slashing ferociously through the crowd, which was moving as one organism in the same direction. Like the herd of cows that converged on the car when Uncle Bubber drove across his ranch lands, they massed and lumbered. Pressed up against each other, exerting powerful force. I was surprised. Angry at the obstacle they presented, yet startled to realize they had been lingering all day precisely in order to speak to my mother. The grieving mother of the dead boy.

Johnny and I torpedoed under the arms holding drinks, dodged cigarettes, dogged our way through, demanding our position, until we stood beside her and she placed a hand on each of our heads.

She didn't speak to us. It was as if she had forgotten that she hadn't spoken to us since breaking the news the night before. We were waiting for something, something very specific, but it was forgotten. She had gone past it already or had never known what it was, and as we stood there beside her it was impossible for me to remember it either. Only my greedy self, bursting open like a seedpod.

She spoke to the grown-ups, who all had a thing to say to her, some formal, stilted condolence. One by one they came to her and took her hand. I watched and listened in a rage. Many of them had sons. They were glad it was Jimmy, not their boy who died. I could see that as if it were written on their foreheads in neon; so obvious their cringing relief, their guilt.

Each one saying the stupid thing, the meaningless thing. Or praising Jimmy without knowing at all who he was, as if he was just a *boy*, any *boy*. It gave me a kind of vertigo—they were killing him again.

My mother gave each person who approached her two or three minutes of her attention. It was very hard for her. She was so thin and pale, her eyes hollowed; she was swaying on her feet. She was like a young tree that had been forced to come inside and speak, black branches sleeved in ice. I loved her with a great distant passion.

Why them and not us? This is what I was thinking as she opened her lips, found words for each person; why him and not me? I knew the hand on my head meant love. You are mine, she was saying, I claim you. I heard that. But I wanted words.

I wanted action. Why didn't the grown-ups—all these grown-ups who professed to care—organize a search party, set off for the underworld? There were entrances on earth, everybody knew that. You could cross its barriers alive: the Greek heroes did. Odysseus, Orpheus. What I had learned from the story of Orpheus was that such a thing was possible; you could rescue someone; you just had to be more careful and disciplined than the poet. I quite literally wanted the adults to sit down now, in a circle against the far wall where nobody was standing (you have to start in an empty place, a place empty except for the gray shadows) and hammer out a plan for rescuing Jimmy. Put their heads together, all that they had learned from so many years on earth, their different lives and jobs; surely somebody must know something of consequence. All these men and women. If they were really connected to us, a community (like the kings of Greece all going to fight for Menelaus) then they must do this now, settle this thing. Find where it was, the entrance to Hades. Who could be appealed to, who must be fought against, who tricked. Why were they delaying? Didn't they see there was no point in living until we had conquered death?

Mommy was only downstairs for an hour, then she went back to bed. We thought surely we could talk to her now. We could lie on her bed and talk to her.

They didn't let us. Always there was some woman—one of our aunts, Nicky—guarding the door, saying don't go in. Mommy was in the blue guest room and as we crept down the hall—two, three, four times—the woman would appear as if from nowhere, alert. "Your mother is resting. Go downstairs now, be good children." It caused a queer twisted pain in my heart. Why was it bad to want to see her? My grief a wrongness while in her it was holy and protected.

Eleven

THE AFTERNOON GREW dark. It had snowed again, then stopped; it was snowing now. I sat under the hall table by the front door, reading the telegrams. There were so many the piles had toppled, sliding off the table to pile up again, like autumn leaves, on the polished floor by the coat closet. Somebody had opened and read them, probably my grandmother. I sat cross-legged and gathered them in my lap. Thin yellow whispery envelopes, like the paper patterns when my mother sewed.

"Sympathy in this time of great sorrow." "Deepest sympathy Fanny and Jugie." "Sincerest sympathy for your loss."

These words, spaced across the fragile paper—impressed into it with a greater force than in a book. Only slight variations in sentiment and tone, yet each one with a look of profound urgency. I was struck by this, and by their brevity and syntax.

I knew that the brevity had to do with money, but it seemed more than that. The sentences that were created this way were pleasing. Words left out so you had to jump over; it was like jumping rope, the glow in your legs after.

All the words important. A name at the end.

Most of the names were strange to me. Again, I couldn't fathom it, the interest that was taken. I knew it had to do with the past, my mother's past, the life before I was born. Before Jimmy was born. I had an inkling now of the sweetness of it—this love sent, in such volume—yet it seemed still an offense to me, on this day of all days, to have to face that there was a time before we were born. My brother, not only dead, but survived by so many elders.

My siblings, interested in reading the first dozen or so telegrams, didn't understand why I couldn't stop reading. "They all say the same thing," Johnny complained.

People were starting to leave now, so the door opened and shut frequently. A little pleasure in watching the legs go by, hearing the good-byes, absorbing gusts of cold air. Grandmommy was here, presiding over the departures, and she didn't bother me. She hadn't, after all, mentioned what I was wearing. I liked that. But mostly I was concerned with the reading. Though the unfamiliar names with their claims on my parents upset me, I still found each parched sentence exquisite. It was the words that were exquisite. The repetition, the spacing. Those particular words—*sympathy*? *Love*? Perhaps. I didn't know what, really. But I liked that word, *sympathy*. It was sinuous yet had bosoms.

The house was almost empty now. Daddy's relatives back in their hotel, most of the neighbors gone. The Arnolds were gone. Grandmommy was here of course, and Nicky; a few others. Half a dozen women talking quietly in the kitchen, cleaning up.

I wandered. Upstairs, downstairs, not knowing where to be. My grandmother fixed me a plate of dinner.

The best thing was to be in motion. To feel the house settling as the strangers left, rooms returning to the lofty solitude that was their nature. The high ceilings, creamy walls, long expanses of floor where the white fringe of the rugs lay like little hairy worms. If you slid your foot under the fringe it fell between toes.

I couldn't find Jimmy's traces. It was probably too late for that. The spirit-fire of his body had been swirled away. Instead I remembered what I could remember, all our years in this house (the day we moved in, how he led the exploration; House-Roaming) and how he liked to swivel in the red Eames chair, feet tucked under; he said he was a yogi, which I thought was like Yogi Bear or Yogi Berra, who lived down the street from us, his son was Johnny's good friend. Jimmy explained what a yogi really was. Why couldn't he be one? in that way he had of being anything he wanted and still perfectly, brilliantly, normal. This was what I couldn't understand: how it could be him, who was the most—as I would say now—at ease in the world. Who was the key to the world.

Remembering his body in motion, shoulders, arms, the play of muscle, the eager obedience of limb to impulse. He would wrestle with Johnny and me in the upstairs hall, placing himself in the middle of the hall while we ran from the far corners, trying to get past him. He usually won, we sometimes won. Johnny won by quickness, slipperiness, feints; I won by bulldozing through, refusing to believe it was possible I could lose. It was Jimmy who pointed this out, our different strategies, how they reflected our personalities; he found it so interesting.

He would laugh telling us; we loved to be told. He wasn't worried we'd beat him for good, even be stronger. So we could bang ourselves against him like puppies, he'd laugh, and when he needed to be alone, go into his room and shut his door. The music drifting out. Rock-and-roll like a trail of crumbs.

The shock of impossibility was still strong, though less frequent. Every half an hour instead of every five minutes.

I must remember. Jimmy with his friends on the roof, that lined-up taut silence of theirs, as if they were tilting way back. On the phone with a girl, his whole face involved. On his bicycle outside the kitchen window, my mother is inside, talking to Nicky. He rides past then does the exact same sequence in reverse, like a movie being rewound; she doesn't notice the first time; he keeps it up until she does. Or the way he looked practicing piano, soft, Charlotte beside him on the bench, their two heads bent together like the infinity sign . . .

The house was emptying. Grandmommy turned the lights off in living room and dining room—those big dark gaps of space, as if I almost missed the crowd. I didn't know where my father was.
My mother was upstairs, Charlotte and Johnny were upstairs. The women in the kitchen cleaned up almost silently; soon they would leave, we'd all go to bed. Not quite yet, we had a few hours—but I could see, it would happen, the day over, another day. Jimmy further behind us.

Did he know it was happening; did he hear the car? How long was the moment; what did he think? How could he believe it? I, Jimmy, am dying. Up in the air. Coming down.

The dishes were being put away. The dish towels were folded, some woman was looking for her purse. I left the kitchen, crossed the hall, and saw my father crying in the stairwell. He was standing in his dark suit, a glass in his hand, in the shadow under the curve of the stairs. Out here where anyone could see—though nobody was in the hall but us; I, in my shorts and T-shirt, barefoot, Daddy in his formal clothes, head bowed.

Daddy was crying. And suddenly I was having a vision. What I saw was *me*. Not my *me*, but his *me*. How did that happen? It was as clear as anything, as a view through a window. Inside the graceful, suited figure I saw an inner architecture, columns and struts, levels, rooms, all of it red and hot as a furnace, glowing; and a scrambling, swift little figure called *me*. *Me.* A ridiculous figure, cartoonish, rushing up and down, trying to be everywhere at once, yet thrillingly energetic, racing, sliding down poles like a fireman, fixing things. In and out of the fiery chambers, as if the owner of it all, yet so little, so silly and rubbery. I saw this as vividly as life, and I knew it, as I had never suspected one could know anything, especially this. Having never really believed in any *me* but my own.

I was awed, and then I wanted to go to him. To hug him around the waist, fling my affection upon him recklessly. I, Margaret, carrier of invisible wrongness, was also Margaret his daughter who could see him. He wouldn't reject me.

He might.

I tried to act, I gave my muscles the command, but they didn't obey.

I struggled, arguing with myself. *His tears mean that he loves us.*

No, his tears mean that he loved Jimmy.

Could he love Jimmy so much and not love me?

Why not? Maybe he wishes it were you that died.

This idea was like a bell chiming, freezing me in place. I didn't really think it was the case, but I couldn't be sure. To even consider it was to be paralyzed, flattened against the plane of my thought.

More than anything, I wanted to move, to respond to my vision, so miraculous, so amazing. To *see*, and then to *act*.

I knew my vision was true. That that was the real Daddy I was seeing, that wild and haunted *me*, but it made no difference. Experience said: To approach him is not safe. And though it was safe, right now, I knew it, I couldn't act on it because I knew it with a part of myself that had no power. That was only an eye. The power was all in the old, locked stubbornness.

As I struggled with myself, in a fury at my lack of control, I began to understood, really for the first time, to see, how deeply at fault my father was. He had done this to me. I was afraid because he had hurt me and hurt me, and that hurt had shaped me; now I was it. It had been done, could not be undone. I was going to make a terrible mistake—walk right past him, no acknowledgment given his tears, no love given at the only moment I knew he could take it in; that we both needed, which I *knew*; and it was his fault.

It was his fault, he was a bad father; yet I so much wanted to be a better girl. For an instant the world had split open and I was not alone. *I love you.* Anything would have been possible in that moment. I saw it as a door I could walk through. Refusing that grace—that moment as in fairy tales when the heroine is presented with a choice, and the wise fairy or talking animal reveals the correct path—made me exquisitely aware of the damage to my soul. As I walked past my father up the stairs, straight-backed like my mother, like Jimmy, neither of us speaking though I was aware of his awareness of me, as I felt in myself the necessity of a silent disdain, I saw inside my heart with the new vision. Saw Margaret as a being stiff with bitterness and fear, twisted by a hideous isolation.

It made me so angry.

THE NEXT DAY there were still people all over the house and that weird partylike atmosphere. I didn't hide but kept moving, roaming from room to room, up and down the hall. The hall was my preferred place because today the grown-ups only used it for passage, except for the part near the front door where they might stand talking. But the back half of the hall, from the kitchen to the porch, was not lingered in, though it equaled any good-size room. The grown-ups came through and I turned my face away; they paused sometimes as if about to speak, but whomever they were going toward, what they carried in their hands, compelled them forward.

I thought of the hall as my ally, ejecting the guests. Its long coolness was the nerve of the downstairs, its thinking part, where my power was strongest. I walked up and down the edge of the rug, bare feet on wool and wood at once, running my hands over the rough canvas or smooth glass of the pictures. (All my mother's pictures, by a variety of artists, were brightly colored, stylized, figurative, symbolic.) The pictures ended about three-quarters of the way to the porch; then there was only the creamy shadowed expanse of wall. Standing there, head tilted back to touch the plaster, feet off the rug, I was almost invisible.

The house, which had seemed alien the night Jimmy died, then so monstrously occupied, impaired, was alive again, fully. I was in communication with it: its spirit was calm. I could look up and see the soaring vastness, the unbroken snow of the remote ceiling, and be reassured. I could live there. Hadn't I always wanted to? Margaret in the white wilderness, the warm wilderness.

The house knew what was real. In its discreet silence, it was the best evidence for life as it should be. I roamed the length of the hall, *movement is pleasure,* shutting and opening my eyes so that any human gait I witnessed was rendered discontinuous. In this manner, I could make people disappear.

Twelve

MY MOTHER CAME downstairs this second day at noon. She didn't look like a branch sleeved in ice anymore, but like herself, very tired and weary. Her face was as soft as the biscuit dough Lucille would knead at my grandmother's house; and her eyes were soft. She spoke to us as if she had not been silent for so long, and I almost forgot that she had been. One day. One night, and the next day. It was almost as if she were still our mother, our same mother, and of course she was—I loved her leapingly—

Mommy told us that the funeral would be the next day, and that Jimmy would be cremated. He had been reading a book called *The American Way of Death*, by Jessica Mitford, a book about the funeral industry. He had said to her, "If I should die, I want to be cremated."

If I should die . . .

He found the book in our library. Our parents, lots of people, were reading it. The funeral industry, my mother said carefully, sometimes cheated people or convinced them to buy what they didn't need. This book exposed that.

We had to consider the possibility that Jimmy had seen his death coming.

"He couldn't have known when," said Johnny.

"Or where. And he couldn't have known for sure or he would have told us."

"He might not have told us if it was something he couldn't do anything about. He wouldn't want us to be upset."

"But he would have said good-bye. He would have said it in such a way that we wouldn't have understood but then, looking back, we would."

Johnny agreed that this was so. We were silent for a moment. Nothing Jimmy had said to us in the last week could be so construed. "He didn't know," I concluded, "but something knew."

"What do you mean?"

"The fact that he was reading that book right before he died means that his death had already been planned to happen."

Charlotte pointed out that lots of people read that book and didn't die. Neither Johnny nor I accepted this logic because its basis was that Jimmy and other people had the same weight in the world.

Johnny was angry at the idea that Jimmy's death could have been predestined; and his anger was like an animal in his body, I could see it moving from his face down to his arms to his fists. Little clenched fists and his nostrils flaring. I understood, but I wasn't angry. Jimmy was already dead; I believed it now; if it was destiny—that might be a good thing.

There were, now, with this idea, two Jimmys: Jimmy alive and Jimmy dead. I didn't think of destiny in regard to my living brother whom I missed so much, I thought of it in regard to his dead spirit. Destiny held that robed-in-purple, princely boy, made a place for him.

Johnny and I both disliked the idea of cremation. Johnny speculated that Jimmy hadn't wanted the worms to get him. I agreed but was still upset: no grave to visit, to cover with flowers. No pale gray stone with his name carved, no winged angel. No honeycakes.

It was a funny word, *cremate*. As if we were turning him into cream.

I complained to my mother about it. The word, I mean. "That's just what they call it, Margaret," she said and I was offended; what did "they" have to do with it, why were "they" everywhere, not only here in this house but in town, writing his too-brief obituary in the local paper—one skinny column! at the hospital, at the funeral home; they were all in it together, the adults.

Hiding him. Putting him in the fire. And shouldn't we be there, watching?

"Why do you want to watch? You want to see Jimmy burn?" asked Charlotte.

It wasn't my idea to burn him. I would bathe him in sweet oil, scent him with spices. Wrap him in white linen. Either do what they did to the pharaohs, so they last forever, and build him a pyramid, or else send him out to sea on a raft made of laurel branches.

That night, late, Johnny and I met again in Jimmy's room. We stood together in the center of the rug, trying to contact him. Our eyes ranged over his bed, his books, his football helmet, his model glue. We waited, somewhat at a loss but neither scared nor shy. Our parents hadn't been in here all day. Nobody had come here, and this dereliction gave us strength.

We talked about the cremation. We assumed Jimmy would have an interest in this subject, if not in us.

"Because of that book you read," we informed him. "She remembered. She took you seriously." I knew I was supposed to admire the fact that my mother was honoring Jimmy's request, and in a way I did, but . . .

If he was just talking, if he didn't *know* he was going to die . . .

He might feel differently now.

"Grandmommy and Nana are upset about it," we continued. "If you don't really want it done, say so."

There was no response. I spoke louder, enunciating, Johnny beside me, big-headed, bright-eyed little brother. How could Jimmy not answer us on a question of such importance? A question that concerned *him*. It disturbed me to think he was busy, indifferent . . . helpless . . .

Johnny suggested maybe we needed to go to the spot where he was killed; that only there could the ghost hear us. That was a good idea, and we talked it over, but, really, it was too difficult. We didn't know where it was exactly, nor had we any way to get there.

Earlier that afternoon a teenage girl who lived across the street from the spot had come over to bring us something: the frames of his glasses, a couple of twisted pieces, in a white envelope.

I didn't see the girl or the glasses; I had been upstairs reading; Charlotte told me. She said the girl's mother drove her, but she came to the door by herself. She just looked like an ordinary girl, and she was nervous. Mom was kind to her, Charlotte went on, because she knew the girl meant well, but that those twisted frames horrified her and she didn't want to look at them.

"What happened to them?" we asked, and Charlotte said of course they were thrown away.

"They were *twisted*, broken. Do you know what that means?"

We knew what it meant. I wanted them. Johnny wanted them. We appreciated what the girl had done and would have done it with her if we could, combing the site for even the broken glass itself, each glittering shard. "If we found the glass," I said, "and glued it all back together, and put it in the frames, then looked through them—"

"Don't say anything like that to Mom," Charlotte said. "You guys have no idea what she's going through."

And then she was unhappy, my sister, that we set ourselves apart from her.

So maybe he couldn't come, maybe he was tethered to the site. Maybe he couldn't even hear us. Who was stopping him? The authorities in this matter were nebulous—rather like the grown-ups in our house all day—beings we instinctively disdained. A supernatural officiousness whose only interest lay in what it held captive, his bright soul.

I tried to make the cats help. Cats, even more than dogs, are supposed to be messengers to the other world. But when I asked them, politely, to go get Jimmy, they merely blinked at me from his bed, where all four of them had been hiding since the house filled up with people.

I picked up Fluffy, Charlotte's ancient black-and-white stump-tailed female, and scolded her, my face inches from her flat old face. She was the eldest, it was her responsibility. She hissed at me and jumped free.

"Jinx will go," said Johnny, putting his plump gray tabby on the floor. Jinx was a good choice. Ricky was too lazy, Charlotte's Gypsy, too feebleminded. But Jinx was good—small, tough, loyal, and possessed of odd traits. She wasn't afraid of water. She'd sit neck-deep in the stuff, bathing with Johnny. He even claimed she could breathe underwater.

"Go ahead, Jinx," I said. "Go to the other world and tell Jimmy we want to talk to him." Was it such a difficult request? We had housed her and fed her her entire life. Johnny had bought her at a fair in New Hampshire one summer with his own money; then we'd talked Mom into letting us keep her and Gypsy. But Jinx sat still where Johnny had placed her. She looked at us placidly, cleaned her face, and jumped up on the bed again.

"It must be impossible," my brother said. "Where did you read that, anyway?"

"It's not impossible. Our cats are all stupid."

We asked Jimmy for a sign.

"Anything," said Johnny. "We'll know."

Back in my bedroom, I worried about this. Johnny thought a sign would be unmistakable. But in *The Silver Chair*, one of the Narnia series, the children miss almost every sign because nothing is what they are expecting. There are words carved in the stone that they pass in a snowstorm, weary and hungry, focused on themselves, and they don't see.

There were also darker stories. For example, "The Monkey's Paw." In this story an old couple gets hold of a magic monkey's paw that grants three wishes. Their first wish is for money—not a lot of money, just a specific sum they need. Then a message comes telling them their son has died in an accident at work, and the death benefit is exactly that amount of money. Of course at that moment they hate the monkey's paw, and they vow to destroy it. But a couple of nights later, in her grief, the mother uses the second wish to ask that her son come back. Nothing happens right away, and they assume that their wish was too big, forbidden. But after a couple of hours they hear a knocking at the door. The mother rushes to answer it but the father, thinking fast, realizes that the couple of hours is exactly what it would take for a corpse, climbing out of its coffin, to walk the six miles to their door. They forgot to ask that he come back alive. The father rubs the paw for the last time, "I wish him back in his grave right now," and the mother opens the door on nothing.

I was aware, with a kind of surprise, that I didn't take it seriously, asking Jimmy to speak to us. If I did, I would be more afraid. And yet it seemed as if I was taking it seriously. It seemed real. I couldn't understand this, but as I lay in bed pondering, a layer of guilt settled into me, like a sheet of tissue between my heart and my skin. It had to do with all this thinking. With the way my thoughts swung behind and looked at themselves, or hovered above themselves, the way that in the last forty-eight hours I had grown a whole skein of thought-matter, new, fascinating, and now was busy making something of it.

This was not the proper way to grieve.

The next morning, when I went downstairs, I found Charlotte and Hattie in the kitchen talking about a thing that had happened earlier. Mommy and Daddy had been in the living room at eight o'clock discussing Jimmy's cremation—maybe at the exact moment it was taking place, they did it early—and a book of matches on the mantel suddenly burst into flame. There was no fire in the fireplace, and nobody near; all by itself the book flared up, and burned.

Charlotte was excited, babbling. Hattie was shaking her head. I asked Hattie if she had seen anything. "I ain't going in that room today," she said. "I'm going to church." She was sorting the cakes and doughnuts people had brought; I took a cinnamon doughnut, ran to find my mother. Mommy confirmed the story calmly, a strange calmness, as if it had happened years ago in another country.

"Where was I?"

"You were still asleep."

"Why?"

"He's telling us the cremation is alight, it's what he wants." As I made her talk about it, each sentence coming out like when you squeeze a teddy bear to get that chest-sound—it took a continual effort—her voice became singsong, and her eyes flickered. Her brown eyes had a light in them today, yellowish. A warm light—there was a warmth in her that came and went now, like waves; I didn't know if it was meant for me. I didn't think so.

I asked her to show me the book of matches, but they'd already been thrown away.

"Where? Which trash can?"

"Oh, I don't know, Margaret, it's *gone*." This made me suspicious—why would anybody throw such a thing away? (Why was she angry at me? I was just asking what was obvious to ask.) I decided she must be hoarding them.

I kept at her but all she would say was what she'd already said: He's telling us it's alright. Alright. Alright. She was going about her business as we talked, I don't remember what exactly; we were in the dining room, in the pantry, she was finding things, arranging and organizing things. Her voice singsong. Calm and secretive. And that strange yellow light streaking her eyes.

I went into the living room, investigated the mantel. Charlotte came in behind me, talking. She wasn't there when it happened but was almost there, she was awake, in the kitchen, they told her first, she had ideas—I tried to shake her out of my awareness. I needed to *feel*.

I looked carefully. The usual figurines—gray pottery, sleek, modern—part of my mother's mysterious semi-alive collection of objets d'art. The silver cigarette box. For years I had been satisfied with that hidden quickening—the beautiful object—satisfied to wait until the wise man came out of the pottery, or the silver box opened its hinged lid by itself. Happy with the gleams of spirit around me, this house devoted to their attendance, with my mother who was, if not precisely in sync with me, still a channel for the magic. It had been enough. It wasn't now. Deeper magic was happening, matches leaping off the mantel all in flame—Jimmy! *Oh, Jimmy*—and I wasn't there. I was sleeping. They had let me sleep.

Nobody seemed to think I had any rights to my own brother. I was put aside, out of the way, they didn't get it, this was happening to me— It didn't matter what happened to me. I had no power, except in my head. There he was mine, entirely mine. I shut my eyes and here he came, strolling from the left side of my brain, laughing. Had anyone else noticed, I wondered, how thoughts always come from the left? Memories from directly in back, and a little down, but thought, imagination, comes from the left. So I could tell the difference. I could tell the difference anyway, my memories were still so pungent. It was easier to toy with thought.

Folding and folding, cocooning mindstuff around this strange event, the burning matches. The words of the story as I had heard it made a crack in reality unlike any that had been before. It wasn't a crack I could go through or see through, it wasn't like a written story, but still, to know about it was so valuable.

My mother, within an hour, had made herself normal again. More normal than she had been since Jimmy died, fussing with me about what I was to wear. Which dress. Which shoes. Stockings. I went along with her anxiously. Why all this elaborate concern, who cared about this, not even funeral (no body) but memorial service? If we were just remembering, we could do it here. In his room.

What if the matches meant: Stay here. I am here.

Oh, where? What were the mechanics of it, that he could manifest one moment, not another? Was it a choice?

I became upset that I didn't have a black dress. My mother said children didn't need to wear black, it wasn't expected. I thought if it was expected that I go, that I wear a fancy dress, that it should be the same kind of dress as the grown-ups. Black for mourning; did she think I wasn't mourning? I asked her. She said no, it's not that, children just don't have to do it, and when would we have taken you to buy a black dress?

"We could dye one of my dresses," I said.

"Don't worry about it."

All the way to the church I brooded. Everything happened without me: the accident itself, the trip to the hospital, the matches. Jimmy was in the other world, and I didn't know what world that was. Weirdness all around me, and here I sat in my pink dress, carried along in the car, as if I were floating. Nothing beneath me.

The first time I'd lit a match it was for church. I was six and had been chosen to light the Christmas candles. Every year a little girl and a little boy walked down the aisle and lit the tapers on the altar.

I'd never lit a match before because it was forbidden. My mother always said we could catch ourselves on fire.

I practiced for days. My siblings said it was nothing, they could all do it, had done it, forbidden or not, even Johnny, nineteen months younger than I. But I went in fear of my mother's words—"catch yourself on fire"—and I trembled each time I struck the match.

I learned how to do it and did it smoothly on the day. I walked down the aisle, all the grown-ups looking, and drew the little stick across the raspy surface.

It surprised me how much I loved it. To be the one moving while the grown-ups, the older kids, sat still, to climb the steps, set flame to the slender wick. Nobody making fun or getting mad, none of the kids stopping me. Candle leaping, glowing, here I was—

Wrong to even remember that today. It was Jimmy's day. Now we were supposed to all be solemn and cry, everybody watching. Charlotte said, "Don't sob, but you should cry a little. Don't make noise or snot, but a few tears will mean you loved Jimmy. Grandmommy will give you a hankie."

I didn't want to think about whether or not I could cry, like an actress on stage. What I wanted to do was shout ugly things—

nasty words, hate. The idea was burning inside me: Jimmy's death was Mommy's and Daddy's fault. They didn't pick him up when he'd specifically asked them to. *He'd asked them to.* My mother: I'd do anything in the world for you children. I'd walk through fire, I'd give my life for you children.

She wouldn't drive across town to pick him up. She cared more about her stupid dinner reservation.

I was terrified these thoughts might show. I might lose control at the church, disgrace myself. *It was Jimmy's memorial service.* Didn't I love him?

The sequence of images again: car, bicycle, does he turn his head? in the sky—

Suddenly, wonderfully, I remembered that religion was concerned with the afterlife. That's what we were going to do! That was the point of church. As well as talking about him alive, the minister, Dr. Fletcher, would tell us where Jimmy had gone, where he was right now.

It was not—when I thought about it—that I expected to necessarily believe Dr. Fletcher, that white-haired, soft-faced old man. After all, as Jimmy had said, nobody really knows, not even adults; it's all theory. I remembered my brother's careful explanation of this. I remembered. But I wanted to hear Dr. Fletcher's opinion. I wanted to hear him talk as my brother used to, laying out the scheme of how things were. I would decide where the truth lay, I understood that was my responsibility, but the minister's voice would give me a push.

I had received very little spiritual instruction. In Sunday school we learned about Moses in the bulrushes, Joseph's many-colored coat, the Pharaoh's dreams. I heard a lot about the baby in the manger but not very much about the crucifixion. The mysterious ways of the Lord, that he giveth and taketh away, were not touched on. I was not raised to fear God but to regard him with a mild interest. The most pressing question I ever had was whether he could watch me in the bathroom.

All that side of my nature was nurtured by fairy tales and magic. My strongest association to the cross was that if you held one up in front of you, Dracula would be foiled. Dracula was far more frightening than the devil. My mother sometimes lent me a little silver cross to wear to bed, and I loved that she did that; her belief kept me safe. The worst thing, I knew, was when nobody believed you, when they said nothing's wrong. Like Cassandra, poor tortured princess. How could they not believe her? I asked. Because that was her fate, my mother said. Apollo shut their minds.

On the side of good I had fairy godmothers, Aslan the Narnian Lion, Ozma of Oz. Until now I had sensed no lacunae in this cosmology. Who would not prefer fairies to angels? Lions to old men? Fairies lived on the earth, sleeping on pillows of moss. Fairies liked pleasure while angels were rigidly good, held in place by their halos. Even in our décor, fairies dominated. Angels went on top of the Christmas tree—faceless, stiff-skirted—while the fairies we had were little china figurines of sinuous, Pre-Raphaelite girls lounging, wings folded. Dresses of blue and rose and violet and yellow. They sat on tabletops in my mother's room, in the guest rooms. I used to ask my mother Which ones are these, what are their names and powers? She pretended it was a mystery. "Someday you'll find out. Maybe they'll tell you."

I loved the little figurines, though they had nothing on the illustrations in our books, because they were here, in New Jersey. I knew people would scoff at the idea of New Jersey as a magical location, although we had gardens, twilight. We had the Long Grass. Something had happened there last year. As I ran in that meadow above our house, the dusk softening around me, my bare toes whirring as they leapt high, suddenly I realized that the only thing keeping me from fairyland was myself. There was a muscle in my mind that I could learn to use to get there, not unlike learning to wiggle your ears. I even knew where the muscle was. If I moved in a particular way, which was a kind of shift in attention—which I suddenly saw how to do—I would be in the other place. It was up to me and always had been. They couldn't manifest here.

Standing in the green grass, breeze picking up. In my cotton dress, barefoot, nine years old. Light dissolving, tree branches turning into sky. Grass stalks bending, painted with shadow, clouds on the move. I am all of it—

I can go—

Go where the company is, they who live at the heart of things. Song in all colors, ribboning the air. No boundaries.

But what was it really, where was I going? What were the rules, could I ever come home? *If they couldn't manifest here, what would happen to my body there?* I glanced at the lights of the kitchen blooming downhill. Thought of my mother at the stove in her white capri pants. And school—school in September, new books.

The light of the house was so yellow, like the yolk of an egg. Spilling out onto the driveway, soft around the edges. Mommy was the center of the light. Cooking my dinner—humming to herself—waiting for me to set the table. I couldn't leave her.

And now Jimmy was dead and I would never go because I was afraid any leaving had to do with death.

The car stopped. As I climbed out, my mother said, "Just follow me, Margaret. There's nothing you have to do but be quiet. Don't worry." Her voice was so sweet. I forgot what I was specifically afraid of doing, and only knew I was afraid of doing something. What if I couldn't be quiet? If my body made noises. Or if there was something I had to do and they just hadn't told me. Something obvious, they assumed I knew.

I would ruin the ceremony. Maybe I'd pee in my pants. Maybe the pee would spurt out whenever they mentioned Jimmy's name.

Could anything be more disgusting? I tested my bladder muscles. They were tight. But then maybe it would be something I didn't expect at all, something I hadn't thought about, protected against, maybe my legs would collapse under me or I'd start barking—

We walked inside the church, took our seats. Everybody looked at us. I stared straight ahead.

Dr. Fletcher didn't talk about Jimmy. He didn't mention his name. Nor did he tell us about the afterlife, no speculation, no news. Nothing about heaven, or angels, or "He's in a better place now." Not even that. What was he saying? I kept struggling to find a place in his words. Something about life. What about death? What about Jimmy? No anecdotes, no stories, and he wasn't even talking to us. He was talking to the air.

I was suffocating with anger, a condition that was almost unbearable. To be angry here, now. In the light of the candles. In the sorrow of the music.

And Jimmy with no grave. This was it.

To close the service, Dr. Fletcher read from a poem that my mother had chosen. I knew she had chosen the poem, she had said so, and that it was therefore of special importance. Shelley's "Adonais," on the death of Keats.

I didn't understand most of it. I liked it better than the sermon but it still seemed too high-flown; I thought it must be how my mother thought, alone in her brain. I saw abstract shapes like the reflections in the bowls of silver spoons, or any gleam on silver. All making a kind of glass forest. There my mother moved, solitary, through her exquisite philosophies.

I read the poem again at home, after the service, read it several times. Gradually I understood. Immortality belonged to poets. Belonged to Keats for being a great poet and, more slyly, to Shelley for elegizing him.

This was painful. Keats died young but not that young. He had time to leave the great poems by which he was known. I had a much harder task because Jimmy had been only fourteen. The few drawings he had left did not capture his genius.

I didn't like Shelley. "Weep for Adonais—he is dead." Why didn't he say My friend, John Keats? Anyway, I thought, if you're a poet yourself, to say that poetry makes a person immortal, well, *that's* pretty obvious.

I thought: Maybe Shelley was glad, a little, that Keats died. And he didn't want to say his name *John Keats*, *John Keats*, because he wanted to be the great poet with all his fancy swirly stuff.

Maybe I'm like that, too.

I'm like that, too, but it's a secret. Nobody has to know.

It was me death was communicating with. Jimmy and I had parallel destinies. His death was the necessary tragedy to make me a great poet, and my poetry would redeem his death. He was the one the invisible world chose to keep close at hand, while I, the dreamier, more passive child, was their agent on earth. I had to admit, it was an elegant transposition.

Thirteen

MOMMY LET US stay out of school a week. I heard my grandmother and Nicky suggest we go back sooner, but she said we didn't have to go back until we were ready. I didn't think I would ever be "ready." Not that it mattered, being in school or not. Still, if there was such a thing as ready, I would never be it.

Yet by Monday, I was. I don't think Johnny was. I enjoyed school more than he did, liked the soft, lamblike old ladies who taught us, liked most of my classmates. Most of all I liked sitting still all day, listening in the company of other children yet freed from the anxieties of social life. I had to speak only now and then, give the right answer which I could usually do, while the teachers worked to fill me with knowledge of all kinds: arithmetic, vocabulary, scientific facts.

Actual school would be fine; but first this business of going back. Everybody knowing what happened. All those eyes. I assumed that my classmates wouldn't know what to say to me, wouldn't say anything at all.

I walked into school intensely self-conscious. I had been

dipped in the waters of death and had come out with this weirdness around me; I would never be the same. Always, I knew, a part of me would be engaged in a search for my brother, as if tracking him across the sky. What would the other kids think of that?

Crossing the threshold. Our low, modern cement school building, set back from the road. Pale green walls, cream-colored floors, wide, cool corridors. Into my classroom. Staring faces. Averted eyes. Then Alison came up to me. "I'm sorry about your brother," she mumbled, looking scared.

Chris was right behind her. "Yeah, I remember him—he was really cool."

They both looked embarrassed. I answered them, words chirping out of my mouth; then they asked how it happened, who the guy was who hit him. I told them what I knew. A few more kids clustered round, and then later in the day, one or two spoke to me privately. I was amazed. In this classroom it was me to whom the tragedy had happened. Even those who didn't speak glanced at me with friendly glances. I recognized that they felt sorry, that they knew who my brother was, that they were putting themselves in my place and felt subdued and awed.

From that moment on it was different at school. They knew who I was, Margaret. It was a most surprising and wonderful result.

For weeks, Johnny and I would meet each other in Jimmy's room. After school, we'd dump our books and shoes, pad barefoot into the sacred chamber. We'd lie on his bed, we'd walk back and forth on the narrow footboard, remembering. Going over and over what we knew, sifting, arranging. Our brother—his character, temperament, likes and dislikes. Which foods he wouldn't eat, what his favorites were. His hatred of spinach, elaborate games to trick himself into eating it. (He would shovel it in with his eyes closed while we were instructed to tell him jokes.) I had an idea—startling—Jimmy ate spinach, it became part of his body. Absorbed. Now he was dead and we were remembering him eating spinach—it was as if *the spinach had absorbed him, too*. Tears came to my eyes as I thought this.

We talked about his friends, his hobbies. His voice, his laugh, his thin between-the-teeth whistle.

One night I imitated that whistle. I thought I sounded just like him, but Johnny said not. I was aware then, forcefully, of the tension, wanting my brother to correct and corroborate my memories, to back and forth with me, but wanting also the freedom to fill in any gap in my remembering with imagination, to re-create Jimmy if need be out of myself.

But that re-creation was not really necessary yet. Jimmy was so fresh in my mind: two weeks ago, four weeks ago, he had been alive! He had eaten breakfast, a bowl of Wheaties. I thought of how wonderful it would be now to see him eat a bowl of Wheaties, and imagined my still-alive brother trying to have breakfast while his family surrounded him, fainting with joy, obsessively watching him lift the spoon to his lips—

He wouldn't understand our weirdness. He'd be a *normal person*. That, more than anything, made me realize how much we'd changed.

◎

MY MOTHER'S PAIN took her like an animal, alone. She was physically present. She got up every morning and I would see her at the kitchen table in her plaid wool bathrobe, hair tangled. She didn't have to get up, we could feed ourselves, walk to school, but she did. She made the effort. But she wore no makeup and her voice, scratchy and hoarse, was like the noise a candle makes when it is dying.

I didn't think she was dying. I didn't know you could die of grief. I didn't fear that but only what had happened, was happening. The mother who once rode the waves of our family life like a great ship was now at sea with the rest of us, solitary and small. She couldn't bring Jimmy back. She had no powers. It was like the moment when Oz comes out from behind the curtain and says, My dear, I am only a man.

She was only a woman. Her frailty, her tenderness touched me to the quick. She was tired, entombed, she moved slowly. I saw the difficult of things—filling a kettle, cooking eggs, as I never had before.

I saw the weight and shape and abstinence of the physical world. How the toast burned and the water wouldn't boil. How stains clung to counter and cloth, and nobody really cared. I wasn't frightened by this. Maybe I even welcomed it. Maybe it made sense. What frightened me was my mother's remoteness.

She didn't talk to us very much. She talked a little bit, her eyes luminous. She had dreamed of Jimmy, Jimmy was in heaven. He was thinking of us, he was alight. Her bony fingers on my shoulders. "He's alight." But she wouldn't elaborate and she didn't want to listen to what I had to say. Or couldn't listen. Her whole face blinking on and off.

Little pieces of time, of conversation—Where is Jimmy, did you dream last night? I ask, hopping around her like a flea. Sometimes soft answers in that guttering voice but more often a tightening so that I know my questions are an intrusion. It's inferior grief I produce, or worse: something not even mine.

The panic this idea produced in me—indescribable. Now, I might say: My mother got herself out of bed, she survived, what more could I expect? But I was too young for that understanding. Too lost in the dissolving world. When my mother asked me, two weeks after he died, what I wanted for my birthday, I said, "I want Jimmy." It was my birthday; I thought I had a margin. She made some curt response and left the room. I interpreted this to mean my grief had become an embarrassment, like a fart.

Inside me it was beautiful, became more beautiful day by day, blooming in the place that would become poetry, the home of fate. I conceived of the idea that my relationship to Jimmy was mystical. He was more than my brother, he was my psychic twin. We were the two artists, the two blue-eyed children.

The color of this idea in its entirety was blue. The blue of the sky on a cloudless day, high up, at three o'clock in the afternoon. That melting blue, the azure. Blue was the color of the soul.

The soul! I trembled to finally know the meaning of that word—what was left, this essence of my brother. He and I had been put on earth together for a reason. We had a task; his part included death. Mine was to make sense of death for the world. It was my understanding that nobody had yet done this.

Blue. I stared into the mirror at my eyes *like his*. In fact, Jimmy's eyes were lighter and cooler, more turquoise. Their shape was different. But I disregarded that. His eyes were blue, my eyes were blue. We were of the same stuff, while Johnny and Charlotte were merely my siblings by accident.

Too stubborn to give up, I tried to explain to my mother about artists, about blue eyes. She looked at me out of her brown eyes. I fell back inside myself in terror. "We all miss Jimmy, Margaret."

That weary voice from its cave of grief. Her son.

MY PARENTS TOOK the boy who killed Jimmy and Grant to court. My mother said he had been speeding; she saw the skid marks. I was offended by this: They want money? How could they accept money for my brother's life? My mother said the money was not the point. The boy had broken the law. He had not even apologized, hadn't come to the house as any decent person would. I didn't understand why she wanted him in our house, or how anyone who'd done what he'd done would dare to come here. Wouldn't we kill him? We wanted to kill him, Johnny and Charlotte and I, we made plans, how Johnny would sneak into his house—pick the locks, feed the dog hamburger with sleeping pills in it—creep up the stairs and slit his lousy throat. Johnny was only a kid, he wouldn't go to jail. If he went to reform school we'd help him escape. He'd live in the woods, I'd bring him sandwiches and bananas. We had it all worked out. How we were going to kill him, our plan; we could carry it out whenever we wished. We could think about it—and we did, for days and weeks, elaborating, refining, as we rode our bikes around the driveway or hunkered down in one of Johnny's forts. But to go to court was another story. Besides the indignity of it, the fact was, Jimmy's death was an accident. The boy was speeding, Mommy said, but in my experience most men and all teenage boys speeded. Daddy did. Jimmy would've. Even I—it was possible—could someday, in a car, kill a person by accident . . .

You wouldn't behave like he has, she said.

I'd run away to the ends of the earth. I'd turn myself into a tree. Go the family's house? Say it was I, I killed your son? No. No. No. No.

I wished my mother would behave nobly. Accept what had happened, blame no one—and leave us alone to murder the boy in our thoughts.

Weren't we doing a good job of it? Johnny and I practiced Indian walking, looked through the kitchen knives. Charlotte had a book that showed just where the jugular vein was. She said it would take only seconds. "We're not really . . ." said Johnny. "It's real," I said. He thought about it, and for once he seemed to know what I meant.

My parents lost the suit. Mommy was very angry. My father seemed only to care about her anger. He came in the door behind her, the day they lost, shrunken. She was wearing high-heeled boots and a big, swirly coat; he looked like a charcoal drawing of a man, a little smudged. Waiting to take her coat. She began to talk about judicial corruption, somebody who knew somebody. We scattered.

Fourteen

MY JOB, IN life, was to make sense of death. Wasn't death the other world, of which I had a natural understanding? Whose country I had always belonged to by affinity?

If there is one world, this visible one of school and automobiles and mothers, and then an invisible one, and then *another* invisible one, the two invisible ones must be connected somehow. Yet they didn't seem to be at all. I knew the stories suggested that going to fairyland protected one from death; certainly it altered time; but the relations were unclear. No story said fairies were immortal, only very, very old. Some stories mentioned that they had no souls, or maybe all the stories mentioned it, but the meaning of *having no soul* differed. In a story like "The Little Mermaid," the pagan joy of life underwater had a price—at death one becomes nothing but foam on the sea. In that worldview, a soul is the great thing, what one needs above all. I knew Jimmy had a soul.

Fairyland, in general, corresponded to imagination, fantasy, dream; I knew that as well as one can know such a thing without giving up the belief that it is a place literally to be found. Fairyland is where what should be, is. Where you are recognized for what you are. But Jimmy wasn't interested in fairyland, would never have wanted to go.

Was he a Christian, then? Of course not. He didn't believe any of that. I couldn't either. Jesus repelled me—that limp body on the cross, eyes rolled up. I preferred almost any of the pagan heroes.

I didn't know what death was, and I *should.* It was a physical pressure, to know. My task, my role, the only one I was given (by default, nobody else interested): keeper of the mysteries. But here was horrible doubt, confusion—the world of the imagination in pieces, no place to go—only the glitter, the byways remaining. Who were the fairies? Did they know my brother? How could they not, if they were real, yet—yet what I was feeling was that there was nothing as real as what Jimmy had been. Fairies were words on the page, stories. Sun in the woods, birdsong. They were only me—I was afraid—

I was clogged with thought as with something physical; nothing made sense. Thought stimulated but unable to find form; banging this way and that; I blamed myself ferociously. Stupid! I would sit down *to figure it out* and suffer the sluggish coiling of what I expected to be a lithe force, building me thought-ships. It never occurred to me that this was too much to expect of myself. A child of ten.

I waited for an epiphany at Easter, but all that happened was that I received a photograph of Jimmy framed in white leather, smiling, in my Easter basket, along with a little red diary. I stared at the photograph but nothing happened. Jimmy smiled without moving; he was cute. I put the picture on my bureau. What I saw was my mother going to the trouble of having the photograph framed, I saw the kindness of her effort, evidence of at least some understanding, and I was frightened by my rage that it was not enough.

I DREAMT ABOUT Jimmy. He was back in the house with us, doing normal things, and then suddenly I would remember that he was dead. As soon as I remembered, he would have to leave, though my pleas would detain him for a minute. He would answer my first question—reassure me that he was fine, death wasn't scary—yet even as he stood there talking, he would fade. His body became silvery and transparent.

Everyone in the family was having these dreams. It was as my mother had said: He was telling us he was alright. I wasn't satisfied.

By the beginning of May, my dreams started taking place outside. I was in the garden, our garden, now an exotic place. Enormous spherical blooms—crimson, tomato-red, purple—grew on all the bushes and in the flowerbeds. The vegetation was profuse, yet very dry and spiky, weird, like plants on Mars. The dryness disturbed me more than the odd colors and shapes; I could feel the parching; it made me anxious.

After a few minutes, Jimmy would come down the round brow of the back hill, walk calmly toward me. I knew now that he was dead; and this was a dream; but I assumed it was a spirit dream, a visit. I wanted to tell him about school, the family, how we missed him, all the details of our days, but he insisted on talking about how he was dead and had to be leaving.

"But you just got here!"

"I came to tell you I'm leaving." We strolled, the brilliant, hotly colored blooms a little sinister yet impressive. I was proud of them: this was my dream. Where he came from—down the hill—was the real afterlife, but this part, the garden, was what I had made.

We passed through the side yard where the mulberry tree was, sat down on the cement wall in front of the house, or we stood on the blue-and-white terrace, under the living-room windows.

Always, in the dream, it was intensely bright, and he was restless. I didn't understand why we couldn't have a leisurely visit. Was heaven so demanding? "What do you do up there?"

"Things."

"What?"

"You wouldn't understand."

Mostly I wanted to talk about myself, ask advice, but whenever I did that he vanished, so I started asking more questions about heaven. This held him the longest, though it also seemed to confuse him. Finally, after several dreams when I'd been very insistent, he said he'd have to talk to somebody, find out what I was allowed to know.

More dreams. He kept forgetting to ask. He reminded me of my friend Alison, who'd forget my invitations. And he'd always leave, going the same way each time, climbing the hill. When I tried to follow, I woke up.

I stopped trying to follow. I walked around the garden alone after he left. Its brilliant dry blooms motionless. Red, purple, neon green.

I was jealous of Jimmy. He was happy and we were not. Awake, the idea of death horrified me, every cell of my body rebelled, but in my dreams I knew only that he had gone somewhere he liked better than here.

It wasn't fair.

Jimmy appeared in a dream to announce he had received permission for me to visit. He seemed nervous, and I felt guilty for insisting; then we were there, walking through a big hall of ocher stone, very peaceful, furnished with rows of wooden tables where men and women in sand-colored robes were working. Their faces were serious, all their movements measured and deliberate, and the ones closest to me appeared to be doing something like painting pictures.

Everybody knew Jimmy. They looked up, smiled at him, greeted him—these were his teachers, I realized—and I could see how proud and pleased he was. I had never seen him so open, his face glowing. He was the youngest person here, and he *looked* young. (I didn't see anyone look that young again until I was forty.)

I knew then that he'd never come back to us. He tried to explain. "I'm doing so many things, great things, I wish I could tell you." I sensed the words on the tip of his tongue, the images he couldn't share. I suspected it was because I didn't know the language, being condemned to life, but preferred instead to think it was stupid grown-ups making rules.

Just tell me.

He didn't seem to mind at all that he was dead.

I sidled closer to the table, tried to see the pictures his teachers were working on. Something scrambled my vision, and I woke up.

Fifteen

WE WERE ALL in our grief, even my father. He was more quiet and subdued than he had ever been. I saw that Mommy's grief scared him. This was odd as it didn't scare me—only made me lonely. She was turned off, but still there, not hurting anyone. Well. Maybe hurting, yes (*blue*). Daddy had blue eyes, and he had been more open, always. Which had not used to be a good thing—the maelstrom inside him—yet now . . .

It seeped into me slowly (I had to recover what from what I had not done when I saw his tears) seeped into me slowly as one might imagine *the warmth of the moon* that maybe now he was approachable. Now or soon. A tiny warm spending through my body; I kept it away. Drew it a little closer. Looked at it.

Soon. In a year? I vacillated between wanting to wait several years, just to be sure, until I was a teenager, and wanting to try right now. To speak to him, offhandedly, go right up and talk.

It could be done. It could be done.

Soon.

My mother would go up to her room after dinner, and Charlotte and Daddy would wash the dishes. I had never seen my father do anything domestic before, but here he was bent over the sink, sleeves rolled up. Yellow electric light behind him, fading evening light coming in through the window in front. Water thundering down, Mommy gone upstairs—is it a little bit like a party in here?

I wanted to help with the dishes but hesitated. I couldn't imagine the three of us working but only myself taking Charlotte's place, which she would never allow. (I imagine something like the goddess Kali, arms and legs whirling like knives.) So I'd wander outside into the green garden, pretending I preferred that—communing with the feathery dusk, having feelings. I always thought of them as peelings, and I saved them, kept them in order.

ONE WEDNESDAY MORNING in June, after school let out, Johnny and I were playing cards. We were sprawled on the floor of his room, putting off the moment when we would go downstairs. There was nothing terrible about going downstairs, it was just Mom and Charlotte, maybe things we were supposed to do, clean up this or that, or just their talk, which was not our talk.

Charlotte was becoming like a grown-up now. She was the eldest, and carried it badly, in our opinion. She wasn't Jimmy. She didn't have his confidence, his grace. Who does she think she is—Jimmy? we would say when she attempted to take charge of us, which she did sometimes on her own initiative, sometimes because our mother told her to. We'd watch her bossy antics with scornful faces. "We don't have to obey you."

"Mom *said*."

"So what?"

We knew it was hard for her, or at least I did; I was glad I wasn't in her shoes. To have to be the eldest, after Jimmy. Who could?

In the past Johnny would often refuse to play with me, holding out for Jimmy or his own friends, but now he seemed to need my company. I did what I could to prolong this state of affairs; I was agreeable to his demands. This morning, for example, he insisted we play in his room, and that we play War. I didn't care for War—it was boring, the entire rules being that the deck is split down the middle, and each round consists of the two players turning up the top card of their pile, higher card winning—but I tolerated it.

It was okay because if you lost it was no reflection on your intelligence. The way it worked between us was, he got to choose the game and I got to tell him, every minute or so, what a stupid game it was.

We heard a squawk from the intercom, then our sister's voice. This was a fairly new thing, intercoms in all the bedrooms, connected to one in the kitchen. The idea was Mom could call us to dinner without having to climb the stairs. In practice it was mostly ignored.

We ignored it this morning. Charlotte said, "Margaret and Johnny, come downstairs." We noticed that her voice sounded odd but that was only a reason to avoid her. Even when our mother came on, "Please come downstairs," we hesitated.

Charlotte burst into the room crying, her body twisted to one side. "Daddy's dead, Daddy's dead. He killed himself."

I stared at her. These words were almost visible, ribboning out of her mouth. A black-and-white ribbon, like newsprint.

Daddy's dead. He killed himself.

Of course this had already happened. We had already seen her like this, the same twist to her body, her agitation, pale, thin hands in motion, as she comes to us with news that is also a kind of plea; we have felt before this refusal, rejection both of the information and her role as messenger, which is too much for her.

It is too much. She can't bear it. Twist in her pelvis, her shoulders, her wrists, as if all her bones and nerves are being braided. I feel for my sister a love that is like the floor caving in beneath me.

But these words she speaks. They make no sense.

When Jimmy died it was life revealed, the face of mortality. Even though it deranged me, I knew its truth. I did what I did with it, but it was real. This was not real. The black letters of her words slid off the screen of my face.

"I saw him," she said. "In the car. He killed himself." Voice shredded, frantic, desperate to tell us what we were suddenly so angry at being told.

We said, we kept saying. "No, he didn't. He *didn't.*"

"You think I would make this up?"

Of course we didn't think she would make it up. Yet we had to get away from her frenzy, crooked sobbing body, telling us, telling us—what does she want from us? We were playing cards. We ran downstairs to petition our mother.

Who was standing in the kitchen. Who was wearing regular Saturday slacks, her hair uncombed. I notice the lack of light in her hair, the pallor of her skin, and that her mouth is bitter. She tonelessly confirms what our sister has said. Yes, your father is dead. Yes, he did it himself. In the car. Late last night. Carbon monoxide poisoning from the exhaust fumes.

It is a mother's fate to be the heart of the world. My soul beat against hers, demanding entrance, and met with nothing. A pitiless nothing, as it seemed to me. She stood there in the knowledge of what was done, and could not be undone.

I can begin to imagine it now, crumbs of it. Her marriage of fifteen years: passion, talk, childbirth, plans. Whatever words had passed between them the night before, the week before. That live circuit suddenly broken. Her hopes, going back to girlhood: husband, partner. Her own father's death when she was just fourteen. Her solitude. Her solitude. Standing upright at the kitchen counter, having already dealt with police, paramedics, and now three traumatized children—her children spun and flung, like cats in a clothes dryer. But at the time I had no understanding. I felt only terror. There was no soft place for me to go.

She gave us the facts. Hattie found him when she came to work. Walking across the driveway, she heard the sound of his car, saw the garage door shut. She became suspicious, went and looked. (Hattie's suspicions. It still amazed me, the nose adults had for this sort of thing.) "So I went out," my mother continued, "and he was dead."

"How did you know?" asked Johnny.

"He was slumped over the wheel," she answered precisely. "I checked his pulse. He was dead. I called the ambulance."

Carbon monoxide poisoning is a very easy death, she told us. All you have to do is roll up the windows in an enclosed space, like a garage, turn the key. You drift off to sleep. No pain. She stressed this, the ease, the lack of pain. It made me think maybe he didn't know.

"It might have been an accident," I said. "Maybe he was just sitting out there for some reason—"

"He killed himself. He always said he was going to do it."

"He did? When?"

"All the time. Whenever the subject came up. At parties. He talked about how to do it. He talked about doing it this way. I always thought if he talked about it, that meant he wouldn't do it." Her voice skittered sideways, a little jagged trail off somewhere I'd never imagined.

"Why?"

"He was emotionally disturbed."

Emotionally disturbed. The words might have meaning, yet

they fit so badly in her mouth. Her real thoughts were not so abstract. What she felt was rage. I could not escape the perception of this. A ferocious, implacable rage, big enough to reach the sky.

I was still in a fictional state. My mind had sealed against the shock rather than opened, as it had when Jimmy died. Jimmy's death had ushered me into an adult world, too big, too dark, full of numinous power—I was staggered, but I was there. Daddy's death did not take me anywhere. Or rather it took me to hell, but I couldn't know that. What I was aware of as I timidly probed my consciousness was that my mind now had an accessible depth of perhaps half an inch. A half an inch beneath my skin I could think, move around, ask questions—below that was a sealed door, black, impassible.

This scared me more than anything. This was *me*, taken away from me. For my whole life what I had depended on, what sustained me, was inner space. My mind my kingdom.

Gone now. Replaced by this wall which forced me out, into the arid day. I was exiled, and in my panic, I, too, became enraged. How dare Mommy be angry? Daddy was dead, poor Daddy. He committed suicide because he was so sad about Jimmy. He was suffering exquisite pain.

I wasn't thinking about how my father chose to leave us. I couldn't think about that. I could only feel a crooning love for him, poor Daddy, poor Daddy, casting myself into his camp: the camp of those who are not stoic, who kill themselves.

Meanwhile I was as stoic, as dry-eyed, as my mother.

The ambulance was still outside, parked in the driveway. There was a police car, too. We could hear the men walking around, the mutter of their walkie-talkies. I caught glimpses of them through the windows: a gurney, a white sheet. Why were the police here? Did they suspect us of murder? In the Alfred Hitchcock stories, suicide was always a cover-up for murder.

Johnny said he wanted to go out and see the body. He started edging for the door.

Mommy grabbed him and held him as he squirmed, her whole body rocking him with a mournful devotion. "You can't—I won't let you—it would be terrible. I know you don't understand, but you can't." It seemed to help her to have this thing to do, hold on to my struggling brother, her woman-strength easily adequate to the task.

Of course I wanted to go outside, too, and I could have managed it while she was holding on to Johnny. But I didn't. If she knew I wanted to see the body—like a little pervert.

I didn't think my mother thought Johnny was a little pervert. She would only think that about me.

After the ambulance departed, and my mother went upstairs, my brother and I ran out the back door, across the driveway, and into the garage. We examined the car, his pale blue VW, sniffing for the odor of gas, looking for clues. The car smelled the way it always did, a thin, acrid plastic odor mixed with cigarette smoke, and the garage smelled of motor oil and metal. There was nothing to see. Just his maps in the glove compartment, butts in the ashtray.

I tried to picture my father in the driver's seat, making the decision. How long did he sit before turning the key? What did he think about? He would have to think about everything, wouldn't he, his whole life? He would have to think about his own death. No pain, she said, easy, like going to sleep. I wouldn't mind going to sleep. But I couldn't understand, really, how he had let himself *die*. At the last moment, wouldn't he turn off the key? Wouldn't his hand do it?

My hand would do it. My hand wanted to do it for him—for his thin wrist, his blunt, delicate fingers. Holding a cigarette, holding a drink. The jumping rhythm of his hands at night. I'll do it. Get out of bed, two, three, in the morning, come out here in the dark—

I wouldn't be afraid of him. Daddy, I would say. Don't do it. I saw myself as like all the daughters on television who run into their father's arms, or curl up on the couch beside him, knees tucked under, asking a favor. Daddy? On TV, the girl always gets what she wants from her father. Fathers are stern with boys but not with girls. It seemed to come as a surprise to me that we had not had such a relationship. As if it were just an error, easy to correct. I merely needed to be a *girl*.

Too late.

I leaned hopelessly against the open car door, bare feet on the greasy cement, keeping watch for our mother or Charlotte as Johnny crawled around, searching under the seats. Nickels. Ballpoint pens. I couldn't stand it that there was never anything left.

Neighbors came in cars and on foot, bearing dishes covered with tin foil. Johnny said we were lucky this time, it was summer, we could stay outside. I was struck by that remark, tucked it away. *Lucky.* We retreated to the farthest point from where we could still see the house—the top of the hill—then crept back halfway down, watching. The party party.

Death: so what. I tried on that shrug—New Jersey sarcastic, what Jimmy had taught us. It still had the scent of him. So what?

I thought what I was feeling, as I watched the neighbors arrive, was jadedness. Yet in fact the repetition seared my mind as the arrival of a god. The event and its shadow. That which is two faced, which meets you coming and going.

We didn't move much. We stood halfway up the hill. It grew hotter very quickly, and there was no breeze.

Charlotte came to join us, picking her way in her low heels across the dry grass. She wore a brown skirt, a cream-colored blouse. I liked this, how she came to us. Johnny and I stood together, dry-eyed and calm, in the same deep weirdness. I imagined my sister was different from us, too mortal.

Daddy sitting alone downstairs, in the brown leather chair, whiskey in hand. All of us asleep, the house belonging to him alone. He broods, he is deeply himself, he gets up, walks through the hall, out the back door. The house lit up, and then the summer dark. Across the driveway, into the car. Acting on will, on desire, on diabolical impulse. I recognized the signature of self-pity, though I didn't know what it was called. I knew it as an inner nectar, survival food, could imagine it like a nimbus around his body. Pretty.

"What are you guys doing out here? Everyone's inside." My sister's eyes and nose were red from crying, and her voice seemed to be flaking apart, like a piece of mica. She told us again about seeing the body. She had run out when Hattie came in crying with the news and had seen Daddy's forehead resting on the steering wheel. His head tipped forward when he lost consciousness. (It was just like going to sleep.) His face was red.

"What color red?"

"The red your face gets if you're gassed," she said sharply. "People's faces turn red."

I wanted to ask what shade exactly—Fire engine? Claret?—but didn't. She went on, "I was washing the dishes with Daddy last night and I thought something was wrong, I had a feeling, but I didn't say anything. Why didn't I say anything?"

Sobs in her voice now. Her voice a rag, twisted and twisted.

I said, "I saw him crying the day after Jimmy died. He was standing alone in the stairwell, crying. I wanted to go up to him, comfort him, but I didn't. I was too scared."

"Scared of what?" said Charlotte angrily.

I didn't reply.

Charlotte went on talking about why she hadn't spoken to Daddy last night, what might have happened if she had. Maybe he just needed someone to be nice to him, needed to be reminded he was loved. It would have been so easy for her to say something—"Are you alight, Daddy?" and maybe changed his entire fate, and ours. Or if she had only woken up, later. Come downstairs in her nightgown, right before he went outside. Said, "Daddy?" Gotten herself a glass of water, he would have seen her, you never know what small thing can make a difference . . .

"Why didn't I wake up?" said Charlotte. "Why didn't I?"

Johnny said nothing. He listened, watching us, his bright eyes darting from one face to another. I was aware of wanting him to say something, contribute in particular to this conversation. Yet I also wanted to protect him, keep Daddy away from him.

I couldn't think. I stood in silence, a long swaying blankness, and after awhile my sister left. We wandered some more. To the top of the garage, back across the hump of the hill, down between the crabapple trees to the garden. The formality of the landscape was our refuge. Stone steps. Stone fountain. We needed to keep moving but couldn't be out of sight of the house.

So hot. So dry. I clung to the idea that he had died here, on our property. Wasn't that better than what happened to Jimmy? Closer, with us, even though we hadn't woken up. The sound of the car in the garage all night. It was almost a comforting sound, like a cat's purr, if I imagined it, the cool dark and Daddy, the car throbbing, not yet gone.

Going slowly. Nobody else here but us.

And Jimmy? What did he think? Was Daddy an intrusion—

He died here with us, wasn't that better?

Johnny went back to the garage to search again. He said if he was alone he might see what he had not seen before.

Nicky, our neighbor, came outside. She wanted to take a walk with me. "Let's take a walk, Margaret." Holding my arm. I had thought at first, when she came in my direction, that she'd been sent by my mother to get me. Instead, "Let's take a walk around the garden."

So we walked. Nicky was a short woman, not much taller than I, with frizzy dark hair, a cute little scrunched-up face. She was wearing blue jeans, a baggy shirt, and sneakers. She walked slowly so I had to walk slowly. She told me my father was a good man who loved me. Her voice was calm and even. "He was a good man, Margaret. He loved you."

I didn't say anything. I was in the dumb alert prickliness of a child being talked to. As if tiny silvery things were all over my body, swimming against my skin. But more powerful than that—I seemed to be melting. As when we had modern dance at school, the teacher put on the record, "Now you are bees, buzzing, buzzing, now you are horses, galloping, galloping," and we could become anything we wanted.

What I was doing, so swiftly, was getting younger. I remembered this self. Tiny girl. Melting like butter. *He loved you.* I glanced at the house, in sudden terror my mother would see.

I went back into the house. My mother was there, downstairs, but only vaguely someone I knew. Like a Greek column—her slim composed beauty, pallor, ineffable remoteness. I realized I was not afraid of her if I put certain things *aside*. Which was, wasn't it, a form of control? Yet once I put them *aside*—things like my father, or melting—I couldn't get them again. They just fell away.

Meanwhile neighbors, friends, cakes, drinks. The doorbell ringing, telegrams piling up on the hall table.

Something in the air it took me a long while to recognize as *disapproval.* Men in suits, women with distant eyes, wandering around our house, not with that poked-forward sympathy of Jimmy's death, but this other thing, vague, staticky— It was funny. Last time I had wanted nothing but to be alone with my family and now we were alone, though the house was full. I kept thinking, *It's just like last time*, but it wasn't— I was reminded of when I would imitate something another sibling had done to much applause and the adults would react to my imitation with embarrassment and censure.

I didn't blame Daddy for being envious of Jimmy's death. For wanting to be loved that much, so everybody cried. I understood, and I worked at summoning the fluid, spontaneous emotion I had felt in February, seeing it now as a gift. Somebody dies, you go all to pieces, your mind throws up memories. *There is a drama your mind stages; it is supposed to happen.*

But where was it? Only a half-inch of me; not enough. I had been in a maelstrom the night Jimmy died—the most horrible feeling I could ever imagine; now I was almost nostalgic for it. That was real; this was not. This was two-dimensional. It was hard to keep myself from just going upstairs to play.

I tried to prime grief, casting around for memories of my father to make myself sad. I felt exactly as if he were hungry—thirsty—and needed my sorrow for his poor parched spirit.

I tried. Remembering Daddy—Daddy? A buzzing confusion, a kind of foamy or cottony blank. Come on. I had to be able to remember. Yesterday, last week, last year. It seemed all the units were empty or filled with this foamy stuff. How could this be—I couldn't remember my father? I found myself blushing, deeply uneasy, I found myself grieving. Not for him but for the inadequacy of my brain.

Which returned, after awhile, to its chill detachment, picking at its thoughts, arranging them in rows. Daddy had *died* to win our love, and nobody would give it. Not even me.

The party went on the requisite too long. People arriving, making drinks. Leaving as quickly as possible. The doorbell ringing, the yellow telegrams piling up, fluttering down off the hall table. I wondered if they were the same telegrams.

I read the telegrams. I was trying to do the same things, have the same emotions, so I read them and maybe they were the same, maybe they weren't. I felt dizzy, not in my body but in my thoughts. I didn't know thoughts could do this—bounce and shiver, or shimmer, like an echo bouncing and changing as it hits different surfaces.

I went to my room, lay on my bed, eating cookies, the sharp crumbs scratching my throat as they went down. The only good thing about death was that there was food.

I couldn't remember my father (how was that possible; I must be insane) so I thought about his names: Daddy, Arthur Chester Diehl, Jugie.

"Daddy's dead," in my sister's voice—

Jugie, short for Junior. That was what the grown-ups called him. When I thought of Jugie, I thought of my father's physicality: his heavy tread, the crackly mid-range North Carolina tones of his voice—a brown music—his home attire of white T-shirt, white boxer shorts, socks. This much I could remember, his squarish flesh, his lively molecules. A background presence. Knowing he was in the house—upstairs, in the library, I didn't have to see him—Jugie. My mother's voice calling him in her wifely tones. How they lived together, how he went to the city in his little VW.

Several times I found my thoughts drifting to Jimmy and I stopped myself. I wasn't allowed to think about Jimmy today. It wasn't fair to Daddy.

Arthur. That was the name on the long envelopes on the hall table at night, the name used on the phone by people who didn't know him. It was also, it just occurred to me, the name of King Arthur. I had even called one of my toys, a glossy china spaniel, King Arthur, and I realized that I must have been naming this toy after my father. I felt, for a second, not numbness, but a crawling embarrassment. *Now that Daddy was dead, he might know everything about me. He might be able to see me—how I lie on my bed eat-*

ing cookies—how I get up now to hide the china dog under clothes in my drawer.

The numbness returned, and with it the guilt. Daddy wanted us to grieve. He had asked, it seemed to me, specifically: mourn me as you did your brother. With that great awe, world inside out. Love me like you loved him, the cherished boy—let me be that now. I can no longer hurt you.

I received the lament, the request, but couldn't respond. Wouldn't. Couldn't.

CHARLOTTE TOLD ME that my aunts thought Daddy's suicide was Mommy's fault. They had said so on the phone. It made me so angry. The accusation was collapsing our mother. Dressed now, though not completely—her feet stockinged—her bitter hardness of the morning was gone; she was whisper-voiced and despairing, not knowing how to face them.

"What can I say?" she said. "He was their brother. They don't know how he was."

That rage, Daddy at the dinner table; we were free of it. Free. Mommy's plaintiveness, her softness, eyes swimming toward us, her dusk-threaded voice. I was seeing what it is to be a widow—your daughters will become Amazons.

"Tell them to go to hell." Daddy's favorite curse. I could say this. She might listen.

Charlotte remarked that since they were Catholics, and Catholics believed suicides went to hell, that's where they must think Daddy was now. Our mother waved a hand—don't think about that—but I was caught, spun around again. They believe he's in hell? Really? I had no vulnerability to the Catholic doctrine, was as certain as a child can be that it was wrong, but the cruelty involved in someone imagining that—about a brother—and still being able to move—attend a funeral, accuse someone else—

Nicky had gone to pick them up at the airport. When we heard the car drive in, when they entered the front door, Charlotte and I were flanking our mother. Daddy's mother was flanked by her two daughters. Mommy was vibrating with distress. I was vibrating with rage. *They think he's in hell. Stupid old pigs, witches, bitches. . .*

Nana was gray and staggering, my mother a gleaming tentative darkness. My mommy, my mommy, my mommy. I'll catch her if she falls, lay her down in the yellow guest room. Or if these aunts dare to be hostile, I'll bite them on the legs. Like the mouse Reepicheep in the Narnia chronicles, only two feet tall, but able to inflict significant damage. That was what I most wanted to happen, my own feral instincts set free. To rush forward in a rage, to snarl and bite. But the two mothers greeted each other politely, the aunts were polite; I drifted away.

Sixteen

LATE ON THE second afternoon, Charlotte informed Johnny and me that there was some question of us going to see our father's body in the funeral home. Nana was going and wanted us along. Our mother didn't think it was a good idea. Charlotte tried to explain to us why Mommy was right— "I saw him, you guys, and I wish I hadn't," but we ignored her. We ran to lobby our mother.

She was sitting at her dressing table, getting ready for the evening's assault of visitors. The bedroom was big, messy, scented, in shadow, but still holding the heat of the day: nobody stopped us from entering. And it was all hers now, this room, we just began to notice; no chance of a man coming in.

What a difference that made. Now it was our room, too; we weren't afraid of bed or window, we could prowl and feel cocky, test ourselves against her. Mother like a trampoline: tough, elastic, welcoming, you bounce on and off the strong fibers of her soul.

Though she wasn't looking strong now. Warm from a bath,

wearing only her slip, hair curling from the damp rising up from her shoulders, our mother seemed impossibly weary. Not angry at all anymore. Her anger was lodged in me like a hard nut, but I couldn't think of it in her presence.

She turned in her chair, soft breasts shifting sideways against the beige silk, and said, "You don't want to see him. I'm only thinking of you. You don't know what it'll be like. Once you see you can never not see.

"I saw my father and I wished I hadn't."

I liked how thrillingly she spoke, trying to convince us. Not telling us what to do, but speaking on our level. And the dark tones of sorrow in her voice—old sorrow, for her father, moved me. Yet I had to oppose her, this was my chance; and Johnny felt the same way. We flopped on her bed, we paced around her room, we argued with the tireless craftiness of children.

"We want to see."

"We can handle it. You don't know what we can handle. We're tough."

"We need to see, we have a right to. We didn't get to see Jimmy."

"You didn't take us to the hospital; you took Charlotte. And Charlotte got to see Daddy, too."

"He's *our* father."

We exhausted her. "I'm only thinking of you," she said, her voice catching in little sobs. Mommy crying. Never seen before. Crying freely, bent forward from the waist. Her sinuous, olive-skinned torso with its narrow shoulders, small-boned, round arms. She's soft and deep, satiny. The expensive lotion she's been slathering on for years scents the air. I feel something like lust for her.

My thoughts rise up in cresting waves.

@

WINNING THE ARGUMENT put the responsibility on me. I was going to see his body, the whole of him (no mangled face, no outer damage at all)—and so? What would it be. What would I do.

I had rejected her testimony, making her cry. I have to be right. I feel my rightness as I feel my own breath, my own weight, yet there is a doubt—*she thinks I'm a pervert, wanting to look at the dead.* I didn't know she cried for her own inability to reach us. For the difficulty of it all, and her own aloneness. I thought she cried because we opposed her, were stronger than she, and she thought our strength an evil, as in *The Lord of the Flies.* Yes; that we bullied her. I suppose we did.

We left her, went to our rooms. Didn't talk to each other; what was there to say? Already, a silence, the sense of what must be hidden. What was already hidden. Daddy a tiny speck, the merest fleck of remembered father inside a huge white growth of mindstuff like boiled bone. Not foamy, not foggy anymore but tumorous.

I was anxious. I was very anxious; I'd only get one chance. I had my own ideas about what this chance meant, and one of them was that if I did it right, I'd get another chance, with Jimmy. I didn't care that he'd been cremated already, ashes scattered. I lived mostly in another world where what mattered was subtle action, where the gods (whom I had not named, who floated into the shapes of one or another of the various characters from literature, the Fates, or Jimmy's teachers from my dream, who had not, and would never, settle, but about whom one could know certain things)—the gods had the final power over things and they existed beyond matter. Their tastes were mine—symbol and myth—they drew pictures in the air, and redrew them as they pleased. I wasn't thinking about it really, it was at the back of my mind, but I kept it there on purpose. I *knew* it was there: this idea of the second chance with the body of my brother. To see him whole again, laid out in a box, like my father, and, once that happened, it would be nothing, the merest flick of a wrist to make him get up and live.

I believed it. Oh yes, I believed it. It seemed impossible not to believe it.

It created a certain pressure. Great anticipation and desire, the need to make a plan. What kind of plan? I couldn't literally plan Jimmy's return to life; besides the fact that I had no idea what there was to be done, three months had taken me too far into his death to let me get specific about it. What I remember is the resentment toward those who wouldn't believe, who'd oppose me even if I succeeded. Not my family, but the rest of the world, the idiots and monsters of "normal life" who would say nobody comes back from the dead, forget it, or make too big a deal if it did happen, not let him just live his life . . .

And of course my father, whom I also loved, was lying across the threshold. Like an electrical wire across a road, sparking.

I sat at my desk, tried to think. *Tomorrow I will see his body. I will see my father. I will see death.*

I got up, looked out the window. Gazed down at the garden, at the narrow stones around the edge where he sometimes stood, having a smoke. The infinite shapes his body could have made in that air.

Looking at the garage where he did it. Letting my mind float over the possible traces of his act, over the greasy sharp scent of motor oil, cool gloom of enclosed space. Had Johnny and I really looked carefully enough? He might have hidden a note inside one of the seat cushions.

But this was what I knew: His suicide itself was the note. If Jimmy's death had been a message from a universe that loved us sternly, Daddy's could only be a message from Daddy. You would think that message obvious. I chose not to see it that way. I saw it as Daddy linking himself up with Jimmy, with sadness, and therefore—in the deepest, most gorgeous sense—with me.

He went to get Jimmy. He failed, but not completely. He left a door open.

The others didn't get it. They couldn't—they weren't meant to understand. The connection was not only with Jimmy and sadness but with magic.

It was not Daddy's time, but he chose death. He walked into what nobody walks into, except the few—Odysseus, Orpheus—knew what nobody knows: the moment of his dying. He chose it, it therefore followed that he could unchoose it. Not easily, of course, this wasn't a game, and he wasn't a Greek hero. He was somebody smaller; I knew that; he needed help . . .

I had the strangest feeling that nobody was watching. Daddy's wizardry had condemned him, not to hell (certainly not to heaven), but to the punishment of the gods' neglect. Wherever he was, it was untended. Could a jailbreak be made?

I believed that it could. It seemed to me a truth, almost scientific: He has seized power by seizing death. He chose to go, he can return. Certain laws have been suspended.

I was so taken by the aspect of my father's will. The force of it made me vibrate.

Something was required of me. The fact that I didn't know what—and no talking bird or fairy godmother appeared to inform me—was a part of my great anxiety. I had to hold certain logical processes at bay; not examine all the clues I had; keep scouring the air for the *other* clues.

I knew magicians worked with matter. This was important. They worked with corpses, though exactly how I wasn't sure. If I could own his body for a little while, do things to it. *Light a fire of fragrant herbs, breathe into its mouth, weight its forehead and knees with stones, lie on it.*

Maybe I thought of these particular things or maybe I thought of nothing, a shining nothing that later became these things. The latter, of course—I was only ten. I remember coming across real magical grimoires later, in my midteens, and saying: Oh, so this is it. What you do. Getting ideas.

I didn't know what to do, only felt the potency of magic and action. The specific gravity of the corpse. Its hope of death held captive, one end of a thread.

I was half my father now. Dead, he was unlocked in me, not in memory but as a vision. My criminal, possibly psychotic father rising to the surface, floating, on his face an expression of great mystery. Here I am, he said. Do with me what you will.

Seventeen

My Aunt Vera drove Nana, Johnny, and me to the funeral home. Vera was a tall, aggressive woman who had always scared me, and now there was this question of Mommy being blamed, so I didn't talk to her. I didn't want to talk to either of them, but Nana talked to me. She turned around in her seat slowly—she was stout and arthritic—black dress rustling, gazed at us. "What are you doing to that boy, Margaret? Are you pinching him? Are you pinching that boy?"

I wasn't pinching him. I was poking him to get his attention. He was pressed against the car door as if trying to become part of it, his face paper-white and clamped shut. I had thought we were doing this together. But Johnny was only with himself.

Wanting to shake him. Force his mind out, make him look at me. "What are you doing?" That voice with its hunger. Why was she so interested? She was supposed to be crying. Or she could pray, that would be appropriate, I wouldn't mind hearing her begging that stupid Catholic god.

Her droopy eyes, pale blue, sticky-looking, slid over me, and I felt something, a shiver—

We were both excited.

At the funeral home the director suggested that I go in first. "The girl." I was very surprised at this—both the primacy and privacy of it. Nor did Nana or Aunt Vera protest. As if the world were finally accommodating itself to me.

My footsteps sounding on the floor. The man showed the way.

There were many rooms; only one held the body. The man ahead of me, his shoulders gliding beneath his suit, head cocked at a stiff angle. I felt as if I had paid him a lot of money, me personally, as when, the summer before, I stole twenty dollars from my mother's purse, and subscribed to every comic book I wanted. I didn't mean to do this, but couldn't resist the advertisements. I kept slipping downstairs, taking another few dollars, then a five, out of her purse left on the kitchen table. Shocked at my own criminality, but caught in it, as if in a conversation with another person. Not wanting to stop. Me, Margaret, my bare nimble legs taking the stairs three at a time, in the cloud of my badness, and some voice—I didn't quite hear it—purring with satisfaction. Egging me on.

My parents caught me when the comics started arriving. We were on vacation, only Daddy was home, collecting the mail. He knew I didn't have the money for so many subscriptions. They confronted me, I confessed. *(Daddy knew! He's the one who saw the comics in their brown paper tubes, my name written over and over on the labels!)* I wasn't sure what I felt about the fact that Daddy knew, though I do remember a wiggle of gladness that he had had to think about me enough to figure out the crime. And mention it to my mother and sit with her when she told me what they'd discovered . . . I was ashamed, of course. My parents thought comics vulgar, and I guess they thought stealing vulgar, too . . .

I confessed my strange greed, the something that came over

me. They didn't seem to know what to do. Mommy asked my opinion. "What do you think your punishment should be?" I had nothing to say. I wanted to talk more about what it felt like, that cloud of thieving energy, how good it felt, and about comics, how I needed the whole collection, Archie and Veronica and Jughead and Superman and Superboy and Lois Lane . . .

They decided that I had to work off the twenty dollars. This sounded reasonable, though I was worried it might take the foreseeable future, but then they gave up. I did a few chores but my mother didn't want to be bothered supervising my lame efforts, and when, after a few weeks, I chanced asking for my allowance again, she paid it without comment. My siblings were outraged—whenever a comic came in the mail: "You stole that, Mom shouldn't let you keep it!" My parents pretended not to hear.

My shoes tapped on the floor. I wondered if Daddy could hear me coming.

The coffin was on a pedestal in the middle of the room. Nothing but acres of floor around him, no chairs or tables, pictures or books. I wondered why the room had to be so big just for the coffin. It was a mark of respect, I supposed; and I was suddenly angry at my knowledge that he was here only temporarily.

I focused on my task. I was in here alone with my father. I was in here alone, not even my father. No, he was here: but I could browse his being without terror. No cruelty would issue from his mouth, no panic leap from his body to mine.

Not even when he was sleeping had I been so safe. Sunday mornings, sometimes, we'd sneak into their room—make sure they were deeply under so we could miss church—he would snore or his eyelids would flicker. The inevitable sibling squeaks, and that sound, like Saran Wrap crumpling, that children always seem to make when they bunch up together, igniting our fear, our anger at each other—"You'll wake them up!" Daddy, even asleep, a hot disturbance, I couldn't look too closely, my eyes might summon him.

But now. I could brood upon his face at my leisure. All mine. It was the anger, it was the shouting that had been taken away.

I walked slowly forward. I beheld his profile. *They weren't lying—he's here!* Nose, lips, chin. Oh, beauty. Then I was standing beside him, Daddy long and still, all his parts, dressed and smooth, tucked into the white satin like—like nothing I'd ever seen before. A man in a box. I looked at his closed eyes and his short wiry hair. It was him. At his cheekbones, skin, his folded hands. His hands. I looked, and looked again.

I remembered now everything I'd forgotten. Ordinary memories back in place: Daddy used to bring me home books—once three volumes of the Oz series, fat books that I read in a day and a half, to impress him, and he was impressed; the rides we took in his car; his jokes. Daddy giving us three-foot-high valentines one year—he bought them in New York City—and my mother jealous at how excited we were, barely glancing at her handmade beauties. How sometimes, when we went out to eat, he'd hand me the bill, ask me to figure the tip. I'd do it in a flash. He'd grin. I thought I must be a genius.

I stared, I slid my eyes over the face, and over again, I changed the angle. His nose, his lips, his chin. I refused to acknowledge that there was nothing to see but those exquisite cold structures. Infinitely empty, offering me such plenitude of nothing. What required storehouses, great hollow tracts that now belonged to me, to preserve that nothingness.

I refused to acknowledge this. I tried to replace ten years of mostly not looking at him, of averting my eyes or avoiding any room where he was, of fathering myself with fear, my yearning thrown ahead of me—replacing all that habitual behavior with a hundred empty stares, one after another.

Years later, in a crowded living room, I would walk right by the open coffin of my aunt, not noticing it because what is there about a corpse to catch your eye? But this was my first one.

I looked. Then I touched him, his cheek. It was grainy and cold and had a texture—what used to be flabbiness when he was a middle-aged man. Now there was no word for it. The cold was not extreme but final. I touched and knew nothing. I touched and nothing happened and that was something, but not what I had any place to know.

I only touched him lightly. What I wanted to do was look inside his clothes. At his chest, above his heart. The tiny nipples. Of course the soul's signature would be hard to find. Why had I expected it on his face? It might be between his toes. A hieroglyph. Almost invisible. Disguised as something else. Obvious to me—

But I was not a girl who could slide her hands under the clothes of a corpse. Not because I was squeamish. I wasn't scared of his body. I was scared the grown-ups would come in and yell at me.

I got more time than I expected. I got five minutes, just me and Daddy. I could have slid a hand under, but I didn't know, I wasn't used to having time specifically for something like this, a sacred moment. I kept thinking it was wrong of me to take it, if my mother was here she wouldn't let me, she'd think it was morbid.

Then Nana came in, wailing; moving with difficulty in her heels, pitching forward. I moved back and she shoveled her arms in, lifted the corpse half out of the coffin. She squashed my father's head to her bosom, stuck it right in between the breasts. "My baby," she cried, "my baby."

She cried and rocked, his body flopping around with the force of her movements. She cradled his face in her hands, kissed and kissed, ruffled his hair. I understood something, then, about that coldness, that stillness. His choice.

Johnny decided not to view the body.

MY FATHER WAS cremated. Nana was angry, claiming that she should have the right to decide about her son as Mommy decided about Jimmy. My mother said she knew what Jugie had wanted, what he had always said, emphatically, that he wanted. It was even in his will. "I don't care personally," she told me, and she was very weary, "but how can I go against his wishes?"

I admired my mother's decision about this, even though I didn't want him cremated. I saw her as noble, vanquishing those who would take away his freedom. She stood up not for my suicidal father but for the young man who broke away from his family. Who came to New York, who believed in literature and jazz. Who was smart and hopeful and passionate, and did not survive.

Still, a grave. A stone. A cemetery: the long hair of the grass. The dead dancing, in the moonlight, in their bones. The dead swimming in the black earth as I swam in my bed, legs thrashing the sheets. And every week we bring flowers, tipping the cut stalks from our arms, round blooms like small suns.

The idea was that such things were ridiculous, sentimental in the worst sense. Soft-headed. My mother didn't feel this strongly, but her indifference was like accord.

I would say now she had no sense of repair. Only of getting beyond. And I find myself waiting for beyond the beyond, the place where they will let me, who will let me, set to work.

I assumed I'd have dreams about my father. I'd have dreams with both Jimmy and Daddy in them, complicated explanatory dreams; I'd learn how it all fit together. Nobody died without coming back, informing the bereaved how to feel.

The dreams were slow in coming. Not that night, or the next, or the next. I was bewildered, and wild to know what was happening. Were they friends? Equals? Was Jimmy of a higher rank, being dead longer, was he helping Daddy—and how did he feel, having Daddy suddenly appear? (My brother would have been mad at me if I'd come. I hadn't even thought about doing so, but still, I was sure, if I'd had the idea, he wouldn't have liked it.)

Daddy would be jealous of how much Jimmy's teachers loved him. He wouldn't be able to help insulting him, the way he always insulted him, and then Jimmy would lose that wonderful happiness he'd found; it made me so anxious.

In fact, I was unable to imagine them getting along. The thought of my father, not dead as I now knew him, but alive again in heaven, *with Jimmy,* agitated me profoundly. It was as if heaven itself would be ripped to pieces, snarling and fighting going on, day after day, no escape. Those monks or angels gliding out of the room, fading . . . Jimmy a little boy again, being hurt by our father.

Frantically, I would push Daddy away—away, away; but then I had to imagine him alone. Locked in a cell deep underground or wandering a deserted outer space.

I tried to imagine a heaven, a garden, just for Daddy, but it didn't work. The angels, or whatever they were, didn't want to be there. They thronged Jimmy's place. And it would never be safe, I realized, letting Daddy near my brother. It was one thing to feel—*poor Daddy, poor Daddy, he missed Jimmy so much he died*—quite another to let him live with him again. I toyed with the idea that Jimmy could help my father become good, but I didn't see why he should have to, and I wasn't sure he was strong enough to. He hadn't been dead very long. And he'd been so happy to get away.

But Daddy alone. I couldn't bear it.

My mother said Daddy didn't believe in an afterlife, he was aiming for oblivion, and it was true that he seemed to be there. Nobody had dreams of him; there was nothing like the matches flaring up on the mantel. Was she saying you got what you wanted in death? Could that possibly be true? My anxiety was telling me something different, which I couldn't quite hear; all I knew, by means of logic, was that there had to be consistency, that something like death could not depend on the whims of desire.

I never did dream of my father. I stopped dreaming about Jimmy, too. What happened was that Jimmy became more dead, sunk down deep, and Daddy became undead, raging around free in my soul.

Eighteen

WE SPENT THE summer at our new house on Sleeper Island in Lake Winnepesaukee in New Hampshire, which none of us had ever seen (we'd been going to the lake for two summers.) Now we were moving in, without Jimmy, without Daddy. It was hard to believe the house was still there, built for a family that no longer existed.

Mommy insisted we were still a family. I had no idea, of course, how difficult this was for her. How it was almost too difficult. All the way up to New Hampshire—we left New Jersey in darkness, four a.m., because she was afraid of the highway traffic—we kids fought and bickered in the car until she pulled over by the side of the road and wept. Until she told us, "I could get into an accident, and we'd all die. Do you understand? We could all die. Or maybe just I would die." I thought she was overdoing it. Trying to scare us, twist the knife—how could we die in a car with our mother? How could our mother die? It was only boys and men who died.

But that was the worst moment. The summer was an idyll, an

interlude, one I barely remember separate from all the summers that followed. Lake, woods, rocks. Pine scent, wave slap, fresh-cut leftover lumber under the house to make things with. Amorous trysts with the green water, deep humming cold, sun-dazzle. Johnny insisting he could drive the boat—he was much too young, the legal age was twelve—assuming all manly tasks. Docking the boat, tying it up, fishing, cleaning the fish. His body seemed to grow more muscular overnight, still small in stature but rugged. I was jealous at how he expanded into the whole territory of masculinity—how definite, how charged his role was—but I had to admit he did it well. Even our mother, though she tried to resist, began relying on him in certain practical matters.

When we got back to Montclair in the fall, Johnny started leaving the house at night. Not quite nine years old, he was staying out until one or two o'clock in the morning, running around the streets with a kid named Jeff. Jeff had no father either, and his mother worked nights. He was on his own, a mild, reedy, red-haired boy, not too bright. Five or six years older than Johnny, he knew the rougher parts of town, knew the kids who hung out at the gas station, yet in all significant ways my brother was the leader.

I thought Jeff looked like a character from the Oz books. Maybe the Scarecrow or the Pumpkinhead—a creature who would get progressively stupider as his head rotted, yet he always put off picking a new one. Jeff's hair was pumpkin colored, and he had a kind of mournful, flimsy air about him. I went to Jeff's house once. Half the furniture was on the stairs. You had to squeeze past a dresser, climb over a rocking chair, to get to the second floor. It was as if had all been frozen at a moment of attempted escape. Escape from Jeff's mother, of course, that squat tough blonde, whom I saw once, heard about often. This person would stand out in the moonlit street at two a.m. waiting for her son. Hands on her hips, low center of gravity, *she took up the whole road*—that tall, thin-necked, drifty boy walking toward her as Johnny pedals away furiously, looking over his shoulder.

When my mother noticed Johnny gone, she and Charlotte would set out in the car to look for him. I don't remember the first time this occurred. Surely it was traumatic—Johnny missing? Bed empty? What has stayed with me is the routine of it. Being left home to answer the phone. My mother's frantic instructions, Charlotte glued to her side, "If he comes back, keep him here. Margaret, are you listening? *Don't let him leave again.*"

How was I supposed to do that? *She* couldn't keep him here.

The station wagon dipping down the hill, big clunky car with its fixed headlights, dinosaur car while my brother was a mammal, little and quick. They never did find him; how could they? He had the whole dark of yards and woods to melt into.

But that wasn't my problem; they didn't ask my advice. Which would have been: Leave him alone. Why shouldn't he run around the streets? He'd had the whole island, the whole lake, and now we were back here, lopped-off family. Mom a little crazy, and the rest of us, too.

When either one alone—my mother or my sister—appealed to me, I couldn't resist, was so thrilled to be wanted. But when they appealed to me together—join the team, youngest member; here, do the peon work—I was stone. Furious.

Once they were gone: solitude. Solitude! In my ten years I'd never been left alone in the house. My first act was to turn up the thermostat to seventy-five, serve myself a bowl of ice cream. Stand in front of the freezer, eating, the frosty air billowing forth while behind me I heard the roar of the furnace kicking in.

I liked the noises of the house. Should I be afraid? I considered it. We'd all begun to hear of what would later be called serial killers. But how could I be afraid, all the danger was out there; and if a murderer should come, the dead were on my side. My father would rise up out of hell to protect me. Jimmy would come with his teachers. It was a pleasure to imagine. Some skunky knife-wielding lowlife with charcoal on his face—and a legion of bright monks, and a suicided man. Daddy snarling up through the floorboards. Air burning with magic.

But mostly I wasn't afraid because this was my house. The house was alive as it had always been; an intelligence. We were old friends.

I had used to think of the brain of the house as being on the third floor (the narrow staircase up was the neck); when I was in one of the little rooms I was in the cerebrum or the cerebellum, in that foamy folded matter like cake batter, waiting to rise. To puff up with the exquisite electricity of thought—*I would be thought of*—I laid myself open to the feelers of the house's I. Now I thought of that consciousness flooding down, humming in the walls and floors.

I wanted to double and triple myself, be in every room at the same time. The bedrooms, the bathrooms, the stairs. Stand at each window. Place my hand on each length of wall. But it was hard to leave the kitchen. Just to sit at the table—any seat I wanted—the whole empty table. I could breathe, I could talk aloud, I could laugh. All by myself, just laughing.

I could watch the dark press up against the windows, slick and black as paint. I could move into that darkness, or I could whisper it toward me. I had powers.

What would come? (Ecstasy of spirit hanging, swaying in the dark. I could bring it all toward me, I could toss myself into it. The invisible like a trapeze swinging in my direction, like a whole jungle gym I could climb, out of this foolish gravity.) What would come?

I spoke.

The dog and the cats came. They tended to scatter when the whole family was home but when I was alone, intoxicating myself with imagination, they'd gather. Stand in a half circle around me, watching with their opaque glances. It embarrassed me a little, yet the sound of my voice was so charming; I was the most delightful of beings. The animals would listen for awhile, then drift away, bored.

When I, too, became bored, I'd climb the stairs to my sister's room. I'd search her drawers, look for anything secret. Letters, diaries, brassieres, Nair. It was a great relief not to be afraid of her anymore, or rather to be afraid in a more normal way. Something crazy in her or in me had changed. She no longer tried to cast me into that underground where I was pinned to the light of her hatred.

One thing in particular that I was looking for in Charlotte's drawer was the dirty book she'd been giggling over with her friend Sue (not to be confused with our dog Sue.) Sue, seventeen, had once been our babysitter. She was blond, pretty, hungry for excitement; the sort of girl who, a couple of years later, would claim she was being kept by Aristotle Onassis. This was before any of us knew who that gentleman was.

The book which Sue had lent Charlotte was called *The Man from S.E.X.* A soft-core parody of the popular TV show *The Man from U.N.C.L.E.*, it featured a mild-mannered sex researcher who is continually mistaken for an agent of the CIA. After one thing and another, he ends up having sex with a beautiful Russian spy, her "slender yet voluptuous" body complete with breasts like melons, nipples like hard berries, and that mysterious triangle called the Delta of Venus.

I was greatly reassured by the fact that this book was comedy. My other source of sexual knowledge was *True Confessions* magazine, with its stories of girls who went too far and suffered forever. Living alone on the bad side of town, known sluts, unwed mothers. Shunned. That was the most frightening aspect, the certainty of these stories that the future of a young, healthy woman could just cease to exist. No possibility of change, rather a swift downpulling of the energy by story's end, a severe flatness that afflicted me on the deepest levels with dread.

So the casual good humor of *The Man from S.E.X.* was a tonic. The burbling jokes, the breezy, lilting paeans to pleasure. I was willing to overlook the stupidity of the women, how they were always ending up naked in embarrassing places, like subway cars, under the control of this mild-mannered chap. How they would fume helplessly, red staining their cheeks to make them look more attractive. Of course, I was used to reading books written from the perspective of men. Years of it had made me feel half male myself.

Mostly I loved the erotic descriptions. The paragraphs that didn't break off at the crucial moment, the amazing vocabulary. This was a time when sexy words still shimmered, when their existence on the page seemed nothing short of miraculous, and I was never sure they'd be there the next day. Reading, I'd glimpse ahead of me one of the significant words; I could feel the heat coming off it.

I could enter that word. It glittered and jumped, like a hooked fish. Reading from beginning to end of the word, threading between the letters, there are worlds between those letters—

I rationed my reading: half an hour a night. Only one of the climaxes. The approach, the flirting, the disrobing of the beauty. Her body unveiled, charged with supernatural allure—the swell of her breasts, dip of her waist, belly rounded over that swanky Delta. I learned to accept male desire as mine, though I had my private desire, too; I was both the girl and the man experiencing the girl. (This works best with books.)

Mostly I read and reread the erotic scenes, but I read the rest of it, too. I had to read both to get the full, peculiar effect—how the sex parts stood out from the text, were not of the story proper. I was intrigued by the disjunction, the smooth stroll of following the story, all the words the same weight, more or less, and me at the same distance, making pictures from the descriptions; then the fall into sex as through a trap door. *Different rules.* My whole body involved—not pictures but sensations—time slowing down, thickening like jam. I loved the plummy sweetness, the hot words oddly mechanical yet so thrilling, jolting me, the paragraph that could be read over and over, never yielding its mystery—then climbing out into the story again. People dressing, talking, a new chapter. Driving the smooth highway of the plot. The sex bits offered the more potent experience; but the story persisted.

When I'd finished my half hour of reading, and my family still wasn't back, I'd take a long bath or roam around the house. No one was watching me. No one was in charge. I was in charge. I had fantasies of the house slipping its moorings, drifting out to sea.

I was grateful when there was math homework to do. Solving algebraic equations: this equals that, figure out how. Explicate the equivalence between this short phrase, that long and bristly one. Some people quailed at the mention of algebra—grown-ups! How could one not love tidy *x* and *y*? And the spilling forth on the other side of overstuffed phrases, parentheses, symbols, operations . . . like a neat little woman in a pillbox hat married to a big disheveled bear of a man, pockets bulging . . .

Numbers and letters, my two favorite things, in the same place. Numbers, which went on to infinity, which you could do so many tricks with; there was even such a thing as imaginary numbers, taken seriously at school. These numbers now in families with the letters which, if you played Scrabble, paid off the most; numbers on top of other numbers, or with that little number at the top right, like an especially brainy person. And as for the work itself, it was just hard enough, I broke a mental sweat, got the glow. Then another problem, sitting there on the page like a Christmas present.

Occasionally I thought about what the women were doing. A

stab of guilt—erased by scorn for how undignified they were being, running around after Johnny. I knew what they were afraid of, could perfectly imagine. But the way to deal with the murderous gods is to lie low and concentrate, increase one's subtle power.

USUALLY JOHNNY WOULD get home first. Hearing the door slam and no car sounds, I'd run quickly downstairs, enjoying the sight

of his defensive posture.

"They're not here. They're out looking."

He'd take off his jacket, the tension in his shoulder blades only slowly relaxing. Seeing my empty dish, he'd serve himself some ice cream, tell me how stupid they were. As if he couldn't take care of himself, as if he didn't know this town inside out, as if they could, in a million years, find him.

I'd feel for them then. Something *could* happen. They were honestly worried. "You know, like Jimmy . . ."

Johnny would shrug. He'd say that Jimmy was too innocent, he trusted the cars not to hit him. He, Johnny, was always on the lookout. He knew where every car was every minute. He was ready to go into the ditch.

"Okay."

It was comical that he thought he knew more than Jimmy. On the other hand, it was true. About this, the way things were now, we all knew more than Jimmy.

It was a good time, the two of us alone in the house. Eating ice cream, inviting the cats up on the table to join us. Their heads would flatten with anxiety as they bit off chunks of vanilla while we explained to them that in our presence there were no rules.

We were always trying to decondition the animals. We thought we wanted them to be free, but I think we enjoyed their confusion. How they slipped into wavery states of being, doing several things at once: what they wanted to do, what we urged them to do, what they'd been trained to do. One impulse after another visible in their bunched muscles, pulsing there. Half leaping onto the table, for example. Missing the table, which was easily reachable, because of this uncertainty. We'd laugh and haul them up and they'd stand, ruffled, twitching their shoulders. Approaching with caution. Charlotte's cat Fluffy was especially interesting this way, because she was old. She had a lot to sort through; nothing was simple in her life. A car had driven over her tail. Fluffy would eat the ice cream but give me the evil eye at the same time, and her stump would vibrate. She'd lick the melted sweet off Ricky's whiskers—my cat all blissed out, eyes closed—yet hiss if she saw me watching. And just when I hated her—feeling injured that she wasn't grateful, *I gave her ice cream, I let her up on the table*—she'd plop into my lap as if she landed here all the time. I'd glance at Ricky, to see if he was jealous. But Ricky was cool. You'd never know.

If I was careful, only casually interested, Johnny might tell me what he and Jeff had been up to. He always kept the story brief. They rode bikes around, met other boys, hid from police cars. He wouldn't say how it felt or what anybody said. I suffered, as ever, a great longing for adventure. To be somebody else! Not exactly, in this case, Johnny, but like Johnny.

Why not live on our bicycles? Forage around town all night, sleep in the woods all day under piles of leaves, our faces rubbed with leaves for camouflage. Or if Charlotte and Mom didn't come home, Johnny and I could sell the flat silver for money. I would cook fried salami sandwiches, bake chocolate chip cookies, make milkshakes. I could also do hotdogs, cinnamon toast. Not that Charlotte and Mom would be dead or anything—they'd be on the high seas, kidnapped, having an okay time. As in the novel, *High Wind in Jamaica.*

But they always did come home. Tense voices outside the door, the influx of gray, dirty despair. Johnny and I going still, our spoons in our hands. We were eating dessert in a warm kitchen, laughing, while they rode around looking for a dead boy.

Johnny's eyes darting, furtive.

Mommy's anguish, even after she saw that Johnny was safe, made her seem mechanical. Her movements were jerky, her words both hollow and swollen. "Can't you understand . . . ?" she would say.

Johnny would yell and run up the back stairs. Sometimes Mommy followed him, with a relentless heavy step, sometimes she sat at the table and cried. Charlotte would swear at Johnny, calling him a selfish little shit, which made Mommy cry harder. She was still upset, in those days, when we used words like *shit.*

I hovered nervously. Slid away the ice cream dishes, though the butterfat still glistened on my lips. When would I be punished for being on his side? I wished they'd do it right away, get it over with. Then maybe I could explain. But explain what? I didn't understand why I couldn't be on her side—not while I was watching her cry. Hiccups of tears, her thin shoulders shaking. She cried like someone who was rusty at it, some awful incompetence making itself known. Why did I have such thoughts . . . why did I have any thoughts . . . her anguish, I was supposed to feel it more. I was supposed to feel only compassion, only love for Mommy. Once upon a time I would have said: I'll do anything in the world for my mommy.

Nineteen

MY MOTHER BEGAN to drink more. Not a lot more: a few cocktails in the late afternoon and evening. She says she was trying to become an alcoholic, seeing it as the only way out of her pain (she didn't succeed), but I didn't know that. I thought her drinking was good.

In my memory, there are alternate evenings: those when Johnny runs away, and Mommy is tense, bitter, and despairing, out in the cold in her car, and the evenings at home with Tanqueray. A sparkle would come to her eyes as she grew mildly tipsy, her voice dipping down into sentiment and affection. It was pain that made her drink, but it wasn't pain that came out. She wasn't lachrymose or whiny. She talked. My gypsy-dark mother in a red cashmere turtleneck at the table long after dinner, complexion flushed. The dishes left unwashed as we discussed the great issues. The philosophy of happiness and right action, the character of the gods. I began to understand that my mother was still a seeker. I learned that one can be all of forty and not know the basic things; more surprisingly, one can be forty and not be surprised that one doesn't know.

Curled on the couch, legs slung up beside her, her round hip scooping the air. She gained weight that year and I liked that, too, woman curves of arm, hip, bosom. On the record player, Frank Sinatra or Peggy Lee.

"I want to be around/to pick up the pieces/when somebody breaks your heart/somebody twice as smart/as me." I loved Peggy's lazy, sensual voice and Frank's frank male energy. My mother told me Frank Sinatra was the Paul McCartney of her youth, that she and her friends adored his skinny Italian waifishness, waited outside the club door, screamed for him . . .

It excited me to watch my mother get excited by the music, begin to sway a little. I learned to make her drinks, and I made them strong. Mommy magic. When she stood up, sometimes, she would dance.

"She acts so stupid," one of my siblings might say. Johnny hated seeing her tipsy, he broke away from her embraces, and Charlotte, as well, was embarrassed. But stupid was what I liked. (Not stupid.) Her thoughts wandering and looping, voice confiding. Oh, tell me, tell me, tell me who you are.

My mother had a mythic self, like a tapestry forest. My own mythic self could live in those woods. I was born of this shy, myopic, poetry-reading girl whose mother wouldn't let her wear her glasses to the dance. Who had to go beautiful and bare-faced, the world all a blur. "I had to wait for the boys to come to me. I couldn't see a thing." Though she wouldn't admit she was beautiful. She would never admit that. As a girl, Mommy said, she was too tall, too dark. "I was funny-looking. June was much cuter than I. She was athletic, popular." I found this fascinating. My Aunt June was nowhere as pretty as my mother. Even in the pictures of them as girls, she wasn't as pretty. My mother had a round sweet smiling face as a child; at fourteen she looked like an Indian maiden on her horse; at sixteen a movie star.

She told me about being sent away from Houston to boarding school in cold Pennsylvania—the Shipley School—where she discovered respect for the life of the mind. She had been rebellious at home, but she was a good girl at school, raising her hand when the principal asked the assembled students, *on their honor,* if any of them had committed the infraction of smoking. Mommy loved that story, not because she was congratulating herself for being so good, but because she was trying to tell us how thrilling it was, that concept *honor*, how it did something to her soul. She wanted us to feel it, too.

I half felt it. I crept around the edges of it, tasting the idea. Not honor per se, but Mommy's honor. A warm spot in her imagination.

She talked about being a bohemian in Greenwich Village after the war, living on Macdougal Street, wearing black ballet slippers. The boys, the jazz joints, the evenings reading Nietzsche. I asked if she had kept the ballet slippers. No. Then I asked her if she would buy me a pair, and she said they weren't fashionable now. She told me how some stuffy men she dated—men from home—were a little scared of her just because of those slippers, and because she read books. Intellectual girls could frighten a man in his business suit.

I thought she should have kept those slippers.

I read Nietzsche, which she did still have. *Thus Spake Zarathustra.* At eleven years old, all I got was the fire. But I liked having the book in my room to dip into, scrambling my brains.

It was such a pleasure how my mother opened up after a few drinks. How the stories came out, sometimes the same ones, sometimes different ones, how she colored the air around her. She had never talked like this when my father was alive. Then she had seemed like a wand of a woman, calm, poised, gracious. Never out of character. But now she was silly, awkward, cute, creaky, a little bit grandiose. I wasn't afraid of this "I" she kept bringing out, I, I, I: It was fine. As she drank her Tanqueray, I drank in her reminiscences, Memphis, Houston, Shipley, Vassar, Greenwich Village. Her father teaching her to swim in the winter by laying her across a chair, making her practice the breaststroke. Hoboes coming to the door every night; the cook gives them supper, which they eat in the yard. The cousins, elderly ladies on their porches in Wilmington, North Carolina, some of them born before the Civil War. Ice-water dinner parties, high-minded conversation. The long-eared hunting dogs of which her father had six or seven. Her father in bed for two years before he died.

It was Daddy's death that made Mommy be like this. It was Daddy's death that loosened everything, afternoon turning into night, dinner, bed, never that moment when the world turns to glass. Even Johnny's expeditions that upset her so much—even her upset—didn't seem to me as bad as the old normality.

I hadn't known it could be like this. Not only afternoons—in the woods, on my bike in the driveway—not only the bloom of yellow light in the kitchen as she begins to cook; not only that but it continues. I don't start thinking of getting my bike out of the way because of the car zooming around the corner. I don't flee to the top of the stairs, to the top of my brain, that high lookout strangely amorous, strangely fractured. Rather there's a sense of vacation every day, as if we weren't going to school.

School was better than it had ever been, too. It was odd. I wasn't afraid of my classmates anymore—or at least the fear lessened so much it seemed like nothing.

On the night in November when the great blackout hit we ate a cold dinner by candlelight: bologna sandwiches, glasses of milk. Johnny and I speculated as to whether Jimmy had caused the blackout. I imagined him like a shadow angel over the city, wings wide. Mommy said Jimmy would never do such a thing; it was dangerous, people got hurt in blackouts; then Johnny said maybe it was an atom bomb that hit New York. "Let's drive in and see."

"Duh," said Charlotte. "No mushroom cloud."

Mommy had a drink or two. She said, "Let's tell stories."

My siblings protested. Charlotte wanted to sit in her room by herself. Johnny wanted to prowl around the basement, looking for the big flashlight lost last year. "If the blackout lasts a week, Mom, we'll need it."

"It won't last a week."

"Rats," said Charlotte.

"There aren't any rats in the basement," said my mother. "Don't be silly."

"I'll take Jinx, she could kill any rat," said my brother.

"She's no bigger than a rat herself," Charlotte said. "She may even be a rat."

"She'd bite its spinal cord, paralyzing it, then eat its face, I taught her how to do that, I'm practicing for you."

"You're such a retard."

Mommy sent us to bed, each with a candle.

"Remember, Margaret, people in the nineteenth century had to do this every night. They could only read as long as the candle lasted." A sidelong smile at me—imagine it, not being able to read!

The most delicious part was that we knew this, Mommy and I, *because we read.* We remembered the heroines being handed the stump of candle—the illustrations of winglike shadow on the looming stair—rays of life-giving light.

MOMMY AND I talked about the afterlife—Jimmy's afterlife. Mommy was wearing his old madras jackets, they just fit, I his pink-and-red shirt. My mother allowed us to pick one thing of his to keep, I chose this. He had bought it himself, nobody liked it but him and me. The clash of pink and red was defiance made lovely, it was futuristic and rock-and-roll, it was heart-colors. I looked good in it, I thought, though not as good as Jimmy had, and Mommy looked good in the madras jackets. Her dark hair now grew to her shoulders.

We discussed seances and reincarnation. My mother explained what the Hindus believed; she talked about someone named Bridey Murphy. I was amazed—how could this half-known truth be lying around? She said that the proof in the Bridey Murphy case was doubtful, that all the experiences people had of ghosts and so forth (the matches on the mantel) were subjective; scientists didn't accept them.

It was strange. I had thought it all of a piece, the grown-up world. Even though I knew better, really, I had persisted in believing this. But as my mother talked about the occult, spiritual systems, theosophy (Madame Blavatsky spinning ectoplasm out of the air like cotton candy), I was happy at the jumbled variety of belief. Enough for me to pick through, find the truth—which it was odd, of course, that nobody had found before me, but then the world was waiting for me, wasn't it? All the centuries of the past leading up to my birth.

My mother told me about Yeats's fairy tales, compiled from contemporary accounts, what were said to be real experiences by Irish people. (Fairy women knocking on the door, having a chat. Men carried off for days of dancing, finding themselves back on the same road, no time passed. The dead returning.) We discussed the Ouija board, table-turning, tarot cards. We asked ourselves what kind of life Jimmy would want to be reborn into—and whether we would know him if we saw him with a different face. He could be in a woman's belly right now. He could even be born already. Was that why he no longer appeared in my dreams?

My mother raised an eyebrow. I wanted to go look at all the babies in town.

We didn't talk about Daddy, his afterlife or lack of it. We didn't talk about the relief; how the afternoons became evening, twilight softening, and she cooked when we were hungry, and we ate casually, chattering. We didn't talk about that, and I decided I could discard him: not my wounded, self-murdering father whom I had folded so tenderly into myself, but the scary live man he had been.

Then, now, always, the table gleams. He writhes in his dark suit. She sits up straight, the lady of noble pedigree. All trembly, I try to eat. He yells. I vanish. He looks at me, no one here. Then he turns his gaze away and I am stunned by the shine of a color, the slant of a taste. My furtive flesh engages itself, turned and coiled in the inner conversation.

Twenty

IN THE EARLY spring, my mother told us she had decided to sell the house and move us to New York City. Johnny needed to go to a psychiatrist and there weren't any good psychiatrists here. Also the house was too big for us now.

Charlotte told me Mommy had to get away from Montclair. Everyone here was a couple and wouldn't invite her to things. "They think she'll steal their husbands," my sister said scornfully.

I had to go with my mother wherever she went, I knew that, but the house was also my mother. Its very walls and floors, its clean smells and high windows. Smooth-barked blossoming trees, soft, uneven earth. The emerald grass of the garden where I jump-roped for hours, counting to a hundred, two hundred, where I sat the cats in the sun to photograph, where I walked with Nicky while she explained to me that my father was a good man, he loved me.

The stone fountain; the stone steps cut in the hill we tobogganed down, Jimmy in the lead, slamming into the flat white cake of the garden. Snow angels, snow in our mittens, snow falling over black rubber boot-tops. Oak and maple leaves pressed between sheets of waxed paper; cracking open with a sneaker the spiked cases of the horse chestnuts. Purple and white lilac, nectar of honeysuckle. The twin crabapples which bore the little sour fruit, flesh twisted around the seam of a wormhole, mulberry tree laden with soft, dark berries. Mulberry tree thinking of its cousins in China, where silkworms were spinning my mother's dresses out of their asses.

How could we leave? Jimmy and Daddy were here. Their traces, bright glints, which were also, strangely, their whole lives. I was always coming across memories as I wandered through the house—memories and hints of things I hadn't known, which I might yet figure out; I had been young but was getting older. We had Jimmy's voice on tape, we had two minutes of him in a home movie. Those we would take with us, but there were other things. I couldn't say exactly what. Also the future, which seemed to me not settled. Jimmy was happy in heaven, but what if he needed to return?

Jimmy might want to visit his room. He might have been doing it all along, and checking on us, too, how could we tell? My mother said, "If he's able to check on us, he can check on us in New York," but I knew she was only humoring me. The idea was preposterous; what did Jimmy know about New York? He'd need to come here, and he'd need for it to be the way it was. It was necessary to wait, even if you—if Mommy—didn't really believe in the possibility of his return. It seemed to me a kind of respect, as when somebody is late to meet you and you don't just run off but stay there, idling on your bike on the sidewalk, giving them time for all the little things that cause delay. You wait, and the sky changes slowly. Then you go home knowing it wasn't your fault.

And Daddy. I couldn't think about him, really, but I knew he was still here. No person but little bits, the glow of his cigarette, the wild shamanic anguish of his hands. The French doors where he used to stand, smoking—his long gazes—his desk in the library. Boxes of books he brought home for me, that his company published. "Margaret, there's something in the car." I hadn't really grieved him. Didn't really miss him— Not yet. I needed to stay here.

I tried to explain all of this to my mother and she replied, "They live in our hearts."

There wasn't room in my heart. It was packed tight and if I tried to fit one more thing in, something terrible would happen. I could see this ahead of me like a car crash one can't avert. Mommy thought I could handle it, but she was wrong.

I will come apart. Nobody believes me. I couldn't believe it would be allowed to happen, my mind—my mind!—being stretched like taffy until the long ribbon let go of itself. What I would say now: panic, dissociation, was then only an image that loomed, as when the dish has left your hand, not yet hit the floor. I tried to warn my mother, but she said Johnny had to go to the psychiatrist, and the psychiatrist was in New York. She said it was too dangerous here where he could run around the streets. In New York there were doormen to keep him from leaving the building; and also the streets were so dangerous he'd be scared to go out at night.

In this she turned out to be correct, but it sounded perverse to me. He needed to be scared? More scared? And what about me? She became agitated, her voice broke into that liquid hurt I couldn't bear causing. She said she couldn't live anymore with the fear of losing Johnny.

O my mommy, nymph of the earth. The hoarse tones of her voice, her shoulders slumped forward. Her dark hair which is growing longer, as if she is getting younger.

Johnny reacted violently to the news of our move. He ran around the house, from the kitchen up the stairs and into

Mommy's room, knocking all the bottles and jars off her dressing table. My mother followed behind him, telling him that she knew he was angry, she understood—a few sentences of psychological interpretation offered, "Your father's death"—and he punched her in the shoulder. She sat on the stairs and wept.

I followed behind Mommy following Johnny. I liked the smash of things, the violation of that too-cluttered dressing table. The excess of it had always been disturbing, as had the heavy perfume of those thick, sticky stuffs. I liked the shock, the badness—bottles on their sides on the carpet, absurd little mascara wands flicked distances, eye shadow upended. Once we were afraid to come into this room. Now Johnny's anger blasted through with muscular determined force; it was the necessary thing. But the punch to her shoulder undid me.

She wept. I couldn't.

WE WERE LEAVING the cats behind. My mother said we couldn't have cats in New York City. Not four cats, not even one cat. She said, "Cats don't love people, Margaret, they only love places. Ricky wouldn't want to go with you."

It was odd how these words coming out of her mouth transformed us both. They made her lips go flat. Where they touched me I went numb, with a little flicker, a little shock.

My mother had never liked cats. She liked dogs—their loyalty, their foolish abasement. Hearts on their paws. She said a cat's purr was only a trick to make you feed it, or a sign of physical pleasure at being stroked, it conveyed no true emotion. "Ricky doesn't love you, Margaret." The sweet, reasonable tones of her voice, repeating this, the numbness spreading. I thought, and it was terror: She must not have a brain or a heart like mine. How could she if she didn't know this obvious fact, that cats could love? Of course

Ricky didn't *speak*; didn't say "I love you," yet he yielded when I needed him to, let me pick him up under his shoulders and stretch his body two feet, three feet, back legs kicking only feebly as his belly lengthened. He would gaze at me from his half-lidded eyes as I declaimed my passion.

I could kiss him on the lips. I could dress him in doll clothes. Not because he *liked* it.

I started reading my favorite books over. Robin Hood, the knights of the round table, Albert Payson Terhune. I also reread the Narnia books and fairy tales, but the adventure stories were what I most craved. Long night marches, sword fights, escapes. Tankards of ale, the leather of horse bridles. Reading. Eyes hooked to the page: All else vanishes. Sensations as of flying over great swathes of land.

My mother might come to my door, "Margaret, you have to . . ." Clean up, vacuum, fold laundry, walk the dog. Murderous thoughts flared up that I had to douse, one by one, in my fishlike gloom.

"In a minute." I wouldn't move

"You never do anything around here."

It was true, I did very little. I did even less than Johnny, who didn't have to do things but did anyway, lifting heavy boxes for Mom, fixing her radio. I found myself unable to pull away from a book; it was as if I were attached, as if I had grown roots into the land of the story and each shift in attention—not to mention actually getting up—required tearing all those roots free. I didn't understand why nobody seemed to know this, how one's brain sends out shoots, sinks them deep in a book's belly. Then you're symbiotic, the words, your thoughts, all twined around together, breathing together.

My mother didn't have the strength to make me do things. She didn't have the will or the force to rip out roots. She made rules, set up punishments, nagged me, but none of it stuck. I was used to obeying her out of love. I wanted obedience to be love.

When I needed something other than reading, I tried to play. I played for hours every day, as I had always done—sometimes getting up in the middle of the night to play—but I was having trouble. What had once been effortless—to see my toys as alive at the same time I knew they weren't really—was now a chore. I felt as if I were using up my last ounces of power in order to fuel the make-believe. I knew this loss of interest was supposed to happen at my age. Eleven was when girls stopped playing with dolls, starting caring more about boys, music, lipstick. I liked those things but I also wanted the dolls, the china animals' company.

I saw myself, sitting cross-legged on the floor of my bedroom, attempting to play when I was too old to play. Why don't you have any friends, you jerk?

I HAD FRIENDS. I had, at last, a best friend, Denise, new that year. Denise was a tall and sarcastic black girl, an eleven-year-old who looked fifteen. She had breasts and hips, long legs, a big, intelligent face. She was the first girl at school I thought might be smarter than I was.

We were both especially good in math. Our teacher gave the class tests every Friday and Denise and I scored 98 or 99 or 100; the other good students rarely broke 95. In victory Denise crowed and strutted, told me I was brain-damaged, hopeless, "You've lost it, girl"; in defeat she was a clown, parading her disappointment.

We hung out, which I had never known how to do before. Idling, relaxed, telling endless stupid jokes. Mental hospitals, retards, dirty underwear. We reveled in our brainpower, bragging. It was powerful to be smart. It was good to be bold. I saw now that the white girls in my class were prim, and that I didn't like prim.

Not being prim, though, meant not being afraid of boys, and I had to lean on Denise for this. I'd follow her around the softball field where the boys were playing as she made outrageous remarks. Threatened to pull boys' pants off, to hang their pants from a tree. They ignored her. They were afraid of her. She was taller than they were, black: I sensed, and felt marvelously protected from, their fright at this angry blackness. I knew what blackness was now, in its essence. It was Denise. Denise Coates in her shirtwaist dresses, her kneesocks. Hair carefully done, brushy and neat, gold barrettes.

I had a best friend. We were always together. She came over to my house, up to my room. She listened earnestly as I talked about Jimmy and show her his picture. I can still see that photograph in her hand, Jimmy's little smiling face, Denise's big, solemn one, the care with which she picks her words. I like it best when she says, "He's really cute." She can't admit that any of the boys at school are cute because of their scorn for her. But Jimmy is safe; she can like Jimmy. My sense of this is very deep and tremulous; I want to cry; I'm nervous that my emotion is wrong, yet I also know that this is an exquisite moment. This is what it means to be *friends*.

I feel shy, yet not in the way of silence. I keep talking, offer her the pleasures of my room, my house. "What do you want to do? We can do anything you want." She won't say. We stroll, she looks at everything for a long time—the books in the library, the paintings and rugs, even the animals—and makes no comment. Her expression is blank, yet I'm aware of how closely she's looking. I can't imagine what she feels.

We go back to my room and sit on the bed. The disparity of our lives is on my mind, but I don't know what to do about it. I can't talk about it—she doesn't. I talk about myself and wait for her to say things. I talk about my mother, she talks about hers. We don't talk about our fathers. She doesn't have one either.

I only went to Denise's house once. It was a warm spring Saturday. Mommy drove me there, and I was a little frightened, having never been in the black section of town. My mother told me again that it was wrong that Negroes had to live in a segregated area, had to be poor, and I wondered why it wasn't wrong, then, that we were rich. Yet I was soothed by my mother's ease. She had no awkwardness about my friendship with Denise, was looking forward to meeting her mother. When we arrived and the two women spoke—Denise's mother short, round, stern-faced—I noticed that the black woman was not at ease. She was polite but didn't invite my mother in.

Denise's house was a little shabby on the outside, and much smaller than ours, but not all that small. It had, I think, five rooms, and a deep, grassy backyard. We sat in the yard, at a table with an umbrella, and Denise's mother brought us lemonade on a tray. Tall frosty glasses. This embarrassed me. None of my other friend's mothers waited on children for an afternoon snack. They'd make it and leave it in the kitchen, or we'd make it ourselves. Denise's mother's behavior reminded me of my grandmother's servants, and I knew it wasn't supposed to.

We talked about school with an odd fervor. We talked about school, that afternoon, as if we'd never get another chance. I heard all of Denise's opinions, expressed more wickedly than before. She talked about how pale Alison was: her skim-milk-white and freckled skin, her pink-rimmed eyes, like a rabbit's. Maybe she was an albino, Denise suggested with a crazy grin. And how thin her wrists! How puny that girl was—she could be broken like a matchstick.

I felt disloyal, but not too much so. Alison was popular, and only a half-friend. To Denise, I guess, only a quarter-friend. But more than that, what made it okay was that when Denise ragged on her, and I nodded eagerly—albino! puny wrists!—her voice was strangely tender.

We sat in the yard, sipping our lemonade, for an hour or so. When her mother came out, removed our empty glasses, I imagined we were in Paris, at an outdoor café. Young women in the sunlight.

I liked Denise's yard because the grass grew longer than in ours. It was long enough to flop over our ankles, to bend into waves with our feet as we idly swished them. And it was darker than ours, not so jewel green but more of a foresty color, quieter.

I thought maybe her mother, serving us, was showing off for my benefit, but not—I realized in a moment—her own courtesy toward a guest; what she was showing off was Denise's high status. In her own home, my friend's implicit grandeur blossomed. She was the eldest, the scholarship girl. Her three younger siblings—skinny and dark, all arms and legs—came circling around, giggling, and she shooed them off casually. They obeyed. She was *Denise*.

Later she showed me her room, where all four kids slept. They piled on top of her as we sat there, the little kids, on the king-size bed. Crawling on our legs—mostly her legs—and on each other, telling me which strip of mattress they each claimed, where their heads went. Demonstrating sleep, *like this*, all laid out in a row, and what big snores Denise made: *like this*, honking. She cleared them out of the room with an anger they didn't take seriously—they kept popping back in with more jokes and giggles—but finally with authority. Then she apologized to me for their presence and complained. I sympathized as she lamented their wriggliness, chattering, nightmares, bed-wetting, yet of course I envied her. To be the eldest. To sleep together, younger ones squirming and snuffling like kittens, their hot bodies, soft flexible little feet.

After dinner, the younger children were sent to bed and Denise and I sat up with her mother. Mrs. Coates brought out a basket of clothes—Denise's clothes for violin camp. Shorts, shirts, underpants, socks. Looking at me sternly, she described the difficult path Denise would take to success in this world, how it all depended on scholarship, on continuous achievement, how this camp was not for fun but an integral part of a well-thought-out plan. Her tone was repressive, anticipating from me—what? sneers?—but I was in fact admiring of her foresight and devotion. Then she said that as a guest in their house I was required to help. I had to sew name tags in Denise's camp clothes, would not be allowed to sit idly. Not allowed. "Anybody who stays in this house has to work. Do you know how to sew?"

What if I didn't? I'd already eaten her food. I couldn't get home by myself. I was helpless, a little white-and-pink girl like an iced cookie. I was so conscious of my corrupt paleness, and how small I was, feet not reaching the floor. Only Denise's embarrassed glance made me feel human.

I knew Denise's mother thought I couldn't sew. She assumed I was useless and was letting me know it. I didn't think it was fair, her springing this particular test; she hadn't asked to me help set or clear the table, which any idiot could do, she had treated me scrupulously as a guest. Now, when it was late, only one thing left to do, she gave me her ultimatum. "Nobody stays in this house if they don't work." I wanted to challenge her back—felt roused to argue in my own defense, even as I felt the full impossible nature of my whiteness *a girl made out of sugar*—but I didn't need to. "I can sew."

Denise's mother watched me closely. I licked the thread, threaded the needle, made a small knot. I chose a garment from the basket, picked up one of the name tags, looked sidelong to see where they wanted it placed—exactly where my mother placed mine, okay—began to sew. I remembered the advice my mother had given me over the years on the importance of small, even stitches, which, in my carelessness at home, I didn't always heed. It wasn't so hard to do it right. I liked my stitches, little footsteps, little broken lines as on perforated paper, one after another. Make them match. At the end, I looped the needle through three times and bit off the thread.

Nobody said anything. Denise looked relieved. I chose another garment, another name tag. I was as fast as Denise, or faster. Her mother tightened her lips. What could she do to me? I was sewing. I was sewing, thinking of Denise at violin camp—would she make other friends?—of the years ahead that her mother had mapped out.

I picked up another garment, kept sewing. I could be white *and* know how to sew. My mother could sew better than anyone—she made her own clothes from the pages of *Vogue*. I let myself remember them, her beautiful lake–blue-and white evening gown, her gray tailored suit with the fabric-covered buttons, and the smocked dresses she made for us with little puffed sleeves. Our red velvet Christmas stockings.

My mother knew I was smart and good. She would explain to me why Mrs. Coates couldn't help feeling the way she did, how wrong it was that Negroes were discriminated against.

I liked doing something so intimate for my friend. Sewing her name on her shirt collar, on the waistband of her white panties. I knew she was embarrassed when I picked up her underwear, but it was as if I were her sister. As if I were her sister and I liked her better than my sister, but I still preferred to be white. Did that make me guilty? I liked my skin, the beige, peach, and olive tints of it.

I only went to Denise's house that once. She came to my house, or we idled after school, walking home so slowly in the late spring sunlight that our very slowness became the excuse to insult each other. Cripple, spastic, retard. We loved those insults—we'd invent dopey variations, spin elaborate chains of invective, dazzling ourselves with our wit. Denise lived on Pleasant Way, which sounded like a euphemism for a mental hospital, and it made me delirious with pleasure to tease her, "You're mental, the men in white coats are coming to take you away," and she'd tease me back. What I wanted to do to boys, how bad I was. I loved to hear it. I loved to hear it, I loved to say it, but we'd always end by reassuring each other that we didn't really mean it. Voices cooing, thrilling sweetness. "I don't *really* think that about you." The sweetness itself half a joke, not quite.

I told Denise that I was moving, of course, and that I didn't want to. She said—carefully, face averted—that she'd miss me and I said I'd miss her. We promised to write. Our friendship wasn't strong enough yet, or I wasn't strong enough, to tell her what it meant to me. To say *I think I'll go crazy. I'm so afraid. My mother doesn't care.* (And the hardest thing of all—knowing that my mother did care. She cared enough so that I couldn't go crazy. I had to stop her from moving us, for her own sake. If I went crazy, she'd be so upset.)

Anyway, I couldn't tell Denise I was afraid. I was white, privileged. Our family could do whatever we wanted, move to New York City. Denise thought New York was cool.

CHARLOTTE SAID NEW York was cool. She'd come into my room, make herself comfortable on my bed, and talk about this, how cool the city was. I was still confused and surprised that she would choose my company, *actually come to my room*, and flattered at how she was coaxing me, as if my opinion mattered. I listened. This would be cool, that would be cool. The school I'd go to, the kids I'd meet. A different kind of kid.

Why would I want a different kind of kid? There was nothing wrong with the people here. Charlotte was unhappy at school, but I'd never been happier. This was strange—I knew—Jimmy and Daddy dead, and I'd never been happier. *In school.* I wasn't afraid of the kids anymore, they knew me, I had Denise. And there were starting to be kissing parties . . .

Charlotte said I'd be unhappy next year when I graduated to Kimberley, the girls school she attended. I'd hate it, she said. All the girls at Kimberley were snobby. Even people who'd been her friends before weren't now.

Why didn't it occur to her, I wondered, that this was *her life*?

But I couldn't say anything. I was afraid she would stop being nice to me if she knew what I believed: that I could be popular at

Kimberley. I was even a little excited at the idea of a girls school. We'd still see the boys, there were always parties and dances, but no boys in class; it sounded chummy. She said it wouldn't only be the girls from Brookside, there'd be others, snobby ones, but I wasn't afraid. Maybe it just seemed obvious that if she wasn't a success there, I would be. That anyplace that suited her couldn't suit me, and vice versa; we had nothing in common.

But the strange thing was how she didn't know this. She acted as if I was just the same as her. After so many years of *Booger, Blubber Baby*, now she was nice—okay—but seeming not to have a clue that I was still so frightened. I didn't tell her.

I let her into my room whenever she needed to talk. I lay back on my pillows with Ricky on my chest. We had an understanding, Ricky and I, we knew what love was: endless observation of the other. He looked at me through half-lidded eyes, sniffed me with his speckled orange nose. I kissed his cat lips, stroked his scar. I investigated every inch of his tail though that made him nervous. I could have told you, then, the precise pattern of his markings, his dimensions, what he ate every day. I liked to lie on my belly watching him drink water.

Charlotte filled her conversation with names of people who lived in the city—the Plumb and Arnold kids—by which she thought to entice me. She had taken it as her job to help Mommy by reconciling me to the move, also she wanted an ally in anticipation. So she recited the names, which only scared me but I had to pretend for now they didn't. Had she forgotten how they all teased me, left me out of games?

Just to hear their names depressed me. To go to their city would be like enduring an eternal weekend, the grown-ups drinking, the games picking up, which I wander out of the range of play. I saw us driving into the city and the light winking out. All the images I had ever absorbed of imprisonment, of goblin's tunnels and giant's kitchens, rose like a dense fog and hovered over that city, fifteen miles, six months, away.

Charlotte's voice—her hopes. She allowed out a musing girlself I was so drawn to, though it filled me with a wraithlike loneliness. I clung to her invisibly, at the cell level, in darkness.

At fourteen, Charlotte looked seventeen. Tall and busty, she had a big, high-cheekboned face, thick curly hair, eyes as brown and glossy as chestnuts. I was smaller than she, always, but now especially so, as if shrunken. Dried up around my own terror, unforgivenness—pressing down upon myself as another part of myself responded, waving in the music of her seduction.

She wanted to be friends now. She said she'd help me get accustomed to the city. I even mentioned the Plumbs not liking me—diffidently, offhandedly—and she said she'd help. But that was because she didn't know ME. If she should ever suspect ME, I NEVER FORGIVE, or ME, the genius who would raise our brother from the dead, for herself alone—if she ever suspected that, Charlotte would also metamorphose. Body of green coils, each coil as thick as a man. Snake slither. We would have to fight to the death.

The hollow of this secret and her voice filling it.

Twenty-one

WE MOVED IN August, after a summer at the lake. We had taken Ricky to the lake with us, my mother yielding finally to my incessant pleading. My siblings had come over to my side, both agreeing that if we could only keep one cat, it should be this one—which thrilled me though I didn't take credit for it. I assumed it was because Ricky was the only male.

Faced with three children united, my mother gave in. I carried him up to New Hampshire in a box, letting him out a few times too often. He'd lie on my lap for a wild-eyed moment, then escape to the front seat, hide under the brake pedal. My mother talked again hysterically of death.

Ricky was nervous at the lake. He had some idea—or no idea, which was worse?—where his harem had gone, and often spent nights in the woods. He'd come home covered with pine needles, hungry, and I'd talk to him as he ate the fish or chicken from my dinner.

I apologized for what had been done to little gray Jinx, to Gypsy, who'd borne his kittens, and stump-tailed Fluffy, how they were taken to the animal shelter where they were probably killed. I told him it was *her* fault—but couldn't quite rid myself of guilt by association. After all, I still lived with her, spent the twilight sunsets sitting with her on the porch watching the blues of the lake deepen as she sipped gin and talked musically. Men would often come by in their boats—sometimes bringing their wives, usually not—and sit with her for the cocktail hour. Then I would bring cheese and crackers for everyone, while she was light and charming and so pretty. In her white pants, her vivid pink-tangerine tops, and deeply tanned skin. Her narrow, arched bare feet, her dark head leaning against the glass of the living-room door. Men would talk to me in order to talk to her, praising me or saying I was like her. She was proud of me, that I could surprise them by how much I'd read, what I thought.

At the end of the summer, for reasons best known to herself, my mother reneged on her promise. She said we had to get rid of Ricky, too. He'd be all right, not have to go to the shelter, neighbors in Montclair wanted him.

I don't remember fighting for him a second time. I thought this was my punishment for loving Ricky best, letting the others be taken away—three girl cats in the back of the car, to their deaths—just as Jimmy's death was my mother's punishment for loving him best.

It was a hot and sticky day in late August when we moved into the apartment of a building on East 79th Street, on the corner of Madison. I followed my mother inside the dim, cavernous, red-carpeted lobby, where we were introduced to the building manager, a small sallow man in a dark suit, who was fretting about something, and the doorman and elevator men in their gray uniforms and German accents. My mother telling us about the rules here; I only half listened. *This is where we live now.* Other residents coming in and out—women in high heels, stiff lacquered hair—giving us disdainful glances. Johnny and I in shorts, sneakers. Charlotte in jeans. I heard my mother say, "You can't hang around down here, can't play here," and understood this to mean that everyone here disliked children.

Then the apartment, an eight-room duplex. I was surprised by how lovely and big it was. "I told you," my mother said. Here was our stuff, still in cardboard boxes, filling the spacious entry hall, the living room with high ceilings, the dining room. Familiar green leather chair standing like an oasis amid the piled sand-brown boxes—its curved arms, ample seat, declining in the middle, the brass fittings catching the light. I sat in it briefly, remembering the island we had just come from. Someday I'd have my own island. Nobody on it but cats.

The living-room curtains were not up yet, the big windows bare to the tumult of 79th Street. Two lanes of traffic, horns blaring. My mother tried to tell us about the park, only a block away, *how lucky we were*, but I knew about the park. Johnny had informed me. Men with knives were in there.

One small rug had been unrolled—Oriental garden with its white fringe, dense blues, and violet-pinks. If I lay on that rug, closed my eyes, would it wrap up around me, transport me home? But this was home. The house in Montclair was empty now. Nobody had wanted to buy it yet, which I found so insulting, though of course I didn't want anybody there.

I remembered coming back to Montclair, years ago, after six weeks at the beach. This was when we were still going to Stone Harbor, before we bought the lake house. I had spent the last day on the beach collecting shells to take home. I found a few pretty scallop shells, but not what I most wanted, a conch shell. Those were only present in pieces, little shiny pink lips or fingernails of shell.

When we got home after so long away, the cool stone steps outside the front door, the airy hall, big staircase with its branching arms were unfamiliar, as if the house had remade itself in our absence. Remade itself exactly the same—it was brand new, the juice of creation still damp, a quiver as when someone tries to stifle a laugh.

I entered my room slowly. Who was living here now? Who was I, sensations gathering around my shoulders like layers of veils, Mommy's net veils and thin silk shawls, like the cloth made of spiderwebs the stories described. I was Margaret in a river of presences, nimbly in motion. Home: the gray white, the creamy white, the blue of walls, the acres of air, silence (family noise downstairs) the whisper welcome of the dull-gold wood floors. I opened my door, pressed my lips against the flesh of my room. Sleek haunch of a china dog, bosomy pillows, blue paisley quilt. And on my bureau, a big, perfect conch shell. Curved and heavy, with the crusted white outside, the deep rose inner spiral. How did it come here? My mother hadn't been here. Nobody had been here.

I put it to my ear and the sea roared. O most bountiful house. What else was it concealing, what gifts in its walls?

My mother told me later that Grandmommy had brought the shell for me. She'd been in the area and had stopped to visit Daddy here, bringing presents for us, just happening to choose this for me. This was a slight disappointment, but only slight. *Everything you need; it is here.* Grandmommy had been simply the conduit.

This was our home now. My mother was talking about the work left to be done—the kitchen wasn't finished, the bedrooms not all painted—and I felt a pull toward her, as if she were a magnet. I was a little piece of iron, flying to attach itself to her body. Yet I couldn't do that because I was still so angry. "Ricky wouldn't like the city," she had said. Of course not. He had a few brains.

I looked around. There was the tall painting by my mother's friend Tom Vincent, bought last year, of a girl turning into a tree. Gray girl, gray tree, immensely foregrounded. She looked solemn yet ordinary, in a simple sleeveless dress, her hands clasped loosely at her middle. You couldn't quite tell where flesh gave way to bark.

My mother had another painting by the same artist, a boy sitting on the branch of a tree, shirtless, back to the viewer, looming sky the crimson of sunset or fire. All the colors were richer in this painting—flesh tones, dark hair. The boy was Jimmy of course, we knew it was Jimmy, were surprised to hear Tom had painted it without our brother in mind. But it didn't matter—it was still Jimmy. An enormous painting, several feet across. I would stand in front of it for minutes, waiting for the boy to turn around.

New York City. I lay awake the first few nights, astonished by the angry roar of the cars, by the groaning, wheezing, rumbling approach of the buses, sigh of brakes, doors clacking open. Who was coming and going at three in the morning? I'd get up and look, see the anonymous tops of heads in the dark that was never dark.

I wasn't exactly afraid of the cars. I imagined them driving up the skin of the building—but I knew they couldn't, they'd topple over backward before reaching the fifth story.

They might get almost to my window. Fall back down, crash, be cleaned up at dawn by the great clanking trucks. The people in those cars were not people. There couldn't be so many people. The cars drove themselves—traffic lights held them still—they surged forward like sharks while I floated on my bed.

My bed, my room. This is where we live now. I was aware of both a great terror—like wet gray felt in my throat—and of the softness of my privilege. I knew from novels what apartments were usually like: people slept on pull-out sofas in the living rooms, the bathtub was in the kitchen. I understood, as I hadn't really before, that it was money which protected me. Which had always protected me, the bigger portion of my mother's power. Whatever happened, we had this money, and it seemed to me corrupt.

Not that I wanted to do without it; on the contrary.

What if we had to live on the first floor, able to be driven over by the cars. What if we were even closer to the park where the criminals had their lairs. I remembered my father coming home from the city, the wild frightened trembling of his hands.

"That had nothing to do with the city. He was emotionally disturbed," my mother said, and those words "emotionally disturbed" reverberated in me. I was emotionally disturbed.

The cars would drive up the skin of the building, headlights beaming my way. The rapists would surge out of the park, following behind the cars. I would fall out of the window and our neighbors would walk over my body in their high heels.

What if we weren't rich? Nobody would take us in. What money bought—big rooms, obsequious doormen, locks—how thin it was, easily pierced through.

Money was only money, it could be lost. And there was nothing beneath our money, no place to fall. Grandmommy, of course, Uncle Bubber—yet it was possible: All money could be lost. What we no longer had was glamor. Glamor in the old sense of the word—a spell, a power.

Maybe a little bit. My mother was still beautiful, confident of her place in the world. Ordering around the painters and delivery men, getting us ready for school. I went to a hairdresser for the first time, had my hair cut Sassoon-style. She let me go to the salon alone, wearing one of my sister's old tweed suits. Nubbly, greenish, it made me look sixteen. And my new hair, swinging around my face. I was even allowed to lighten it, at home, with Summer Blonde, a foul purple liquid in a mud-brown plastic bottle in a bright cardboard box. The dye seethed and chattered in my hair, sending fingers of acid into my skull. "It's eating into my brain," I said. And my sister replied, "All part of the plan," and then apologized. "Don't worry. It's supposed to heat up like that, it won't hurt you. You're gonna look gorgeous." Charlotte was being so nice these days and I didn't know how to handle it. I loved it, loved looking at her slouching on the toilet in her khaki shorts, her long curvy legs up on the edge of the bathtub, smoking a Winston, smoke coming out of her nose. I loved her kindness and sort of believed in it—she didn't have Jimmy anymore, why shouldn't she like me?—but it made me feel weak. I had spent years girding myself to do battle, to win, and now she wasn't interested in fighting anymore.

We had a little glamor, we were Diehls, but our protection was wavering. The city was like the tree of knowledge—so many people, so many people really alive in the world, and cruelty and death. Nobody in charge. There were police but they didn't stop the Mafia. There was government but it didn't help the black people. Nobody stopped the cars.

THE APARTMENT HAD a back door and a front door. The back door was off the kitchen and led to flights of sturdy gray painted stairs. We weren't allowed to use it; it was only for service people. This was a rule of the building. You could also use it for escape in the event of a fire. Both our democratic principles and our proprietary feelings were offended. Why did the maid have to walk up all those stairs? And why couldn't we run down them? We hated going out the front way into the public corridor, then ringing for the elevator, waiting for the elevator, our hearts sinking at the sound of its creaking approach. The elevator was manned by plump, sweet-tempered Herbert in his gray uniform. He operated it slowly and carefully, hand on the polished lever. It took a very long time to ride down.

Sometimes you just wanted to go out, see what the day was like, come back inside. If you were bored you might take a short stroll, half a block. How could you make a man bring his elevator up for that? We were kids. We'd had maids, but they'd never jumped at our summons. They did their own jobs and, when they felt like it, they tormented us. Prune-faced Evelyn, whom my mother hired for a while to help with the ironing, used to whack us hard with the mop handle whenever we came into the kitchen.

Now we had to make polite conversation, the kind of talk that made us squirm. *How are you? I am fine.* At least it was better than: *How do you do*? which had to be answered: *How do you do*? which I could never get used to.

We liked Herbert and the doorman, Joe, and they liked us. Herbert fell in love with Sue, always crooning to her, "My little girlfriend," in his guttural accent, asking about her when she wasn't with us. "And how is Sue?" the name drawn out with a long quiver in the middle, his translucent eyelids half closing. "How has Sue been feeling?" Shimmer of sentiment on his round old face, smile poised for our answer. How should we know? She hated the city, like us. She was scared all the time—she thought she had to wait to pee because she was being punished. Begging us with her eyes, bladder about to burst (we ignored her) creeping and cringing around, absorbing the flares of our hostility. How could a grown man be in love with a dog? But we liked him for it.

We liked him, but we didn't want to be liked. We wanted to be alone. We were starving for our solitude, for ourselves—being able to muse, bare feet on the doorstep, during the passage from inside to out.

In and out. House and yard. Bare feet on wood floors, on flagstone, on grass. Is anything better? Long dreamy afternoons on our bikes—in the bushes, in the woods—were gone; now every time we left home we suffered the breakup the sight of strangers engendered. In the hall, the elevator, the lobby, we had to hold our minds rigid, poised for attack. Yes, we were obsessively private children, too isolated from our kind, but we had our reasons.

And why couldn't our new maid, Neithie, ride up in the elevator? Even her child, who came with her occasionally, had to walk up the back way. "I agree," said our mother. "I think it's wrong."

Long speech concerning her liberal politics. So why did we live here?

The city wasn't entirely bad. I was attracted, after the first shock, to its harsh music, the silver-gray-blue verticals, odd visual treats: glittering sidewalks, colored awnings, taxicabs, overpacked candy stores. I loved the smell of those candy stores: sugar and newsprint, dense aroma of tobacco. And I learned to appreciate the cynical eyes of the vendors, that dark, knowing disinterest in me. In Montclair all the shopowners seemed paternal, even—or especially—the mean ones; but these news and candy sellers were not paternal. They took my quarters and turned away.

Even candy bars smelled different, the city imprinted in the waxed paper.

THE FIRST MONTH or two, while the kitchen was being renovated, our mother took us out to dinner several nights a week. We'd go down the block to Stark's coffeeshop, order hamburgers or sandwiches and chocolate mint sodas. That was the beginning of the inflationary era: the ice cream sodas went from thirty cents to sixty-five in three or four jumps over two years. I remember noting it with a morbid fascination. It didn't affect us much—our mother just gave us more pocket money, and in fact we came out ahead, exploiting inflation for quite absurd rises in allowance. Yet it stayed with me as a feature of the city. Time moves so quickly there is no making peace with it. There is no sobriety.

Johnny would generally misbehave at the table—or rather misbehave the most egregiously. He had eating rituals now, always ordering the same things, eating them in the same order, and he'd erupt if he were challenged or teased, which we couldn't resist doing. Just the sound of him, ordering a tunafish sandwich for the fiftieth time. His voice almost mechanical, his body movements repetitive. We'd tease. If not me, Charlotte.

He'd shout, knock over his chair. Throw something. Run out of the restaurant.

Or if that didn't happen my sister would whine about having to spend time with us. A whole hour of her evening, never-to-be-found-again evening of her fifteenth year. She would drape herself over her chair, threaten to smoke a cigarette—"But you don't smoke," our mother would say—act as if the most exciting events were going on just beyond our sight. They were going on, and she could be part of them. She had a life.

What she had was our old babysitter Sue Witte, who sometimes took her out on a Saturday night—to the Copacabana, of all places, where I guess my sister stood to the side miserably drinking Coke while Sue danced—or shopping in the Village. She had her friend Annie Plumb, our cousin Roberta. More friends than I had, but she was hardly besieged with invitations. She seemed to think merely being in our presence would damage her chances. I hoped so. I wanted to keep her home. I was falling in love with her again. I wanted her to teach me things.

When Charlotte was in a bad mood she was bossy. We resented that ferociously and made a point of refusing to obey her whenever she was left in charge. Our mother would go to the bathroom and we'd start eating with our fingers, or putting our faces down to the plate to eat. Charlotte would turn beet red. "You guys are so disgusting. Everyone's looking at you. They don't think I'm disgusting, they think you're disgusting."

"As if we care," said Johnny.

I liked the energy of the battle; sometimes it didn't seem much different from the concord I could only imagine. If it was battle or silence, I'd take battle. Still, I didn't understand. I provoked my siblings. I was good at the superior putdown, especially of Johnny, attitude of aloof disdain—I wore it like a witch costume, reveling in its slinky power—yet it always surprised me that my brother took it seriously. I did it to feel better, not to make him feel worse.

So we would behave as we behaved, and our mother would say, "Why are you-all behaving so badly? Do you hate me?" In our anxiety, our hatred, we would laugh. Then her voice would turn peculiar, like a record on the wrong speed, and we would make fun of her until she had no choice but to get angry, too.

I liked it best when she got so angry she left us in the restaurant. It was like what she had threatened to do this summer, on the way to the lake, leave us by the side of the road, except that we were fine here, a few blocks from home. She got to make her gesture, and we got to tease each other more viciously, wait in a kind of giddiness for the waiters to throw us out.

They never did. They ignored us, muttering, as we threw french fries and stuck our straws into the hamburgers.

Then Charlotte would leave us, too. "*I'm* going home, I'm expecting a phone call, I don't get paid to babysit you guys."

Tranquility after her imperial snarliness departed. Johnny would finish his meal in silence, in methodical order. I'd look at him with painful affection—his tough, sinewy little body, his boyness as hard and bright as quartz—want to express it with an insult which I'd choke down. Then, perhaps, a betraying thought (why isn't he more like Jimmy, older, more talkative) which I'd also choke down; I'd grow lonely and miss the females.

I knew what they were doing. They were on the phone, making plans to get away from us with boyfriends. Johnny hated their power over him; I hated that they got all the men. I was constantly overwhelmed with the feeling of scarcity, imminent loss—it hit in great toxic waves—and their romantic lives triggered this over and over. My mother's real romantic life, my sister's fumbling beginnings.

I wasn't about to confess this torment to them. I couldn't, it was too deep and painful. I knew what they'd say—"But, Margaret, you're too young. In a couple of years . . ." and that wasn't the point. It had nothing to do with youth. Agony to imagine them out flirting. I would never. I was all wrong inside, not a girl.

Last spring, before we left, a couple of Jimmy's friends had come over to say good-bye. They called first so we knew they were coming, and then they came. Spike, who had seen him last, Michael, his old best friend. They rang the front doorbell, we let them in, they brought the April day inside on their sweaters. They stood in the living room for a few minutes, talking to us all gravely, cheerfully, tall blond Spike in his white cable-knit, his husky shoulders.

Spike had a gift for my mother—a candid of Jimmy taken on his last day alive. He was grinning wildly, glasses askew, the sort of expression never captured in my mother's photographs. I stared at it as if it would come alive if I looked hard enough. "You're getting your fingerprints all over it," Johnny said.

We were all standing there, then Charlotte got to take the boys away. It happened so quickly. She was chatting vivaciously while I was hanging around in glassy silence, gazing at Spike's straw-blond hair, easy smile. At the white glow of the sweater over his big chest, his mouth moving. Spike was the confident one; he did the talking. And Charlotte was talking—her tall, gregarious heat, why was I shy and she not, it wasn't fair; she asked them to come look at something in the library, and they went.

My mother saw me hesitate, as if to follow, and invited me into the kitchen with her. That way mothers invite you so you're startled, you obey without thinking. Trotting behind her into the vast humming lightness of our kitchen I realized with horror what my mother saw: not representatives of Jimmy who belonged to us all, but *boys Charlotte's age.*

Belonging therefore to Charlotte.

It was agony having Michael and Spike in the house, not in my presence. I felt it all down my body, a grinding and swollen ache. I sat still at the table, answering my mother's self-conscious chat, and made plans of wild revenge against my sister, as if she were a tiger biting my head. Also wondering Why does my mother not care? She must hate me, why does she hate me? I don't hate her.

Maybe I will.

Sliding into darkness. All I had against it was the memory of Jimmy. Jimmy and me—linked by destiny.

With Johnny beside me, I would pay the bill, pocket the change, scoop great handfuls of mints from the bowl beside the cash register. He'd take the matches and the toothpicks.

Sometimes we wouldn't go back to the apartment right away. We'd saunter into shops. The drugstore was open until eight. I loved how bright it was—a soft brightness of glass counters, candy-colored makeup displays, floral scarves and ribbons (later, paper dresses!), bottles of shampoo. The drugstore had a rich, talcumy smell, not like the cold glowing heaviness of department stores, or the medicinal old-man smell of the drugstore in Montclair. It was like a woman's bedroom, but not my mother's. The mix was different. The saleswomen were blond, polite, unbothered; they didn't ask me if I hated them.

I'd finger the lipsticks: Yardley's Slicker, which evoked Paul McCartney—Jane Asher daydreams. I wasn't allowed to wear lipstick yet but I bought these anyway, $1.50 apiece, slowly accumulating a collection. Johnny would investigate hemorrhoid aids, any kind of cutting device, and explain to me the principles of shoplifting. How it's all in the stance, the poise, in a quickness of hand practiced carefully at home.

Later, we would practice. First at home, then at the hardware store. His theory was if you take something no adult could imagine a kid wanting—like screws and bolts—you have a chance to learn while not being on suspicion.

It made me laugh how the adults *were* suspicious but didn't believe their suspicions, couldn't bring themselves to follow us around the aisles of greasy hardware parts. They stood up front behind the counters, asking us repeatedly what we needed. "Just looking," we'd say, "just looking," as we drifted past the shelves full of boxes of odd-shaped items. "Now," Johnny would hiss as soon as we were out of the line of sight, and I'd grab a handful of the first thing I saw.

Back in Johnny's room we'd sit on his bed, he'd tell me what everything was for, how he could use it someday, building this, building that, and I wouldn't listen. I'd run my fingers over the grooves of screws, insert a pinkie in a bolt.

We began to steal from our mother. We had stolen from her before (most notoriously I had) to buy the comic books, but it was a rare event. Now we did it regularly. She would come in from shopping, she went shopping all the time, stand her black patent-leather purse on the table. This was a sleek rectangle that she stuffed too full so it bulged on both sides and often fell over. Something about the sight of that swollen shiny thing, tipped on its belly, helpless, made me furious. Why didn't she buy a big enough purse? Why did she shop so much?

One of us would watch the door, the other snick open the gold clasp. She carried a lot of cash, seventy or one hundred dollars. I'd take a few ones, maybe a five. Johnny might take a ten. She never missed it. Often, especially as time passed, Johnny didn't take anything but only counted the money. He might do this twice in a day, his fingers quickly sorting the bills. And then he'd tell her, "You have eighty-five dollars."

"Oh . . . good." She might add, "Well, just leave it there," not in accusation or even concern. In mild bewilderment. With her ridiculous innocence.

We were both so angry at her for moving us here. And still angry with grief, torn up inside, which she knew. But the anger that was at her, for what she had done, was a fact my mother forgot as often as possible. There was a certain expression she wore when she had cleared her mind, when she looked at us without seeing: her features isolated, dreamy islands on her face, and the flesh between like the primordial clay. It disturbed Johnny; it disturbed me. It made us want to hurt her, which made us feel guilty. And it sparked in me its opposite—fervid memory. (Or so I thought; as an adult I have learned to feel on my own face that blank safekeeping.)

Twenty-two

AT THE END of September, we started school. Johnny and I were going to a school called the Town School on 76th Street near the East River. The school was in a tall, narrow townhouse, four floors of classrooms separated by flights of gun-metal gray stairs. I was frightened walking down the long block from York Avenue, sticking close to my brother (we refused to allow our mother to come with us), frightened going in the building; but I had no idea how frightened. After all, this was school. I'd always liked school. And Charlotte kept telling me: New York kids are cool. You're *lucky* to live here. Don't worry.

In the school building, Johnny and I split up, went to our separate classes. That was hard. He didn't look back. I walked up the stairs and found the correct room, barely glancing to the left or right. Took a seat in the front (if you sit in the front row, kids can't turn and look at you.) The teacher asked who I was and I told him; he repeated my name in a tone of voice that made me dislike him immediately. A voice riddled with mockery, a smarmy, impersonal mockery that continued on as he spoke—a little speech welcoming the class. He told us his name was Mr. Caruso but he wasn't *that* Caruso. He simpered, his lips pressed together, big brown eyes rolling. I was aware of a severe disappointment. I'd only ever had one male teacher before, a sweet guy who taught math at Brookside. Mr. Caruso made me anxious, but I thought: School is school. Desks, pencils, assignments. I'd get good grades. There'd be other teachers.

And then the first class was over. I thought I'd ease into the group slowly, observe, but I was surrounded. Boys and girls in their uniforms, in a circle around me. I came from where? Was that the suburbs? I was a Gentile, wasn't I? Faint amusement, which I didn't understand. I didn't come from the suburbs, I came from Montclair. And what was a Gentile? The kids were only curious, not unfriendly, yet I became profoundly disoriented by their insistence on my strangeness.

All of the faces looking at me. Sharper, more direct than I was used to. In front of me, crowding, to the sides, making the circle.

They had never heard of my town. *They had never heard of my town.* At that realization, which I hadn't remotely anticipated, it was as if Montclair ceased to be. As if it were utterly a fiction, and my life there a shadow life, torn carelessly by those children's gaze.

The kids kept teasing me gently about the suburbs. I heard the gentleness, the good humor, wanted desperately to respond. *Who are you, they were saying. We're willing to like you, you interest us. Who are you?*

I was struggling. *Montclair.* It was Jimmy they were talking about, where he lived and died. They didn't know that. They had no idea. As if he were dying again. It was all in the word *Montclair*, which they countered with their own word, *suburb.* (Rows and rows of identical houses, identical people. You're not anybody there.)

I didn't know what to say. I said nothing. So they abandoned that subject and somebody asked, "What does your father do?"

I had forgotten, they all had fathers; they thought I had one, too. A man at his job right now, in this very city. In his shirt and tie. The little bristles on his cheeks. His square hands, trembling lightly.

"My father's dead."

Pause. "How did he die?"

"Suicide."

As I spoke the word I had to struggle to remain conscious. The room was going dark, each pale face losing dimension, hanging like paper decorations in the airless air. It was like the harsh flatness of the morning Daddy died but taken to a new extreme. No half inch of self. No self at all.

Why had they all gone silent?

Suicide. Flag of my country. The world had become an afterimage of itself, without mass or depth. Not a metaphor: what I was seeing. The other kids flattened to nothing, as in cartoons. But no color. No reality. And yet this was reality: How does one question visual perception at eleven years old?

I have a memory of myself turning around, walking with thunderous steps to the corner, standing in the corner facing the wall. I didn't do that, only part of me did.

Then somebody said something and I said something. Whatever they asked, I answered, in two or three words, then subsided, soulless and ready to be killed for that.

How could they not kill me. I quivered with the expectation of it. No thought about reasons, unlikelihood, only the bare knowledge of my fate. I was such a thing of evil as they had never seen before. They were children, I was something ancient and black. Not black like black people, who were warm and brown, but burnt black, stone black, dead black. I was one of those monsters made in the early days of the earth; I simply hadn't remembered. I wasn't a child. I was thousands of years old. Older. One of the mistakes, supposed to be kept imprisoned. I knew the cold weight of almost-eternity. I remembered it now. Surely they could see.

I was trying to act normal. I stood my ground, did not retreat. There was a part of me that said: You are in school, seventh grade, you're Margaret. Harmless. I blinked my eyes, I opened my mouth. I told them about Jimmy. I had to tell them about Jimmy because he must not be forgotten. I saw clearly how my whole life people would ask about my father, because everyone has a father. His absence would be noted. No matter how long he was dead, they would say: And your father? What does he do? But they'd never know about Jimmy unless I told them.

But as I spoke the whole story seemed preposterous. An older brother? Why should I have had one, who did I think I was? Hopeless attempt to invoke the person—his ordinary liveliness and mythic splendor—just by giving his name.

I said it, forced myself. I had a brother, his name was Jimmy; he died. Hit by a car. Riding a bicycle. I don't know what they said back. All I knew was nothingness, desperate sizzle of self clinging to the cliff of the body. All I knew was how grievously I had failed. Jimmy had never existed—or only in a parallel universe, not here, never here, this New York, city of soot and verticals, of children insisting I know about Jews and Gentiles, which I could not sort out right now, it was too much, and their ridicule of the suburbs where Jimmy was normal, where he was the very measure of normality, now utterly disappeared.

Here were different measures. Sharp faces—not unfriendly, but sharp, quick, on the mark. So different.

Too much.

The day went on. I moved, a great monster of stone, in a dead world strangely intermixed with some other. All day long, in class and out, boys and girls around me like fireflies. Flittery. I couldn't dislike them, I longed for them, their whirling gossipy gaiety as they caught up with each other, chattered about the summer, groaned at the new books—knew that I longed, suffered shame at my performance—but on that day these more ordinary feelings became fused with the traumatic so that henceforth I experienced it all together.

I went home and my mother asked me how school was, and I said fine. It was fine now. I was Margaret again as she looked at me, a small plump girl in glasses. Charlotte wanted to know what the boys were like, and that was harder; there was a pain at my side like fire, but I told her. This one, that one, names, descriptions. Mom and Charlotte said I looked nice in my uniform. They told me I was lucky the colors of the uniform suited me. Charlotte said the style made me look thinner.

Facing them—wild beneath the surface. What I had been, for the past seven hours, *a monster*; how could they not know? I worked to preserve the crust of my privacy but didn't really believe in it. They knew. They knew and didn't care. It was even their fault, they did it on purpose so I couldn't compete with them. No, it was my fault. This was what I *was*. My only hope was that everyone might be as blind as they, that I might be, alone in the world, the one who knew.

And maybe tomorrow everything would be different.

It was different, but not enough. There was still a blackness at the edges of my vision. The world flattened out unpredictably and I loomed, to my inner eye, monstrous.

Acute mental illness means losing what is most familiar: oneself. I had had flashes of this before—when Jimmy died, when Daddy died—and premonitions of it the previous spring but never before had to live in it, day after day, the settled menacing weirdness. Shame, an envelope of soupy fog, terror, an unceasing vibration—what I am now used to, what I medicate, talk myself out of, ignore—were then the great secrets of the universe, the great experiences I surrendered to in a kind of ecstasy of loneliness, falling into myself, into pain, as if the embrace would bring some reward. The reward, of course, being knowledge; knowledge for which I would be praised by the parents I used to have, the father who brought the books, the mother who told me my test scores. Knowledge and endurance: where I could get a grip.

Nobody hurt me at that school. I have no tales of being scapegoated, or even mildly tormented. On the contrary. Blond motherly Laura and gossipy Chloe invited me along to the candy store, made a place for me at lunch. Smart, poetry-writing Meryl investigated me for a while, then ignored me without malice. Danny, our class clown/politician/courtier, flirted charmingly.

I was spared, day after day, and I was grateful. I learned that these were nice kids; nicer, in general, than the ones in Montclair. Even when it became apparent I would never really unbend, never put forth personality like the other blossoming girls, I was tolerated. Liked, perhaps, for not being much of a threat. Liked, perhaps, for my occasional lapse into wit. Or maybe liked for what everybody else could see clearly: I was a nice enough girl, human.

I didn't think so.

I knew what humans were like: fluid, thoughts constantly on the dance. Thought came through like honey through the wax of the honeycomb, in golden drops. You talked or listened, did whatever, savoring those drops, and when you got a chance, sank back into yourself deeply. In Montclair, sometimes, I used to just lie on the windowseat thinking. Or if I was doing something else while I was thinking, I would pause in the middle of the action, to savor the completion of my idea. I loved the sensation of thought, the miracle of its geometry. I could slide underneath my thoughts, I could look at them from above. I could try to chase them, to get ahead—and then they would stop, blink out. I could slow down, deliberately not thinking about what I was thinking about, and then a pressure build up that I felt between my legs. My thoughts wanted to be watched. I knew that. I watched them. And they were never the same (my fantasies were repetitive, but that was a different operation.) My thoughts moved, always, onward.

I wasn't like that anymore. Not for the hours at school, and only flickeringly at home. My Margaret-consciousness was a mere skin or scum, the name I answered to, my role—then there was the being of lead. The one whose criminal soul was rooted in the bowels of time. Who could howl if she chose, who had once howled, for thousands, for thousands of years.

Nobody was unkind—I couldn't even pretend that they were. It would have been easier to be able to hate.

I did hate the teachers, who were all loud and sarcastic—rough—but I didn't think the teachers were my problem. My problem was me. At school, after two or three encounters—a little conversation with one girl about homework, hanging on the fringes of a gossiping group—I would be so worn down by the immense mental effort, the monstrous weight of being me, I would creep back to my desk and lay my head down. Eyes shut. The world over me like a river.

Five minutes' social effort at recess, then my head on my desk. Fifteen minutes at lunch, then my head on my desk. The physical and perceptual effects of my terror grew less after a few weeks at school, but I was still deeply impaired. And shocked to motionlessness: The worst could happen again.

I had always been shy, had always known I was shy. My mother talked to me about it from the very beginning of my school life, saying it was fine to be shy, she had been, too. You grow out of it, she said. Don't worry.

But this wasn't shy. Shy was having something to say and being timid about it. Shy was that confusion of how a personality, which is inside, can come out; it was fear of there being a step missing. But you were still a girl like other girls, if you were shy. You just didn't get to be popular.

I not only didn't know what to say, I had no thoughts while I was in the presence of other kids. Obviously, I had thoughts—how else would I remember—but the sensation was of profound emptiness, of being in an empty room, a small room, in terror of losing the last bit of light, myself. Clinging to that spark of light, that handhold of consciousness. Holding myself rigid. Clinging.

Trying—not to speak a thing I wanted to say—but so deeply beyond that, trying to figure out language, where it came from, if a sentence spoken by a kid was spoken that way for the first time and if not who owned the words? Standing there in my emptiness, hoping to be a girl, *please ignore me until I become human,* letting a casual statement ring in my head. Tearing it apart, like tearing apart a flower, clutter of vowels and odd accents, tender debris. What did it mean, was there a secret, and again: Who owned the words? If I used them who would hurt me?

I knew I was afraid, of course, but didn't recognize this whole experience as the shape of terror. I thought the fear was the result of this other thing, being this thing. One who had no insides. The only conclusion I could come to was that I wasn't human. The fact that I felt human at home (even if lonely and angry) didn't seem entirely relevant. I would have liked to think the girl I was at home was real, and sometimes did; but I was hard on myself: School was the world.

If I wasn't human, what was I? I wasn't a ghost or an animal. I wasn't a robot, I bled. (Unless I was a very advanced robot, from another planet, perfectly mimicking human flesh—was that possible? Who could know?)

I could be a changeling, those ugly babies fairies left in the cradle when they stole a human child. That made the most sense: how I could appear human, how unhappy I was, my old longing for fairyland.

It fit, but I didn't believe in fairyland now. You couldn't live in New York City and believe in things like that. Johnny didn't need to argue with me anymore—"Have you ever seen a fairy? What do they look like? Where do they live? Show me. You can't, can you? It's all lies." How I used to laugh at him, delicious knowledge welling up in me: proof! The spring evening air, tinted pink, the rustle of the trees, leaf-shimmer, life-shimmer; my own body aloft in long grass. I was a violin and they played me. In the little rooms on the third floor, they played me. In the garden making snow angels, cold swish of arms, they were playing.

But not here. Here the cars were everywhere, belching exhaust; soot piled up on my windowsill; pavement covered the earth. Clearly there were no other powers on earth but grown-ups. It was a grief that felt like folly.

I decided I was an alien, seeded into this body at birth, crafted to pass as human until my mission became clear to me. They had done such a good job on my body nobody had known, not even doctors. But they had made one mistake, their technology not quite up to the challenges of human puberty.

It made sense, that puberty would derail me. The definition of a species is those who can mate with each other. My brain hurt with the effort of trying to examine itself. If I had been fascinated, when Jimmy died, by the windows opening into my thoughts—the fluidity of memory, its mercurial duplicity, or the enormous engorgement of grief—now I was frustrated by the secrets my mind kept, the dense tangle in my skull that might possibly be wires.

The aliens were canny. If I cut myself, I bled. My brain might look like other brains—gray matter, as it was called. But it would break down soon. It was breaking down now. At some point, systemic failure. That was when I couldn't pretend to be Margaret anymore. When "margaret" would peel off like a shed skin, crumble and blow away, and I be left, I be left, this anguished cylinder. The enemy.

The one thing I couldn't do was tell my mother. She wouldn't feel sorry for me, she'd be angry. Even if I hadn't been deceiving her on purpose, still, living in her house all these years, she thought I was wonderful, her little girl, etcetera, letting her feed me, dress me—

And all the time, not her child at all. Who wouldn't be angry? Who wouldn't be horrified—seeing the alien flesh beneath the melting skin? Disgust, terror . . . but mostly I thought, anger. That I presumed. That I had come in. That I had sat with the real children, like one of the family.

On the other hand, she remembered my birth. She remembered being pregnant with me, and when I was just born—I was born on St. Patrick's Day in a Catholic hospital and the nurses all called me Patricia. "No, she is Margaret," my mother said. "Margaret." I could see in my own face features like hers and Daddy's. I could see resemblances to my siblings. I wanted to ask if it were possible—could a person look like a person but not be a person, not only in stories, but really; but she wouldn't take me seriously. And if she did?

I couldn't risk it. Human or not, I wanted to survive. Even if I were one of a destructive alien race, pledged to take over the planet, kill everyone; even then.

@

CONSTANT EFFORT TO cover up. It consumed me utterly for a year, somewhat less so for the next twenty. Taking so much energy to hold in. All day in school covering up, covering up. Something happens—a little thing—fear of exposure—I start to come apart. Feel the me of me begin to shift: blackness or blankness. Clamp down. Hold. Focus my will.

I had been human, I could remember it. In Montclair, in the garden, in the pink dusk—*that* was me. Who was this? Not me really, but I took care of her. Kept her face bland and smooth, fed her, moved her around. Ignored the unpleasant teachers, waited for the time to be over. For all the time to be over—until when?—when I was somebody else.

Nibbling away at the edges of the hours, as I nibbed away at the edges of my classmates' society. There were two things that mattered that year—I could scavenge a little friendship, a walk to the candy store; and time did pass. I waited each day for the end of the day, time alone in my bedroom; and then the next morning for the end of the next day. It was hard labor.

Time at school was hated time, I did everything I could to kill it. Time at home was a drug, I tried everything I could think of to stretch it. I tried unconsciousness, which eased the pain but spent the time too quickly, then superconsciousness to fix the moment of solitude. Three o'clock Sunday afternoon. If I concentrate hard enough, it can't get any later. If I wedge myself inside the minutes, the seconds, remember Zeno's paradox, how motion is impossible— Before you can cross a certain distance, you have to cross half the distance. And before you can cross that smaller distance, you have to cross half of it. And so on, and so on; the fact that space is infinitely divisible means that you can never move at all.

Time must work the same way.

It's called it a paradox because the two sides of it—logic, physical reality—are incompatible. But didn't that mean I could jump to the other side; live the logic, as it were?

I spent hours trying. Glaring at the clock, making myself dizzy as my will sliced the time, and sliced again, as my muscles stiffened. The minutes passed, but I convinced myself that they were slowing down. I clung to the fact that it was not-yet-Monday and everything else about the day or my mood disappeared, didn't count.

Charlotte, Johnny, my mother out doing things, like people. I lie in my room, on my bed, trying to overpower time. Wrestle it into submission by working on myself as one of its functioning parts . . .

I was worried that my recognition of the fact that I wasn't human meant that the disguise was breaking down. It hadn't started to show yet physically, but that didn't mean it wouldn't. I needed to know what to expect before my body started doing something horrid and violent. If I didn't know when it would happen and it started happening—if they who had seeded me here were no longer in charge, helping, had even died—how could I hide from the humans? The police? I was in the city, there was nowhere to go. But if I could find out, if I could make sure that I really wasn't human, maybe I should get away somehow, into the woods.

I looked human still. I kept coming back to that. My face in the mirror, my arms, my legs. I was relieved by digestion, bowel movements. I was greatly relieved when I got my period, though I had a scare at first—the color wasn't what I expected. It was dark, not the bright red of a skinned elbow. I went with trepidation to ask my mother, trotting into her room. "Mom, look, is this—?"

"Yes," she said with a cursory glance, she was busy talking to Charlotte. "Go in the bathroom and your sister will show you how to use a napkin."

I was embarrassed. I had made her look at the stain, which was brown like shit. She had already explained the whole thing to me, years ago.

But the point was, I got my period like regular girls. I ate and went to the bathroom. Maybe even if I wasn't human, I was a good enough fake.

My alien-comrades might never come. Their spaceship might have broken down ten thousand light-years away. If they had been attacked or hit by a meteorite, if cold space had claimed them, their whole civilization could be dead.

I still wondered occasionally if I was a changeling, those babies who cry and cry, who grow big but never up. They can't; they don't have souls. How cruel I had been to want to be taken by the fairies—that meant a changeling would have had to be left in my place. Some poor fairy-child who meant no harm, whose parents didn't love her.

If I was a changeling who thought she was a human child waiting for the fairies to come, but really waiting for them to come *back*—

It was too absurd. I embarrassed myself thinking about it. And the stuff about aliens was stupid, too; I had been born, people saw it. I had been to the doctor many times. I must be human.

If I am human, I am crazy. Insane. Mad. Mad—mysterious word. Somehow maternal, fiery but compact, tied up. I thought I was an alien or a changeling the way mad people think they're Marie Antoinette. Madness means what feels like reality isn't.

This made sense but couldn't satisfy. The idea had no depth, somehow. By its nature, I thought, it couldn't satisfy: If I was mad, how would I know it for sure? I would have no way of knowing anything for sure. What this meant was everyone else would be right. When you're mad you have to surrender. The men in white coats carry you off. You live on the funny farm, stuck in your delusions, entirely mistaken—in a straitjacket—and they—who? they, everyone—laugh at you.

Twenty-three

I GOT OUT of school at four each afternoon. I would walk with a few girls to the little candy store on the corner of York Avenue, a flock of us in dark blue wool jumpers buying strings of red licorice and those square, foil-wrapped chocolates called Ice Cubes. I had more pocket money than anyone else and bought eight or ten small squares of chocolate, giving a few away.

Am I buying friends? I wondered. No. I wanted to give them chocolate. And though they accepted graciously, they didn't act any different toward me, which was all right. I liked seeing, from my island, their sharp white teeth biting.

Those girls. I watched them. Laura like a Jewish Fragonard, girl on a swing, tiny feet tipped up, Laura laughing so her slim body shook. Boys competed to make Laura laugh because of the way it inhabited her whole body, how she bent her head helplessly, and glanced sidelong—Laura the mistress of the sidelong glance. And Chloe the gossip with her alabaster skin, rosy mouth, and bold charm. Chloe was constantly "forgetting" to wear her uniform, coming to school in white wool, or peach silk over her plump, pampered body. The teachers loved to tease her about this, and she played her part, round eyes widening as she told the absurd story over again. The fine dark hair on the back of Terry's arms. Terry's velvety gaze, her shyness like mine used to be, that of a girl who's in her place, who follows. Terry's big nose, like a building that gives shade—all the Jewish kids hated their noses, I loved them. My mother had a nose like that, substantial, beautiful, anchoring the face in itself. Laura's fluttery eyelashes, dusted with gold. (Laura the mistress of the fluttery-eyelash glance.) Chloe's small wobbly chin, the blue pulse in the column of her neck. Skinny Meryl with her high cheekbones, her body-heat and sharp elbows. Meryl exploding in laughter, or complaining blushes, then on to the next thing, eyes always roving. Meryl was the one I most wanted to be, except that she was competitive. Openly competitive. Brilliant and high-spirited.

I knew I couldn't be like that. If I ever get through this, I thought, become human again, I'll conquer through love. Only love. An idea that soothed like butter. Jimmy and I. I am his handmaiden. He teaches me things. Or maybe I would live alone—Island of the Blue Dolphins—ruling a society of animals. Build my own small hut, plant a garden, housekeeping the secured space. Dark blue ocean, pale blue sky. Tree branches moving in the wind.

Sitting on the bus, familiar throbbing motion, things were better. With each inch away from the school building, I grew stronger. I liked being on my own in the city, looking out the window at the streets going by. Block after block of shops and apartments; I was learning my way around, getting used to crowds and traffic. I had more freedom than the other girls. They had to go right home after school; I had to be home by five or six. I supposed. My mother had never said, exactly—or she'd say something and forget what she said. All the rules were scrambled now.

My mother never knew when she'd be home herself. She spent

her afternoons shopping—I could never understand how this activity could take so much time. Our maid Neithie did most of the housework, unlike in Montclair, when even having a full-time maid did not free my mother from work. And then she had had to drive us places, while now we went by ourselves, mostly, on buses or by cab. So what was she doing? She was dating. What else? What do ladies do? What is the point of being a grown-up?

Once or twice I went to Laura's apartment after school, lay on the bed in her dark bedroom with her pretty, giggly little sister. Laura was easy to talk to but it didn't mean much; she talked to everyone. Continuous chat about nothing in particular. I lay there soaking up the feeling of normalcy, as if I could bank it. I missed having a real friend. But to get any closer to Laura, one had to dominate, one had to press, and though I had that in me, I didn't know I had it in me.

It occurs to me now that I didn't want to get home before my mother did, although at the time I thought the opposite. I thought I wanted to be safe in my room before she came in, but in fact I dawdled. I'd get off at Madison, walk down two blocks to the G and M pastry shop, my goal. Not go in right away. Look in the other windows, maybe put my face in the cold scented glow of the drugstore, or read the well-known menu at Stark's. Think back with nostalgia to my first weeks in the city, before school started, when Johnny and I would roam the neighborhood, east to Second Avenue, shoplifting from the hardware stores, weaving in and out of the secondhand stops. These junky establishments were always guarded by an old woman sitting in a low chair, often a fat little dog at her feet, and most of them didn't like children. "No children allowed," they would say, and we'd go in anyway, a quick sweep, making disdainful remarks about the quality of the merchandise. It hurt our feelings, their attitude—we loved junk. There used to be a dump behind the house in Montclair when we first moved in. Our parents didn't like it, Jimmy told us it lowered property values, but Johnny and I wandered the mountain of old toasters, car parts, and broken toys in bliss, accompanied by a silent girl from the other side of the hill. All the time my mother was redoing the garden into the orderly paradise it became, Johnny and I climbed the hill to the dump, gathering treasure we could never take home.

Now Johnny had friends from school; he spent his afternoons with them, in his room or at their apartments. I didn't go to Second Avenue anymore. When I was feeling adventurous I went to Lexington, bought Milk Duds or Tootsie Rolls at the newsstand, mostly for the sake of that newsy tobacco-y smell and the flat-eyed stare of the man with the cigar, somehow a delight.

Men were short in New York, sometimes hardly taller than me. They were grumpy but not frightening. They liked my money and would count it carefully, coins on their broad palms, and if I asked where something was, they'd indicate with a flick of their eyes.

Sometimes I looked down the maw of the subway, which I hadn't yet ridden. My mother said it was too dangerous so I'd watch the people coming up, white people, black people, Puerto Ricans, a great variety of shoes. The smell was especially strong there. I didn't yet know this was the smell of urine—it was so mixed with other smells, doughnuts and chewing gum, exhaust fumes, cigarettes, hair oil. I didn't know what it was but I liked it, from this distance, standing by the bars of the entrance, looking in.

But I couldn't linger because if I did, some man would talk to me. Not the safe, stolid kind of man, who wanted my money, but the furtive kind, with the hungry eyes. "Are you lost? Do you need a token for the subway? What are you waiting for?" Those men meant I had to turn around, walk quickly toward Park. If I let them get too close they'd touch me, long eellike fingers reaching out to pinch off a corner of my youth. Once I had been tricked by one of these men. He said he was an immigrant, couldn't speak English well. His wife was sick and he had to buy her some clothes. He needed me to write something down for him—the names of women's clothes. "This," he said, rubbing my blouse. "This," fingering my skirt at my hip. I stood there in a doorway writing for a minute or two before I was absolutely sure what he was doing, his fingers walking toward the split of my legs, then hurried off, with apologies, in the five o'clock dark, somehow fearfully certain that our doorman, two blocks away, had seen what happened, known what it was in me that invited this . . .

It wasn't as if I was an innocent. I knew all about these men.

G and M Pastry. It was a tiny place, a little scooped-out den of buttery, sugary creations, shelves covering the four walls. Only the doorway to the back, and the front door, were free of the displayed goods. Several blue-smocked, guttural-voiced women trotted back and forth, serving customers cookies, strudels, tortes, creampuffs, eclairs, napoleons. Packing pink boxes, tying them with string.

These bakery workers were the only women in New York who reminded me of my lamblike old-lady teachers at Brookside: but these women were more mysterious. They were German—not in a comical way, like our doorman Herbert, or the TV show *Hogan's Heroes*, nor like the Nazis who killed Anne Frank, but German as my father's father had been, as fairy tales were, European.

The women darted around the small shop in their neat lace-up shoes, breasting through air dense with spice and sweet, sliding the heavy iced cakes on their paper doilies into waxed cardboard. Lifting out the fawn-brown cookies one by one with their spidery fingers—or moving, carefully, the wobbly napoleons—all the while nodding, nodding, at the demands of the tall, high-heeled, fur-coat-wearing East Side ladies.

I hated those ladies. They swept in, their perfume ruining the air, their fur coats shoving me sideways. A whole wing of a coat could flare out, press its hairs into my face. Fur. It should only be worn by women as wild as the animals themselves. The East Side ladies were always served first. Regardless of when I arrived, I had to wait until the shop emptied out, the bakery women rewarding my patience with little tidbits popped into my mouth. I resented having to wait. I was spending money, too, wasn't I? It was because I was a child. I didn't feel like a child. Yet I let them seduce me with the broken-off bits, half cookies, jammy mouthfuls, leaving a silk of butter on my lips.

They liked me best.

That such a place as this existed, and I was in it. Peering at the shelves, examining different confections—all that labor of pastry making, nut-chopping, butter measuring. The glaze on the brown crusts, the crimp along the edges, the plump fruit lying in place, pretty side up. At G and M, no expense was spared. The cakes bulged with cream, the chocolate was dark and thick, the air itself had layers of mocha, praline, apricot, marzipan. This was baking as it was supposed to be and if some of it was exotic to me—all the nuts, the jam between cake layers—I was ready for it. It was the dance of the sugarplums from the Nutcracker. I had seen the ballet half a dozen times, and last year, at school in Montclair, I had starred in a play based on the same story the ballet was based on.

The bakery ladies popped sweet tidbits in my mouth. So quick—no chance to say Thank you. They smiled at me, whirled off. I was deciding: what to buy? What to eat in the sacred solitude of my bed, the glorious relief of the day over?

Cookies—I got more of them for my money.

Napoleons—that flaky pastry, yellow custard and whipped cream, the whole shivering rectangle.

Creampuffs—not so interesting except for the name, from *The Rootabaga Stories* by Carl Sandburg; "The Village of Creampuff," a little girl who is fed creampuffs by her adoring uncles.

The East Side women were buying cakes for their dinner parties. Six, eight, ten people who would eat a thin slice after rich meat and bottles of wine. While smoking cigarettes. I had nothing but contempt for this. Cakes were to be eaten in private. Even one of these big tortes, sacher torte, linzer torte, should be consumed alone; I imagined a woman like a wolf licking red crumbs off her lips, chocolate smeared on her chin—in her room dense with feminine stuff, silks and scents, pleated lampshades—while the dinner guests downstairs were given only cutlery.

It was exciting to imagine being so powerful, purse full of money, house of one's own, but only for a second or two. I had a horror of the grown-up body, grown-up mind. I'd rather be Clara, rising from her bed in her white nightgown, running down the stairs to where the Christmas tree twinkled, and the nutcracker came alive.

I imagined this shop, after hours, as a kind of theater. Sometimes, if I arrived too late, the door was locked and I would gaze in the window as the women cleaned up, offering me a smile and a shake of the head. There were so many of them for such a little store; they were so busy. I would stand back against the outside wall so they wouldn't see me lingering, keep watching. The front light would go out, leaving only the blue glow of the back kitchen. Which cakes did they eat then? Ones I'd already seen for days, growing staler on the shelves, or one that had been kept hidden? The hundred-layer cake. . . .

I couldn't see the kitchen from outside; only the glow. It was a theater, I just didn't have a ticket. My face and hands growing cold; cars with their headlights on. The women would be talking in German, which was the secret language of the birds, drinking coffee, their shoes off; I wondered, did they ever speak of me?

I always bought the same thing at the G and M bakery, or almost always. Finally waited on, I would hesitate and the little plump woman would suggest lace cookies. I liked that: lace cookies. They must think me lacy. I got the lace cookies sometimes, to please them—they were brittle and nutty, got stuck in my teeth—and once or twice a napoleon or a creampuff, but what I usually got was eclairs.

I'd buy four of them: smooth logs covered entirely in chocolate, bottoms too—a quarter of an inch thick—and heavy with yellow custard. Twenty-five cents apiece. Four fit neatly in the pink box, no extra room, covered with a gauze of tissue. The women worked carefully laying them in. I was soothed by the vision of their round ends like shoulders nestled against the cardboard; the dense and even frosting. Pink string wound around the box, then it was mine.

I paid my dollar and said good-night, walked out—were they laughing at me? For buying sweets every day? I had gotten fat, but it was mostly covered by my coat.

I was fat. I could see it in the mirror, I could measure it with a tape measure. My mother and sister offered advice. "Eat only meat, skim milk, and vegetables."

"Don't eat anything but cantaloupe for two weeks."

Johnny liked my fat. He would beg me to show it to him—my bulging belly—let him plunge his hands in the folds. He'd squeeze it together, let it flow apart. I'd be lying on my bed, shirt pulled up and tucked beneath my breasts so only the hill of belly showed. Squeeze, let go, squeeze. One roll swallows another. It reminded me of when we were very young, Charlotte and I used to play with his penis in the bathtub, pushing the little poker back into the hollow of his groin. "Making it disappear," we called it and loved that, how the wormlike bud was sucked in, then, let alone, uncoiled slowly, as if on a spring. So I knew how he felt as he manipulated, how charming was the bouncy plasticity of flesh. I, too, if I hadn't had to worry about what kids at school thought, what my mother thought, if I didn't feel a kind of shock and terror of it coming true—I'm fat! I'm fat! Blubber Baby!—would have loved my belly without reservation. Its round pumpkin-fullness, its silky impenetrable sheen.

Once I left the bakery, I felt a little depressed. I missed its symphonic odor, crowded shelves. And something changed between me and the women when I handed over the money—a kind of shame hit.

I wasn't their girl.

I'd walk the two blocks home, turn the corner, enter our building. The eternal embarrassment of that, having to answer the doorman's musical "Good afternoon," then the same thing in the elevator with even more talk. I hated it, hated it, I felt like an animal being herded around with sticks. The vibration of my self-consciousness hiding flushes of rage—their pink bald heads, I could slice them like ham, their puppet movements, I could break their arms—which, when I noticed them in myself caused a confused sorrow. Why was I so bad? Eloise lived in a hotel and didn't hate the elevator men. I didn't really hate Herbert, who was asking me again, "And how is Sue?"

Herbert peering at me, waving good-bye, elevator door thankfully shut. Of course I didn't hate him. He was nice.

And then I couldn't linger in the hall because the neighbors might come out. I really did hate them—they disdained us. Their eyes flickered over our clothes or our mother's clothes and they actually lifted their lips a little in scorn. Our mother wouldn't let us bark at them, or act like spastics, or any of the other good ideas we had. We couldn't pour molasses under their doors. So we had to ignore them, but they were ignoring us already—so what good was that?

Then inside the apartment. Different bad feelings. I'd charge up the stairs, hide my eclairs under the pillow. Even if my mother called to me when I came in she wouldn't make it into the hall before I got out of sight, or into my room before the booty was gone. She might say, "Why didn't you stop when I called you? I've told you not to run up the stairs. It's rude, Margaret, not to speak when you come in."

I had to hide my treasure. This wasn't a candy bar or two I could keep in my pocket. I was a fox with a chicken dangling from his mouth. But what my mother saw was a girl who needed to learn the social graces.

It was agonizing—especially now, right after school and the building gauntlet—to have to face her continuing ignorance. She still thought I was her daughter in the regular way; I would keep learning from her as I had done at three, mastering buttonholes. Didn't she know what I would give to still be that—a regular girl—and here she was angry and hurt, as if I was injuring her. "You're so rude to me, Margaret."

Was I? I couldn't think about it. The pressure of my grief at school, about school, had reached its very limit, as it did most afternoons; I had to be alone to repair myself. I needed to protect my sweets, and then, in peace, to eat them, allow their healing powers in. Sugar and chocolate, yellow custard. They worked from the inside out, suppressing madness. Wasn't I smart to invent this cure, instead of ending up in a padded cell?

Mommy would follow me upstairs, I'd be sitting on my bed. The box was hidden now, under my pillow, that was fine, but her words about my rudeness were so piercing. That I had hurt her—the tremolo in her voice—her appeal . . . I'd sit still, head bent, shielding myself. She thought she just had to say more, demonstrate her unhappiness, get through to me . . . it made me panicky. Sometimes I'd rush into my bathroom and slam the door.

"Don't run away from me. Don't shut the door in my face."

"Will you leave me alone? I have to take a piss."

"Don't use language like that. . . . You could have said, 'I have to go to the bathroom, excuse me a minute.' I'm just trying to talk to you, Margaret. I'm your mother. . . ."

My nails digging into my arms in the bathroom, teeth biting the air. Aren't I insane to feel such rage forking through my body? If I wasn't insane yet, I would be soon. Is that what she wanted? No. She was so stupid, she had to leave. *Help me—make her leave.* Raking the air with my teeth. And this panic her presence engendered itself such a grief to me, I remembered very well how it used to be between us. . . .

And she kept saying, I know you're unhappy, talk to me, I can't help you if you won't talk to me—

How could I say: *You sold my house, you killed my cat, I will never forgive you?* What would we do then? She wouldn't want to help me then. How could I say: *I'm not really a person inside. I'm crazy. I'm crazy, Mom, I can't go to school or learn the social graces.* I had my pride. Or it had me. To admit to her my failure—the breadth and depth of it—was out of the question. She wouldn't love me then. She thought she would, but she was wrong. She didn't know what I was.

I needed my sweets, I had to be alone. School had rent me in a dozen places, all throbbing now. Every period between classes when I either spoke to someone and tortured myself with the idiocy of what I had said or didn't speak to someone and then the darkness loomed created a gap that now had to be closed. I knew how to close it. I had taught myself. Chocolate. Yellow custard. This was to my mother's benefit as well as mine, someday I might be a person again, make her proud, if she'd leave me to it.

Instead she came in here, told me I was rude. Mommy, I'm dying, I wanted to say, but only as a last measure, as I died. (But then I'd be like Daddy, and her contempt would exile me forever.) To just say it—the words wouldn't form.

Please go, Mommy, please go, please. If you love me. I love you. Leave me alone. Please.

"I'll leave you alone, since that's what you seem to want. Margaret—you know you can always talk to me. I'm your mother, I love you."

Why did she hurt me so?

She went away, shut the door behind her. I sealed off all memory of her distress and my own. I opened the bakery box, let the smell drift out, picked up whatever novel I was reading. My eyes hooked to the first sentence. My hand brought the eclair to my lips, I bit through chocolate and pastry. My eyes swept to the right, down, left, right again as the explosions of sweetness spread out from my tongue. The dark intelligence of chocolate doubling and tripling my own. The eggy consolation of custard, the amorality of sugar. Spirit guides, all counseling pleasure, privacy, descent.

The corridors of my body were a universe where I had work to do. Each bite of sweetness was labor. The book held my mind in company while the food traveled my blood, skimming toward the hurt places. I was no longer looking for what I used to look for, the climax of pleasure in taste, but something deeper and dreamier. Dreamier but precise. Pleasure was part of it, the richness of the dissolving chocolate, the cool gobs of custard plopping down, but it was a means to an end, and this end invisible. I didn't know how memory was killed but that's what I was doing, choking off and silencing each agonizing moment.

Otherwise they'd just keep coming back. All night. I'd relive them over and over, electric prods of humiliation, because of whatever I had said or not said in any social encounter. How awkward, alien, stupid I was. Seized and shaken by this self-hatred—my whole body in a clamp, rigid, feeling as if I was dying, or wanting to die—over and over. Like squirts of acid. Who could take it? I had to kill it.

In a couple of hours I was fine. My stomach felt heavy and rubbery, I was dizzy, yet mostly I felt a sense of accomplishment. My mind in one piece again, armored. Safety.

ON THE AFTERNOONS when my mother and I didn't have a scene—when I'd had time to come upstairs, put my sweets away before she came home, so I could greet her nicely, if weakly, when she tapped at my door—I would go into her room after I'd silenced the shame. I'd spend a half an hour or forty-five minutes with her while she got ready for her date. She went out almost every night.

I liked being in her room, my soul quieted by the river of chocolate in my veins, and the schoolday vanished, like a letter torn into pieces. Now I could be Margaret, girl of the house. Third child, mild one, Mommy-loving, crowding beside her on her dressing-table chair or acting as her handmaid, bringing shoes and dresses from her closet.

It takes her a long time to make up. She sits in bra and panties, creaming her face, applying foundation, rouge, eye shadow and mascara, lipstick. She does her hair. She is most at ease before the mirror, though she complains about her looks. "I'm so ugly . . . I'm so old." I tell her she is beautiful, as of course she is, though I do notice the signs of age. Someday I will be more beautiful.

But she's still got it. Her soft limber body in its dainty undergarments smells of the warmth of her bath, of her creams and lotions, of the dark loose curls of her hair. Her hair is like the darkness just above the grass that the grasshoppers drink for their supper. I would like to be a grasshopper—a tiny jeweled grasshopper—and live in it, an ornament, secretly alive. Would I? No. Yes. I barely think of it, the thought wings by. I am amazed that I can have such thoughts at all.

She brushes and brushes her hair, a hundred strokes, combs it and pins it in place. Then stares at herself—no smile, no twinkle—and so misses her own charm. She ought to flirt with herself in the mirror, as I do. Instead she gazes as if her face were a strange woman at the door.

Sometimes we talk. We chat, we discuss color and style, or books, or I lie back on her amazingly soft bed, the satin comforter puffy and slippery, and talk about school from the perspective of one who sees all, knows all, is smarter than all the teachers.

This isn't hard. I am smart; I can criticize, I can talk about it as if it all makes sense, as if I am in her world, and I think she believes me. She explains the frustrations of schoolteachers—it's not much of a life—suggests that maybe I threaten them with my ideas. I don't think so. They just don't like me, except for Mr. Valenti, the sadist, who likes me because I'm blond. But it doesn't matter. I talk; I'm aware of floating high above my fear, sentences coming out round and well-formed, convincing her again that I'm superior, that she is—that if she is, I am—if I am, she is.

Then the doorbell rings, and Mommy goes downstairs to her date.

Silence when she leaves the room. I have only a minute. Her perfume hangs in the air. I lie on the slippery bed as if she were still here, rolling over on the beige pillows—that luxury of space and airiness, maid-clean bedclothes, money spent casually, that I thought would last forever. Or sit at her dressing table, investigating lipsticks, brushing my hair. I am her daughter. I see a little of her in me. I can fall into the dream that has no name, the dream of the odor of her makeup, the shape of her tortoiseshell combs.

◎

I HAVE A few minutes but that's all. Mommy always insisted we come down to greet her boyfriend, the slim southern corporate lawyer she had known since her youth, or the other men she dated occasionally. We had to be polite, shake his hand, say, "How do you do?" Answer any questions he chose to ask. Nobody wanted this. We wanted to stay in our rooms. She insisted.

I felt physically ill at the thought of it. The men she dated weren't enemies to me, yet I found their presence unbearable. It's easy now to speculate that I couldn't tolerate any reminder of what had happened to my father, or that I was jealous, or both, and I'm sure these things are true, but that wasn't how I experienced it. It was far more inchoate and frightening. Something wrapped around me would begin to unravel—I felt larval, tearful—and then a fierce, hot, mad xenophobia. Strangers—*strangers.* Almost a passion, this hatred, Johnny and I drugged on ourselves, on our mother, on familiarity, acidic burn of repulsion. *Strangers.*

Especially strange men. How dare she let them in. How dare she make us speak to them.

"Come downstairs," my mother would insist. "You have to be courteous."

Something, it seemed to me, excessive in her insistence on courtesy. As if it mattered more than anything else we had to learn, almost as much as our very survival. Maybe she did think so, maybe she was right. Maybe it was the only thing she knew how to teach. Courtesy, good breeding. If you know how to behave, all else follows. I thought it was insane. Didn't she know we were crazy?

"You have to come down," she hissed, never more adamant, and we would. Johnny rocketing into the room where the adults sat, spitting like a firecracker. Rude? You want to see rude? Long strings of insults, variations on the man's peculiar name, would uncurl from his mouth. He was dancing a Krishna dance. He was a boy-monkey dancing.

The couch and coffee table were against the far wall of the big living room, under the windows; there was a kind of natural stage for my brother to perform on. Sweeping down the stairs—whir of his bare feet—across the hall and in to caper on the expanse of vivid rug. Beautiful insults, long rhythmic chants of them, like swung beads, like the gifts of a genius Tourette. My mother would protest, he'd insult her, too. Then the man, red-faced spluttering, rising from his seat. "You can't talk to your mother that way, young man—"

Johnny a dervish, spinning and leaping. No old man could catch him—and anyway our mother's whimpering, "Don't hit him, that's what his father did," would upset the man who didn't want to hit the boy, yet whose hands were moving of their own accord, jerking and twitching.

I stood to the side, in love with Johnny's badness and wishing I could be, for just a minute, on stage. ("Look, you guys, I'm crazy, too; don't hit me, that what's my father did.") Yet I also felt sorry for the man. Some part of me drawn to him, to both of them, the overdressed couple on the couch. Mommy in her perfume, Rudi Gernreich dress, knee-high raspberry-pink boots; slim, southern-voiced man in a suit, lighting her cigarettes.

This softness of mine embarrassed me. I should be like Johnny, pure hate, except that I can't be like Johnny, only he is allowed. And I don't want to be like Charlotte, the responsible one who would come down and chat with the man in a teenage way. I wanted to curl up under their feet like a cat. Under the sofa. Let the hatred flake off slowly—it would take a few hours—then be invited out to talk about myself. No, not talk. Too hard. Leap up like a cat, walk along the back of the sofa, sniff delicately at their hair. (So embarrassed, always, at knowing this about myself. Soft. Girly.)

I had to chat politely, then go. They'd have a drink, he'd take her out to dinner. How long adults could spend over dinner! My mother especially. All the drinks first of course, the coffee after, but even her eating, her chewing, took place several orders of magnitude more slowly than with us. She would sink back into the elegant, talky comfort of a restaurant as if it were an ancestral home, as if you might see her, in a tableau at the Museum of Natural History, in her faux diamonds and jet beads, glittery clothes, at table with dessert fork raised. I enjoyed going out with her in my later teens—loved the food and wine, the conversation, but would be ready for sleep long before she had her coffee. Made dizzy by her snakelike slowness over food. That first year, I remember an obscure resentment, suspicion: They aren't really just going out to dinner. They're gone too long. Where are they having sex? Not that I care.

As Jimmy had taught me: Be cool.

Mommy thinks I'm rude. It doesn't matter. As long as I'm cool, which feels good, the sleek, incurving power of it, a rush—

I can't do violence. But I can do cool.

I watched the grown-ups leave. After a drink or two, after Johnny's exhausting scene, the man would get Mommy's coat, she'd slide her arms in gratefully. "I'll be back by——," she'd say brightly. "Neithie will give you dinner. Answer the phone if it rings."

"And if it doesn't?"

"What?"

"Never mind."

Once Mommy and the man were gone, the oppression lifted. She became absurd, we'd make fun of her miniskirts, her boots, her ocean of perfume. Just the way she held herself—I'm ready!—anxiously adorned and oddly stiff, like a Christmas tree. Her metallic mesh evening purse clanking, lipsticks rolling out the oversize holes.

Mommy was gone. We went into the kitchen to hang out with Neithie, clamor for our dinner.

"When's it going to be ready? Whenwhenwhen?"

Not that we cared, particularly. We were rarely hungry anymore, having money to buy sweets. (We didn't only steal it. Our mother gave us loads of money. She didn't know what children needed to get around New York, so erred on the side of too much. And never kept track. I liked this, of course, but it made me feel funny, like not having a bedtime anymore. I missed my old fifty cents, that had to last a week.) We weren't hungry for food, but we were hungry for the easy whiny yapping of children bugging a woman. And Neithie didn't mind—she was lonely, too.

Neithie was slim and young, light-skinned and light on her feet, good-natured. Her teeth were bad; she hid them when she laughed. That hand over her big soft lips and few rabbity teeth made her seem shy, which she wasn't. She was relaxed and goofy and gay, her gaiety increasing with her consumption of scotch-and-milk. She sipped slowly at this concoction all afternoon, hiding her glass behind a row of my mother's cookbooks. After Mommy left, she drank openly, Johnny or I refilling her glass. "You really want milk in it? That's weird."

"It's good," she said. "It's so good. It's just what I like."

Neithie always burned the food. She burned it because she didn't know how to cook, she'd never cooked in her life before taking this job. It hadn't occurred to my mother that a young black woman might not know how to cook, and Neithie had had no wish to enlighten her. She nodded her head at my mother's instructions, then asked Charlotte and me for help. I knew some things from having watched my mother, and I passed the knowledge on to the best of my ability. I wasn't sure about cooking times. But then even when I was sure, when it became obvious through painful experience, Neithie kept overcooking the food. I think it made her feel like she was doing it properly to do it a considerable time. She liked the reassurance of the hamburger's lengthy sojourn in the pan, that background sizzle, like music; as I recall we had hamburgers every night, though that can't be right. It didn't matter. I had eaten so much already, Johnny would eat a hamburger in any condition, and Charlotte was dieting. Half the time my sister wouldn't even come down to dinner. It was just Johnny, Neithie, and me.

While Neithie cooked the hamburgers dry, I'd call the Little Garden Superette, where my mother also had a charge account, and order a quart of coffee ice cream and a box of Pepperidge Farm Milano cookies. Our mother never noticed what we charged, though she would remark in amazement how high her grocery bills were. She thought it was due to Manhattan prices. The balding old deli man would climb three flights to deliver the small paper bag which I began to feel guilty about, after the thrill wore off. Still, what could be better than picking up a phone, ordering whatever I wanted? It wasn't my fault the apartment people wouldn't let the old man use the elevator. Besides, he was a white man, which made it better. I liked to see Neithie handing him a quarter. Pulling it out of her pocket, her insouciance, grown-up toss of her head. I thought she deserved the experience. (The quarter was from the stash my mother left for unspecified emergencies. We tried to get at this money for other things, but Neithie was careful with it. Only the quarter for the deli man. "Or else you'll have to tell your mama you done took it.")

Booty safely in hand—and never taking for granted the luxury of it, marveling—*an old man walking up three flights to bring us cookies!* we would linger in our de facto dining room: the little, square, overheated breakfast nook between the kitchen and the back door. This was where we ate all our meals. It was furnished with and completely filled by the two white plastic café tables that used to be on the porch in the old house so when the four of us ate together, we'd eat two by two. But Mom was out, Charlotte upstairs—just Johnny and Neithie and me at one table, eating ice cream, drinking scotch, as we entertained her.

We told stories about, imitated, our mother, her boyfriends, our teachers, the doorman. Neithie swooped her whole head down when she laughed. She seemed unused to our brand of wit, and we loved showing it off to her, coming up with more and more outrageous word-pictures. Mr. Younger, Johnny's tall, slim, yet eggishly curved homeroom teacher (mincing, disdainful); we described him in insect terms, sticky insides, little legs languidly waving. And the vigorous sadist Mr. Valenti, science teacher: Johnny did a madman grimace, teeth and eyes popping out. Mr. Caruso—that preening, yellow-faced—but it was enough, in those days, to call him a faggot. "The guy's a faggot." And Neithie would laugh. It was almost too easy to make her laugh.

She grew tipsy but not drunk, at least not so we noticed. Her body was naturally floppy like a Gumby or a ragdoll, long-waisted, high-breasted, and if she lost a little muscle function, it didn't seem out of character. She liked her scotch; that was all. I approved of people drinking. Especially women. They got looser and sweeter. They laughed.

The way Neithie sipped her drink, mouth pooched out to receive the milky scotch—eyes half closed—reminded me of our cats lapping cream. That privacy, delicacy. . . . Where were our cats? Were they all dead? Was Ricky in the woods right now starving, freezing?

I imagined Ricky's whole head in my mouth—I would keep it open very wide—licking the ice cream off my tongue. His scratchy tongue hurts me, but I stay still.

Neithie left at eight, or a little later; her husband picked her up. I thought that was fine—a man coming and waiting for you as you put your coat on, taking you home. Her husband was considerably older than she was and, though she seemed subdued in his presence, there was also a hint of sassiness, some streak of girlishness I envied. He stood grave and still, a dark, solid man just inside the back door, holding his hat against his overcoat; she swished her hips a little, flounced, as she gathered her things. And the scotch and milk, I thought, folded over and in, sinking down into the secret recesses of her body. I knew all about that—hidden cargo. It lit the insides of her cheeks and temples; I noticed the stiff way she held her head, even as her hips danced, as if carrying a glass carefully so it would not spill.

Her husband was patient. He would nod to us politely when he came in. Sometimes he didn't come in. If we were still eating our dessert, he stayed in the shadow just on the other side of the door. His politeness was not like the deference I was used to from black men. It had more reserve in it and more sadness. I wanted him to come in, to sit down with us. But this was something I couldn't even imagine saying.

Not infrequently Neithie's boyfriend came for her instead, and then she left early. She left early, purple lipstick newly applied, with the young man, of whom I remember nothing. She wouldn't even say good-bye to us when the boyfriend came. Her excitement was a hard excitement, her eyes fixed above our heads. Twenty minutes later, her husband would knock on the door. Heavy dark face, dark overcoat. He made no fuss.

I wanted to say I'm sorry, but I was too embarrassed. I wanted to say She's bad, isn't she? but she was my friend. I said nothing. I felt implicated—also knew in some cloudy way that it was another aspect of my privilege that allowed me to see this man's shame as I wouldn't see a white man's. I stood there politely waiting in case he wanted to say more to me, which he never did. He'd nod his head, put his hat back on, and turn toward the stairs. He walked very slowly down.

I was awed by the power of Neithie. Her daring.

Neithie didn't talk to us about her life. She laughed and laughed at our stories—seemed sometimes even younger than we were, wondering at our tales of private school, and savoring, I believe, the exotic details of our arrogance—but she offered no stories of her own. She explained neither husband nor lover; she just went out, like our mother went out, like women did. Years later she was murdered by a man, not her husband; he threw her off a roof.

Twenty-four

After Neithie left, Johnny and Charlotte would spend the evenings in their rooms, doors locked. Johnny, over the course of a year, acquired three locks for his door, which he affixed with great care, as if any of us were lock pickers.

I had sympathy for his need for locks. It was clear to me that enormous pressure was on him—he was the *boy*. It was almost a glow around him. The way our mother acted, as if he was the most traumatized, because in our minds he was the most at risk. His running away in Montclair, his violence here—he was constantly throwing tantrums, running through the house hitting people or knocking over and breaking things in our mother's room—yet I knew that violence isn't necessarily the worst thing. He was the most at risk by fate. Mommy kept telling us what people told her, friends, doctors, about how a boy feels, the needs a boy has, for a father. The damage that can be done to him, the delicate machinery of his pysche. The fact that she knew from her own experience how a girl feels losing a father (my mother's father died when she was fourteen, of tuberculosis) was never spoken of—I had a hard time even remembering it. It was as if girls couldn't be hurt too much, we hadn't that machinery.

It was easy to resent Johnny's specialness, and Charlotte and I did. We wanted to hurt him for having that quality that called forth our mother's full compassion. Yet we also felt sorry for him. The boy. The boy. Like something made of gold, the heir to the throne whom the demons chase. Also, he wasn't Jimmy. He wasn't Daddy. It wasn't his fault we saw their ghosts in him—that our need found in his features, his energy, an echo. Of course it was craziness.

I knew it. I didn't think we had any choice. I felt scornful of my mother, who claimed not to know it, who denied it. It didn't surprise me, that our emotions were perverse.

What would you expect?

I would stand outside Johnny's door, try to talk my way in. I was lonely, and his fierce solitude radiated heat; I loved that ferocity because I wasn't afraid of it. He was the only person in the universe I could allow to hear me beg.

About half the time, he'd let me in. Unlock the five locks—anger making his shoulders, his head stiff—return to what he was doing. I didn't quite get it, how he could be so sociable downstairs, so intractable here. I'd lie on his bed chattering, while he lay on the carpet in his usual position, on his stomach, propped up on his elbows, reading *Popular Mechanics*.

Johnny had the smallest bedroom, which he had chosen. He liked it because it was at the end of the hall, a little cubbyhole tucked away by itself. His room had carpeting, where he had also chosen—the rest of us had rugs, which were classier but Johnny didn't care about that—and a single bed under the window. It was always warm in there, and smelled of model glue. The floor was usually covered by something in pieces.

I liked that masculine clutter—wires and screwdrivers, photographs of cars and Ursula Andress, lots of books of matches, firecrackers hidden under the bed, unidentifiable bits of black plastic and round rubber rings, the sealed packages of radio, flashlight, remote-control airplane batteries.

Johnny mostly didn't answer what I said. I spoke to the air, long sentences; I conversed. Sometimes Sue would look up at me curiously, as if even a dog knew a person should be answered. I talked, I was amazed at how well I talked, I had ideas, opinions, wasn't anyone impressed? I was impressed. I couldn't do this at school.

Johnny never showed any interest that I remember. Not in his room. He'd suffer my talking—suffer my silence when I ran down, my presence that wasn't, I knew, really quiet, I was all over the place, my soul exuding stuff—then he'd say suddenly, sharply, "Get out of here."

I'd ignore him. My loneliness was like a ship going down; I couldn't deliberately climb back onto it. I'd stay, rolling around on his bed, throwing off sparks of anxiety while he withdrew further inside the nutlike carapace of his body. His dark bedspread, his snug carpet, the heat blasting out of the radiators—why should I leave? I admired the sheen of light on his brown hair, not staticky and flyaway like my hair, or thick and curly like my sister's, but in-between hair, strong and silky, unfortunately cut too short. A preppie cut he hated; he cultivated the front wing of it that could fall into his eyes—those wide-set brown defiant eyes. Add his long mouth which gave him Daddy's infectious grin, tiny retroussé nose: His face was the perfection of little brother. Like the mouse Reepicheep in the Narnia chronicles, bravely wielding his sword on behalf of the good Narnians.

He'd tell me again, "Get out of here." Sometimes I had to hit him.

I could win a fistfight with Johnny. I was inches taller, thirty pounds heavier. It was satisfying to beat him, but then he'd come in my room at night when I was nearly asleep, throw lighted matches at me. The swiftness of the passage extinguished the flame, yet I was worried: What if it didn't? He'd throw three or four, standing poised for flight on my threshold, his little manic face lit up. Charring holes in my quilt. Once or twice he came after me with a baseball bat. Smacked my arm or shoulder, "Your head will be next." I didn't think it was fair. The older gets to abuse the younger, those are the rules. (I fought with Charlotte too, sometimes, gasping with the joy of finally landing a punch, inflicting pain, but she always won. She sat on my chest and pulled my hair, she chased me into my room and drooled spit on me. I suffered her winning for the one moment of my fist connecting to her flesh.) Johnny changed the rules. I had too much imagination, too much respect for his wildness. Yes, I could also throw lighted matches, get a baseball bat—but then? I had no doubt he'd escalate up to nuclear weapons. And what if I really hurt him? I stopped picking fights.

No. I couldn't do that. He was my only intimate, fractured as our relationship was. The only person I didn't feel shame around, no matter how badly I behaved. What I did was shift the terms of the battle. When he started trying to kick me out of his room, when I felt the steep cant of the ship of my loneliness, I'd pretend to go into a trance. I'd cross my eyes, shimmy my arms in front of me, advance on him with delicious slowness.

"I'm going to kill you," I'd intone. "I'm going to killll you."

Singsong voice, all spooky effects, I half-hypnotized myself as I backed him into a corner.

"I'm—going—to—kill—you." My brother white-faced and still. The men in our family had died by some invisible magic or predatory fate; wasn't he was slated to be next? I had reminded him of this possibility often enough. It was my obsession, my terror—I assumed we all shared it—in any case, I made him share it. I won't die next; you will die next. Saving myself, yes, getting ready to lose him, yes, and of course, most desperate of all: If you guess the game, they have to change it. But now I wasn't desperate, now I was playing with it. My hands moved, my fingers curled; I was weaving spells in the air; I could feel the lines of power. Later, reading *Kubla Khan*, I would be reminded of that sweet derangement. "His flashing eyes, his floating hair." The same druggy rhythm in my voice, words like a dance. This symbolic moment.

"Kill you," I said, hands not touching, then touching his neck—my snake flicker fingers—just barely circling his flesh. He's frozen, I'm ecstatic. My will is a dark syrup. Holding the world in a ring of power—the whole universe a flaming circle around this point *me*—then overcome with tenderness.

"*Never* kill you," I cry, and my voice runs butter: sweet, sweet.

"I lo-ove you," I croon in my big-sister voice, my crone-sister tongue, "loo-oove you." These words break the spell, he lunges away (why does he leave me?), punches me in the stomach.

I'm a little shaken, yet relieved. He's tough. "You were afraid," I say, retreating.

"I was not."

Forced back into my own room, solitude. "You were afraid."

I am always afraid. It's so much a part of my life I can't imagine living without it. I see through it, move through it, all my social encounters take place in its chambers. It's a shadow that goes ahead of me; it's almost a separate being. I come to think it is a separate being—what must be appeased. All my rituals, my avoidances, gifts for the fear. I know it can't be spoken of. What other people mean by fear is a mood or a feeling, a temporary reaction to danger, a mistake: what I know is the god. Protean and demanding, it rules my behavior utterly and I become accustomed to its control. I adapt.

We were all adapting. My mother had her lovers, my brother his locks. My sister was in ninth grade, beginning to date. I knew

I would never have a boyfriend. Maybe kisses—I could handle parties like the parties we had in Montclair, spin-the-bottle, but they didn't have those kind of parties here. People were friends, they talked, then went out on dates, and I couldn't do that. I would see Charlotte in her room, sitting on her bed, the boy in a chair (Mom said: Leave the door open), talking. Or they would go out for a walk, have a soda. She didn't really have a boyfriend either, only these beginnings—one date, two. Still, I knew it would happen. She wasn't damaged the way I was. Something in her still supple, not afraid, while for me the while idea of *boys* held such a terrifying glamor it was like that moment when the class circled me and said *Where are you from? What does your father do*?

I knew I wouldn't get over it. Still, I bit down on hope. Flooding myself again and again with its intoxicating music.

Twenty-five

IN THE SPRING, Johnny began to sit on the ledge outside his bedroom window, threatening suicide. This ledge, five stories above ground, was roomy for a ten-year-old. He could sit at his ease, legs dangling, survey the street. Traffic.

The first few times he did this it was simply what any boy of his kind would do, finding such a perch outside his bedroom window. Idling, dropping pennies. I said, "What if a penny fell on somebody's head?" We knew if you did that from the Empire State Building, you could kill someone. We didn't know what would happen from here.

"Probably just make a little dent. Like a little saucer. Then the guy could keep pennies on top of his head."

Johnny was seen, our mother told. The building manager was quite upset. (He was often upset with us.)

The ledge became Johnny's weapon. My mother would tell him to clean up his room, he'd go out on the ledge. She'd say, "You have to,"—out on the ledge. My mother reminds me now that she remained calm. Didn't cry, scream, or threaten but reasoned with him carefully, keeping the volume low. She's correct, though I barely noticed, being so attuned to the hysteria beneath her skin.

Johnny says he was never contemplating a jump. He was merely making her crazy; anyway, he liked the ledge. He invited me out and I was tempted—look at her, Margaret Diehl, sitting five stories above traffic! But my physical timidity has never allowed that kind of thing. I wasn't really afraid for my brother—I trusted him, he was nimble—but I could see myself sliding off immediately, as if my bottom were greased.

When Johnny sat on the ledge, Mommy gave in to his demands. She freed him from household chores and obligations. She said, "I know he's manipulating me, and it's terrible for him to get away with it, but what else can I do? He doesn't realize he could fall."

Her soft, ragged terror. The pleading swoop of her voice. No tears, no, but such a vibration.

My sister and I talked about the Simon and Garfunkel song: the boy on the ledge, the crowd gathering below, the desperate mother. The song that ends, "He flew away." I remember Charlotte interpreting the chorus "Oh, my Grace, ain't got no hiding place," as referring to both what the boy was thinking and what the crowd was thinking—no hiding place from witnessing such events.

I was impressed by her sensitivity. I wasn't aware of wanting a hiding place. The drama of Johnny's ledge games was intoxicating to me—that he would dare to refer to this thing, suicide, in front of our mother, dare to use it.

SUICIDE

I would say it aloud to myself, pronouncing each letter. Getting between the letters, the *u* and the *i*, the *i* and the *c*. It derived from Latin, which I was learning at school. It began with an *s*, like *school*, like *somnambulist*. Like *sinister*—which also came from the Latin and originally meant left, which, because it wasn't right, was devilish. Like *shudder*. Like *sex*.

U for underground or "The Fall of the House of Usher." *I* of course was *I*. *C*—cruelty or creation. *I* again. *D* for Diehl. No, *d* for death. *D* for desire. And *e*—the End.

A long word, a dense text. I could meditate on it as the Jewish mystics mediated on the Hebrew words of the Old Testament, determined to crack the very letters for meaning. Meaning!—that marrow, I believed for decades I would get it, taste its darkness on my most secret tongue. The meaning of life, of death: No one has yet untangled it? Of course it can be found, of course it waits for me, and there is even, perhaps, help, a cadre or cabal of the wise. For now I had the word. I loved to hear it spoken, or even referred to, as Johnny did, gesturally. SUICIDE. The heart of it was between the *u* and the *i*, the sticky place.

Johnny was a boy, so he could get away with suicide. Pretend suicide—yes—but still get away with it. She didn't hate him as she had Daddy or would me, for hurting her so badly (if I dared to mention it); boys didn't mean to hurt anybody. Boys were innocence.

When Johnny was on the ledge, he was captive and needed me. He couldn't move until Mommy gave in, and sometimes their battle went on for a while, so he couldn't reach for something he wanted in his room, or cover any contraband. I carried out these actions, fetched and hid. (Hid his *Playboy*, any thieved unexplainable items.) It was also my job to be mediator between camps. Demands, negotiations, my mother's surrenders, which filled me with longing.

He also needed someone to complain to about Charlotte's threats—she took the opposite course from our mother, she said, "If you jump and survive, I'll bash your brains in, if you die, I'll follow you into hell and punish you in the next life." If our mother wasn't listening (gone to her room on the theory that Johnny might come back in without her witness) Charlotte would say, "Go ahead, jump, see if we care—"

Johnny needed me there to agree with him that he didn't have to jump to prove her reverse psychology wrong, that in fact by not jumping he was psyching her out, though of course what she was aiming for was to get him inside, raging, swinging at her so she could grab him, which is usually what happened.

Then Charlotte would tie him up in a sheet, throw him in the bathtub. What a day when she came up with this idea! All the crackling of her own anxiety, her take-charge personality powerfully taking charge. "He's out of control, Mom. This is what we have to do, like a straitjacket in a mental hospital. I'm sorry." She was giddy, vengeful, barely plausible—and our mother, wringing her hands, weak from getting her heart back—our mother, exhausted as adults get in these moments, unlike us—disappeared backward. "Don't hurt him." Going to lie down. I'd help my sister tie up Johnny, who fought us savagely and uselessly. We made a strong team, a witch-team. I was worried about my betrayal of him; I had been on his side five minutes ago; but as soon as he came in, as soon as he started raging, I was angry, too: Who did he think he *was*?

Always breaking things. Always scaring us. Always getting the attention. The two of us stood there beside the tub as the cold water roared over his bound and thrashing form—"It'll bring him to his senses"—occasionally poking at him with our feet like Third World women doing laundry. Giggling. Poker faces if our mother came in. "Just a little longer, Ma. Don't worry. We won't drown him."

"I know you won't drown him, I'm worried he'll catch cold. Don't make it too cold."

"He needs the cold." Charlotte so authoritative. I like her certainty, it makes me feel safe. She's stronger than our mother, saner than Johnny. We're the ones who have to take care of things. Thrashing the laundry, shoving it with our feet; he tries to bite our toes. When we let him go he won't speak to anyone for days.

I feel guilty that I am not more distressed by it all. That I crave the drama, find it so interesting. In my defense I would say I knew Johnny wouldn't fall, much less jump, but what this means I don't know. I would watch him sitting out there in his solitude, and feel energized by the vicarious danger. Feel enlivened by the fear raging around me; at least it's not me that's afraid, this time. Laughing a little at how Johnny is trapped by his act, unable to come in until he's won ground. Often I lounge on his bed reading his magazines, "It's so warm in here!" while he has to sit on the narrow concrete ledge, suffering manfully.

Mostly, I think, enjoying our whole family together, working for a common goal, as on a canoeing vacation. Margaret, Charlotte, Mom: Get the boy inside. (Nobody out on dates or in his or her room.) I did my part—nonchalant persuasion—"You might as well . . ." they did theirs.

Boy in danger; save the boy.

Done.

And I feel much better as, later, my mother felt better after divorcing her second husband. Going through it again with nobody dying. But I still felt guilty. How did I *know* he wouldn't fall?

LATE AT NIGHT when I couldn't sleep I'd go into my bathroom and talk into the mirror. I'd watch myself—mouth moving, eyes aglow—and be so pleased this body, this soul, belonged to me. The creaminess of my skin—the mystery of my eyes. Even I didn't know what was behind them. I could look at myself and not know; not know. They beckoned me in. The human person is a door.

The more I gazed, the stranger, dreamier, my mood became. I was never frightened by this but welcomed it, welcomed any signal, as I thought of it, from the other world. And at the extreme pitch I was living at, things happened so easily. Several times lights appeared in the room, or rather glowing balls of different colors floating—blue, gold, violet—lazily around my head; I knew they were intelligent. They were beings with powers: This was their first manifestation. I watched them, deeply pleased. Were they going to open up? Grow bigger? No, they just drifted, yet they were watching me, too. I arranged myself in a cordial being-looked-at pose.

Another time the glass of the mirror began to sweat and droop. I had been staring into it for a long time, consciously calling on the magic behind my eyes, raising the inner voice: *Come on, come on.* The glass sagged, like Saran Wrap, first around the edges. If I kept looking, I knew, I'd be pulled inside. I lingered enough to feel the touch of it, a sucking force on my neck and shoulders, yes, it was getting stronger, accelerating, *dragging me in;* then turned my gaze away. I wasn't scared; I was aroused, thrilled at the high-wire challenge. Playing with the powers. They're here; they want me. They weren't benevolent; nor yet malevolent; they were powers. One becomes an adept, and then they are tools.

But I knew I wasn't an adept yet. I was a child. I was merely noting their presence, succored by it—there is room in the world for me to use my talents, magic *works*—but not foolish enough to walk into that melting mirror. I had things to do first. To learn.

Twenty-six

IT'S BEEN THIRTY years since I was that child. I grew, trading in sweets for marijuana, LSD, Southern Comfort, had visions, had sex, went to college, wrote poetry, got married to an older man with four children, drank far too much red wine, stayed up all night talking to the dead, published two novels. I'm still married. My stepchildren are grown. I've spent this year going to their weddings.

And I've never stopped being that child. A few years ago, watching my old friends turn middle-aged, I thought *When will I grow up*? Of course many of us wonder that. In my case, thirty years of hypnotized waiting for what, for whom, can never return, has sucked up enormous rations of energy. As I started writing this memoir, I thought: The withered child who opens her mouth to speak, spits out the dust that was her tongue. The house of the body re-forming itself until the front door and the back door become mere inner thresholds, and the windows all face each other. Until the wait itself is a sexual presence, a heaviness in the limbs. And when I said to myself at last—Well, I mistook the nature of the world; the past does not return; I am not being preserved for special knowledge of the unseen; this is it, get on with it, girl—such rage, such grief, as subsides only very slowly.

I HAD TWO selves in my youth, the drunk and the sober, and the sober paid the bills for the other's strutting boldness. Which I do not regret. To feel emotional connection was so exotic to me in my youth. I imagined it as a sacrament, kept holy all the moments, late-night drunken conversations or passionate one-night stands, that opened me briefly to another person. I would brood over those windows of contact like a dragon his gold. What was said in the clear hour between too few drinks and too many. What action I performed half unconsciously, leaving my signature in the air.

I was shy, skittish, sarcastic, arrogant, depressed. Ragingly bewildered. I was smart in school, but knew nothing at all about how the world worked. I couldn't attend. I was somewhere else.

In my thirties, attending AA meetings, I began to learn how common extreme loneliness is. The details of my childhood, my adolescence and sexual confusion, the precise nature and extent of continuing fears—all of that was mine, but to have such stuff and be alone with it was only life. Those who always knew this, or knew it past the age of sixteen, may not be able to appreciate my intense happiness at finally getting it. I experienced again that awe I felt watching my father cry, seeing the *me* inside him. Sitting in the big basement of the Soho meeting, in that odd intimate detachment, I was able to hear without alcohol the simple fact of other people's lives.

Madness is distance from this fact. Madness is turning the information other people give out into dreams, occult sightings, messages from oneself.

I loved that madness because I made it. It was my first production, so painstakingly created. I didn't set it aside for a long time, for a long time; even in therapy, trying to have sanity *as well.*

I feel nostalgic now for those early days of realizing that isolation was not the only game in town. That I didn't have to savor every crumb of drunken contact, carrying it around like the peasant in the Monty Python movie hoarding a moldy potato.

MY FATHER, THE suicide. That blank infects the entire past, it is who he was from the beginning. My mother says he loved to talk about it; he was always asking people how they'd do it. Most people had no answer, and he'd regale them with his scenarios.

Vigor, a seeming common sense surrounding an inescapable passion: that's how I imagine Daddy's relation to his death. I see him in the middle of those suburban gatherings like some goofball from hell, like the salesman that he was, erupting in enthusiasm for his favorite subject. You just turn on the car in a closed garage! Not as painful as going to the dentist! My father, shocked when people talked about sex in public, was not shy about suicide.

I hold him in thought as if by doing so he will not die, condemning myself to carry the leathery egg of his despair. The suicide's daughter. She who stares fixedly at the corpse in the kitchen so time cannot pass, the body not decay.

The man lies as if asleep, dressed in a white shirt. His face shaven, shoes tied. The faint unblemished perfume of his body. No mother, no sister or brother in this story. Maybe a dog, thin and rust-colored, watching me as I watch my father.

When I edge away from this fixity, I encounter the blank. The man who took himself apart, who removed his image from the mirror.

In college, writing poetry, I invented a father who drove his car into death. Who drove down the long tunnel, then was ferried deep into the earth in an elevator of molten rock. Everything glowing with that red heat in blackness; his hands dancing their trembly dance on the wheel.

He had powers over death. He slipped sideways through the prison bars, a knife in his teeth. He left a dummy in bed to fool the authorities. He was on a mission.

This mission somehow contained within that act of weakness from which we averted our eyes. It was the hot center of something soft and wicked, obscene. I knew about that—how the true magicks must be wrapped in putrid cloths for safekeeping.

Yet the world would not countenance powers over death. There is a place between life and death for those who dare, a place of stasis, where the prison bars are webbed and blue; they are made of time and cannot be broken. My father is suspended there. He hangs from the ceiling in his blue cage, naked but for a pair of shorts, his only companion an invisible girl who sits in the corner, reading.

She reads fairy tales, mythology, poetry, and fiction. Books on Christianity, Zen, the Tao, Gurdjieff. Aleister Crowley and Aldous Huxley. Freud, Jung, the post-Freudians, post-Jungians. Bill W. At first she reads for pleasure, then for wisdom, and then because she doesn't know how to do anything else.

TO GROW UP in the image of a father who unmakes himself. Of a mother who holds on, whose fierce survival instincts fill me with awe and hunger. A mother who values family love above all things, but who can't bear too much raw feeling. A father whose feeling was like lava, and was buried in it.

I had, of course, to be like her. Like her (and secretly like him) and then slowly, agonizingly, like myself. But even though I was always aware what a relief it was that he died—the mood in our house, that last year in Montclair, even with Jimmy dead and Johnny on the streets, such a *relief* to me—I didn't know what to do with the absence.

Now that I am past forty, I understand why adults in the middle of their lives want to die: how little it could possibly have to do with a child's unworthiness. It has to do with all the things I didn't know about him, will never know. And yet, not knowing, I know. I lived with him ten years, absorbed his terror and his shame. I have only to observe myself to find the reasons for his suicide: sudden eruptions of rage, scalding self-hatred, the cell-deep sensitivity that is itself—even in a writer, who can use such a quality—a source of profound embarrassment.

TRAGEDY HAS ITS fans. Extreme experience is hypnotic, creating its own texture in the brain. Posttraumatic stress, or something more like religion: This was where the veil of illusion was rent. Jimmy's death, Daddy's death, the two together, one two-part event, was the biggest thing that had happened, or has happened to me. Like a meteorite pinning my life under it—not me, exactly, I've always been free to go, but my *life*, the story. Turning back to look, and look again. That which has created me.

What can one life reveal about anything? The intersection of necessity and chance makes an image one learns to put in the company of other images—quilt of lives I have observed, been involved in, read about; yet the irreducible quality of the subjective confounds. Here is reality. One wants to solve a life as one does an algebra problem, finding the identity of all unknowns. Or that's what I wanted, and still want. The belief that we have a fate, that there are something like gods—so attractive. Is it possible? I remember that school where I dreamt Jimmy went, where he was happy.

Yet the danger of spiritual seeking is just that: I am drawn into the idea that this world, this life, can never be as good as another. I refuse to wait for death as I once waited for fairlyland, yet often I find myself doing exactly that. Last year I was lying in bed, ill, in the depths of a depression brought on by the writing of this book. My depressions have always had a seductive element, tied as they are to the beloved dead. I was in a gloom that was both gray and silver, the grayness all depression sufferers know, shot through with this melancholic, musical silver. I imagined—though that word isn't strong enough—Jimmy and Daddy together, climbing a series of low hills. They were almost the same size, like brothers. I saw them as beings of light from the early days, when our souls were new and the flesh-suit newly chosen.

Jimmy and Daddy climbing the low hills, the green hills, while I'm stuck here alone, prey to exquisite yearning. And sullen about it, like a child left home from a party.

IT'S ALWAYS BEEN harder to grieve my brother than my father. Daddy's death cut off what was happening naturally, and when I tried to get back to it couldn't find the thread. My father was someone I could identify with in adulthood, while Jimmy . . . Jimmy was the one of us untouched by death. Always the sanest, happiest child in the family, eager, generous. To remember him is to doubt I can ever approximate such wholeness; and even without envy (I am sometimes without envy) I don't know how to love him humanly. I fall into a dazzle which makes me feel defensive—nobody will believe me, *you won't*, you'll say he was only a kid, like other kids. . . .

My sister's younger daughter had a picture of Jimmy on her wall for awhile. One day she told me that a friend of hers, another eight-year-old, had asked who was that cute boy. My niece told the truth but I wanted her not to have. I wanted that other girl to go away thinking this was a boy she might one day meet, that she could love. I wanted Jimmy to have the experience of being desired again by someone not in his family.

Once I had a child's mind, which values survival above all things, jettisons whatever impedes. But one gets lonely for what has been lost. Swimming the dark sea, looking for the thrown-away, the foolish heart thinking not only to regain the cast-off pain but the boy himself, who fell out of the sky.

Nobody promises that.

The books, the therapists, they say: You find yourself. And then having found, having put together yourself, you are ready for the world.

Is Jimmy in the world? No, he is not in the world. Or one can say he is in sunlight, laughter, other little boys—I used to imagine I'd have a son, I'd name him Jimmy.

I worried about it, having a son: He'd be somebody else. Would I be disappointed? In the event, I've had no children. I have stepchildren. I didn't expect them to be Jimmy. Yet all the time they were growing up, I wondered: Which will die? Not necessarily a boy, though I was much more afraid for the boys. I didn't believe it possible for four children to grow to adulthood, nobody lost.

Last week I had a dream.

Jimmy was back (I knew it was a dream, but so what. I hadn't dreamed of him in thirty years!) and I was so happy, following him around. He said Lay off. He said You're getting boring, still obsessed with me. I said I can't help it, I'm so glad to see you, can't I express it?

Get out of here, he said.

I thought: He's trying to make me not like him so I'll get better; it's a ruse. He's not really mean like this. He'll come round.

Slow learner.

About the Author

Margaret Diehl is the author of two novels, *Men* and *Me & You*. She lives in New York.